Analytics Optimization with Columnstore Indexes in Microsoft SQL Server

Optimizing OLAP Workloads

Edward Pollack

Apress®

Analytics Optimization with Columnstore Indexes in Microsoft SQL Server:
Optimizing OLAP Workloads

Edward Pollack
Albany, NY, USA

ISBN-13 (pbk): 978-1-4842-8047-8   ISBN-13 (electronic): 978-1-4842-8048-5
https://doi.org/10.1007/978-1-4842-8048-5

Managing Director, Apress Media LLC: Welmoed Spahr
Acquisitions Editor: Jonathan Gennick
Development Editor: Laura Berendson
Coordinating Editor: Jill Balzano

Cover image designed by Freepik (www.freepik.com)

Distributed to the book trade worldwide by Springer Science+Business Media LLC, 1 New York Plaza, Suite 4600, New York, NY 10004. Phone 1-800-SPRINGER, fax (201) 348-4505, e-mail orders-ny@springer-sbm.com, or visit www.springeronline.com. Apress Media, LLC is a California LLC and the sole member (owner) is Springer Science + Business Media Finance Inc (SSBM Finance Inc). SSBM Finance Inc is a **Delaware** corporation.

For information on translations, please e-mail booktranslations@springernature.com; for reprint, paperback, or audio rights, please e-mail bookpermissions@springernature.com.

Apress titles may be purchased in bulk for academic, corporate, or promotional use. eBook versions and licenses are also available for most titles. For more information, reference our Print and eBook Bulk Sales web page at http://www.apress.com/bulk-sales.

Any source code or other supplementary material referenced by the author in this book is available to readers on GitHub at https://github.com/Apress/analytics-optimization-w-columnstore-indexes-in-microsoft-sql-server.

Printed on acid-free paper

For Theresa, Nolan, and Oliver, without whom none of this would be possible.

Table of Contents

About the Author xi

About the Technical Reviewer xiii

Acknowledgments xv

Introduction xvii

Chapter 1: Introduction to Analytic Data in a Transactional Database 1
Where Should Analytic Data Reside? 1
Analytic Data Size 2
Analytic Data Structure 4
Analytic Data Sources 5
    Data Warehouse 6
    Unstructured Data 6
    Third-Party Analytics Software 6
    OLAP Data in an OLTP Table in a Transactional Database 7
    OLAP Data in an Analytic Table in a Transactional Database 8

Chapter 2: Transactional vs. Analytic Workloads 11
Transactional Data 11
Analytic Data 14
The Need for Two Systems.. 18
Building Better Analytic Data Structures.. 19

Chapter 3: What Are Columnstore Indexes? 21
The Limits of Transactional Data Storage 21
Introducing Columnstore Indexes 24

Benefits of Columnstore Indexes in SQL Server 26

    Native Analytic Data in SQL Server.. 26

    Scalability.. 27

    Exceptional Compression 29

    Faster Analytic Reads.. 30

    Faster Data Loads.. 30

Chapter 4: Columnstore Index Architecture **33**

    Sample Data... 33

    Rowgroups and Segments.. 36

    The Delta Store 40

    The Delete Bitmap... 41

    Nonclustered Columnstore Index Architecture... 42

    Physical Data on Pages.. 43

    Summarizing Differences... 47

Chapter 5: Columnstore Compression **49**

    Basics of Columnstore Compression 49

    Columnstore Compression Algorithms... 51

        Value Encoding... 51

        Dictionary Encoding... 54

        Should String Data Be Normalized? 60

        Row Order (Vertipaq) Optimization 62

        Other Compression Algorithms.. 65

        Columnstore Archive Compression.. 68

        The Compression Life Cycle 71

Chapter 6: Columnstore Metadata **73**

    Available Columnstore Metadata 73

        Rowgroup Metadata 73

        Segment Metadata 75

        Rowgroup Physical Metadata... 79

Rowgroup Operational Statistics 84

Columnstore Index Memory Usage 89

Internal Columnstore Index Objects 93

Chapter 7: Batch Execution 97

Row Mode Execution 97

Batch Mode Execution 100

How Does Batch Mode Work? 105

Batch Mode vs. Row Mode Performance 107

Chapter 8: Bulk Loading Data 111

Bulk Load Processes Explained 111

Bulk Loading into Columnstore Indexes 112

Performance of Bulk Loading into Columnstore Indexes 114

Trickle Insert vs. Staged Insert 118

Other Data Load Considerations 119

Drop Nonclustered Indexes During Data Loads 119

Columnstore Reorganize Operations with Each Data Load 120

Summary 122

Chapter 9: Delete and Update Operations 123

The Cost of Modifying Data 123

Delete Operations 125

Update Operations 128

Chapter 10: Segment and Rowgroup Elimination 137

Segment Elimination 137

Rowgroup Elimination 142

Combining Segment and Rowgroup Elimination 154

Chapter 11: Partitioning 157

Maintain Hot/Warm/Cold Data 157

Faster Data Movement/Migration 158

Partition Elimination 159

Database Maintenance 160

Partitioning in Action 161

Partitioning Guidelines 175

    Partition and Rowgroup Sizing 175

    Partition Column Choice 176

    Storage Choice 176

Additional Benefits 177

Chapter 12: Nonclustered Columnstore Indexes on Rowstore Tables 179

Use Rowstore Indexes 180

Separate OLAP and OLTP Processes 183

Nonclustered Columnstore Indexes 185

Managing Hot, Warm, and Cold Transactional Data 187

    Compression Delay 188

    Filtered Nonclustered Columnstore Indexes 195

    Code Changes 199

Vertipaq Optimization for Nonclustered Columnstore Indexes 199

Testing Nonclustered Columnstore Indexes 203

Don't Forget to Drop Unneeded Indexes! 204

Chapter 13: Nonclustered Rowstore Indexes on Columnstore Tables 207

Using Nonclustered Rowstore Indexes 207

Enforcing Constraints 212

Filtered Nonclustered Rowstore Indexes 214

Enabling Vertipaq Optimization 216

    Add Filters to Nonclustered Rowstore Indexes 216

    Perform Periodic Index Maintenance 216

Indexed Views 218

Compression for Nonclustered Rowstore Indexes 220

Nonclustered Rowstore Index Guidance 222

Chapter 14: Columnstore Index Maintenance 225

What Causes Fragmentation? 225

How Much Fragmentation Is Too Much? 228

    Quantifying Deleted Rows 228

    Detailing Unordered Data 230

The No-Maintenance Columnstore Index 236

Columnstore Reorganize 237

Reorganize to Remove Delta Rowgroups 239

Columnstore Rebuild 242

Columnstore Reorder and Rebuild 245

Columnstore Index Maintenance by Partition 246

Index Maintenance in Nonclustered Columnstore Indexes 247

Chapter 15: Columnstore Index Performance 249

Columnstore Metadata Reads 249

Columnstore Data Reads 253

Memory Sizing 254

Dictionary Size and Dictionary Pressure 257

    Normalizing Wide Columns 258

    Add or Change the Columnstore Sorting Column 259

    Partitioning 259

Columnstore Indexes on Temporary Tables 260

Memory-Optimized Columnstore Indexes 264

    Demonstrating Memory-Optimized Columnstore Indexes 264

Optimization Strategies 274

Index 275

About the Author

Edward Pollack has over 20 years of experience in database and systems administration, architecture, and development, becoming an advocate for designing efficient data structures that can withstand the test of time. He has spoken at many events, such as SQL Saturdays, PASS Data Community Summit, Dativerse, and at many user groups and is the organizer of SQL Saturday Albany. Edward has authored many articles, as well as the book *Dynamic SQL: Applications, Performance, and Security*, and a chapter in *Expert T-SQL Window Functions in SQL Server*. His first patent was issued in 2021, focused on the compression of geographical data for use by analytic systems.

In his free time, Ed enjoys video games, sci-fi and fantasy, traveling, and baking. He lives in the sometimes-frozen icescape of Albany, NY, with his wife Theresa and sons Nolan and Oliver, and a mountain of (his) video game plushies that help break the fall when tripping on (their) toys.

About the Technical Reviewer

Borbala Toth-Apathy is a database professional with nearly 20 years of experience in the IT field. She has an MSc in Computer Science – unsurprisingly, as she's been writing code from a young age.

Specializing in databases after her degree, nowadays, she is designing and building data warehouses. Her secret passion is data analytics.

In her free time, she likes calisthenics or yoga, nature, puzzles, and crafts.

Acknowledgments

A big shout-out to the SQL Server community and the many speakers, organizers, colleagues, and others who have supported and advised me over the years and provided opportunities to grow both personally and professionally.

A book doesn't happen without dedicated reviewers and editors. Speakers do not get the opportunity to share their knowledge and grow without organizers, sponsors, and volunteers that provide those chances. Articles are not written without companies, editors, and services to support and encourage that work.

To everyone that has provided those opportunities to be a part of your events, publications, and groups: Thank you!!!

Introduction

Analytic data is an ever-present challenge for developers, analysts, and data professionals. Its rapid growth coupled with the constant organizational need for speedy answers to complex questions leads to the question of how massive amounts of data can be stored efficiently enough to allow for real-time analytics.

What Is This Book?

This book uses columnstore indexes as a tool to address the challenge of storing different types of analytic data efficiently. Applications such as data warehousing, logging, reporting, analytics, and data science can all be solved by effective use of columnstore indexes. In addition, real-time operational analytics can be accomplished with this tool.

Analytics Optimization with Columnstore Indexes in Microsoft SQL Server is structured into three functionally different sections:

- Chapters 1 and 2: Introduction to analytic data and its challenges

- Chapters 3 and 4: Columnstore index basics and architecture

- Chapters 5–15: Deep dives into features, architecture, and best practices

The goal is to provide enough theory, architecture, use cases, and code to enable the immediate use of this feature in solving real-world problems.

Each chapter tackles a specific feature or data architecture need from a high-level overview, then delving into extensive detail. While not all professionals may need to know precisely how columnstore indexes compress their data, having that knowledge available will provide value in the future when the need to improve performance arises.

Most examples in this book are derived from data in the WideWorldImportersDW and WideWorldImporters databases. On their own, they do not provide enough data to allow for meaningful examples of analytic data. To augment this, new tables are created, copied, and modified to allow for objects that are large and interesting enough to be useful in demonstrating columnstore indexes. While real-world tables can easily contain tens of billions of rows, the examples in this book settle for about 25 million rows. This provides a healthy compromise between effective test data and tables that are so large that building them takes a very long time.

Intended Audience

This book is intended for data professionals, architects, and developers as a tool to tame reporting and analytic data quickly, inexpensively, and effectively. Topics in this book range from introductory to quite advanced, allowing it to be used as a tool by both beginners and those with years of data architecture experience under their belts.

Those who have little experience with columnstore storage technologies will learn everything needed to implement this feature for the first time and begin realizing its benefits. Data experts can use the feature and architecture details, as well as demonstrations provided throughout this book as a tool to optimize existing data structures.

Columnstore indexes are not only for reporting and analytic data. They can also be used to table the complex organizational need for real-time operational analytics. When analytic and transactional workloads mix, the risk exists for latency, blocking, locking, and deadlocking. Developers and data professionals that work with mixed workloads can benefit greatly from the use of columnstore indexes to help cover each workload effectively. In addition to improving performance, these efforts can avoid the need to purchase or architect new systems to manage portions of a mixed workload.

Why Columnstore Indexes?

There are many solutions available that help tame analytic data, but most require investing heavily in new hardware, software, technologies, and architecture. Not all organizations can (or should) feel forced into investing immense resources in new solutions unless there is a truly compelling reason to do so.

Columnstore indexes can be implemented in SQL Server using existing hardware and licenses, allowing for analytic data solutions to be realized without a significant investment of time and resources. This allows for easier QA and testing of the feature without the need to commit to it up front.

In addition to providing a robust solution, columnstore indexes are based on mature technology that has underpinned many other data storage products (such as PowerPivot and SSAS) for years. Despite their maturity, columnstore indexes in SQL Server evolve and improve with each new version that is released.

Contacting the Author

This book is incomplete without readers, and this experience is only truly meaningful when I am available to answer questions and accept feedback. The thoughts that are shared with me at conferences, industry events, and through electronic means provide ways to grow and improve, as well as ideas worthy of consideration.

Feel free to contact me about this book, its topic, or related thoughts via Twitter (@EdwardPollack) or email (ed@edwardpollack.com).

CHAPTER 1

Introduction to Analytic Data in a Transactional Database

Analytic data, by its nature, can be large and challenging to maintain and can grow quickly over time. Similarly, its use increases with time as analysts and data scientists find more ways to crunch it. There is a great convenience to having analytic data in close proximity to its underlying transactional sources. Utility is also gained by choosing a location for analytic data that can withstand the test of time, thus avoiding the need for costly migrations if the data is unable to scale appropriately.

Where Should Analytic Data Reside?

Until the advent of columnstore indexes, storing analytic data in a transactional database in SQL Server was cumbersome and required tricks and compromises to make it performant enough for the rigors of analytics. Other technologies and services were incorporated as a way to work around these limitations.

There are a variety of places that analytic data can be stored, such as

- Data warehouse (SQL Server Analysis Services, RedShift, etc.)

- Unstructured data (data lake using Hadoop, Hive, etc.)

- Third-party analytics software

- OLTP tables in a relational/transactional database

- OLAP tables in a relational/transactional database

© Edward Pollack 2022

E. Pollack, *Analytics Optimization with Columnstore Indexes in Microsoft SQL Server*,
https://doi.org/10.1007/978-1-4842-8048-5_1

Each of these options has advantages and disadvantages, but before diving into specifics, it is important to review analytic data and how it looks.

Note that OLAP stands for "online analytic processing" and references analytic tables and data, whereas OLTP stands for "online transactional processing" and refers to transactional tables and data.

Analytic Data Size

Typical analytic data has significantly higher row counts than its source transactional data. This may be due to tracking many metrics in extensive detail, or it may be due to tracking those details in repeated samples over a long period of time. If a transactional log table adds a million rows per day, then 365 million rows will be captured per year. Figure 1-1 shows the dramatic effect that time can have on data and how a small data set can grow very quickly when sampled regularly.

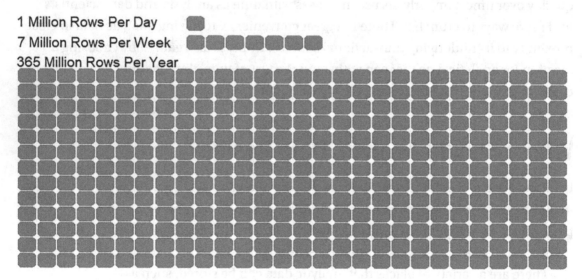

Figure 1-1. *Illustration of the growth of data when the time dimension is added*

Analytic data can also be quite wide. Even a small table can have many calculated metrics derived from it, allowing its OLAP counterpart to contain significantly more columns. For example, consider the hypothetical sales order table in Listing 1-1.

Listing 1-1. An Example of a Transactional Sales Order Table

```
CREATE TABLE dbo.SalesOrder
(       SalesOrderId INT NOT NULL IDENTITY(1,1) CONSTRAINT PK_SalesOrder
        PRIMARY KEY CLUSTERED, ProductDetailList INT NOT NULL CONSTRAINT
        FK_SalesOrder_ProductDetail FOREIGN KEY REFERENCES dbo.ProductDetail,
        CustomerId INT NOT NULL CONSTRAINT FK_SalesOrder_Customer FOREIGN
        KEY REFERENCES dbo.Customer,
        OrderTime DATETIME2(3) NOT NULL,
        SalesAmount DECIMAL(18,4) NOT NULL,
        TaxRate DECIMAL(6,4) NOT NULL,
        ShipTime DATETIME2(3) NULL,
        ReceivedTime DATETIME2(3) NULL);
```

This table in Listing 1-1 contains only eight columns that provide information on orders, including the customer, product details, and timing/cost. After some time and deliberation, an analytic team creates a data warehouse–style fact table based off of this transactional table, as seen in Listing 1-2.

Listing 1-2. An Example of an Analytic Sales Order Table

```
CREATE TABLE fact.SalesOrderMetrics
(       OrderDate DATE NOT NULL,
        CustomerID INT NOT NULL,
        OrderCount INT NOT NULL,
        SalesAmountTotal DECIMAL(20,4) NOT NULL,
        SalesAmountMin DECIMAL(20,4) NOT NULL,
        SalesAmountMax DECIMAL(20,4) NOT NULL,
        AverageTaxRate DECIMAL(6,4) NOT NULL,
        MinTaxRate DECIMAL(6,4) NOT NULL,
        MaxTaxRate DECIMAL(6,4) NOT NULL,
        AverageHoursFromOrdertoShip DECIMAL(6,2) NULL,
        AverageHoursFromShiptoReceive DECIMAL(6,2) NULL,
        MinimumSecondsBetweenOrders INT NULL,
        MaximumSecondsBetweenOrders INT NULL);
```

Note that the analytic table in Listing 1-2 has a variety of additional metrics that are used to summarize data elements as the source data is transformed from detail data into daily aggregate data. Analysts could easily add many more columns if an organizational need existed for them.

Because of these details, analytic data can easily grow and encompass millions or billions of rows in a destination table. Similarly, an analytic table could contain far more columns than its source transactional data. As a result, it should not be surprising that an analytic table can potentially have many rows and/or many columns. Even a table that is architected to not be wide (many columns) or deep (many rows) can change over time as an organization grows and evolves. Therefore, having plans to manage larger data can be beneficial, even if those plans are not implemented when an analytics project is first completed.

Analytic Data Structure

Analytic data will typically be comprised of one of two kinds of data:

- Statistical metrics

- Detail data

Statistical metrics are numeric fields that can be aggregated into meaningful derived metrics. These may be dates, durations, measurements, rates, and more. In general, these data types use fixed-length data types, are relatively small, and have a predictable storage footprint.

Detail data consists of text-based data types, such as VARCHAR, JSON, XML, and other types of markup. This data is typically not used directly in metrics or statistics, but instead is further crunched for analysis after the fact. While detail data is important, it is not the focus of this book. If a dimension exists with a large text-based data type, it is worth considering the normalization of that column to reduce its footprint and allow for easier management of detail values.

For example, the table in Listing 1-3 contains a large text column.

Listing 1-3. Example of a Table with a Wide Text Column

```
CREATE TABLE dbo.WebAccessLog
(       LogId INT NOT NULL,
        LogTime DATETIME2(3) NOT NULL,
        LogSource VARCHAR(250) NOT NULL,
        ErrorCode BIGINT NOT NULL);
```

Assuming that the data in the *LogSource* column is repeated often, normalizing it into its own dimension table would save computing resources and allow for easier analysis of distinct values or a subset of values, when needed. Listing 1-4 illustrates this table after *LogSource* is normalized.

Listing 1-4. Normalization of a Text Column into a Lookup Table

```
CREATE TABLE dbo.LogSource
(       LogSourceId SMALLINT NOT NULL IDENTITY(1,1) CONSTRAINT PK_LogSource
        PRIMARY KEY CLUSTERED, LogSource VARCHAR(250) NOT NULL);
```

```
CREATE TABLE dbo.WebAccessLog
(       LogId INT NOT NULL,
        LogTime DATETIME2(3) NOT NULL,
        LogSourceId SMALLINT NOT NULL,
        ErrorCode BIGINT NOT NULL);
```

The *LogSource* column, which had been represented with a 250 character string, now uses a SMALLINT to reference the lookup table *LogSource* instead. When normalizing a column, ensure that the data type for the lookup key is neither too small (and could run out of values) nor too large (wasting space). Normalizing dimensions is not always a necessary action, but it can be beneficial when dimension values are often repeated and the need to reference them is frequent.

Analytic Data Sources

Where can analytic data be stored, and how can it be known that this decision is being made effectively? With a brief review of analytic data out of the way, this question of where to store analytic data can be explored in a bit more detail.

Data Warehouse

A data warehouse is a classic repository for OLAP data structures. Decades of experience have gone into the development of exceptionally effective data warehousing software with nearly every major data platform having its own proprietary warehousing solution.

Solutions such as Microsoft's Azure Synapse, Amazon RedShift, and Google BigQuery are examples of data warehousing solutions that are served up with the intent of being used alongside other data storage components that these organizations offer.

The upside of using these technologies is that they are prebuilt, ready to use, and are optimized for analytic data. The downside of these systems is that they involve learning a new architecture, new scripting languages, and gaining enough expertise to maintain them over time. Larger organizations can often afford to specialize in this regard, but even then, the desire to increase complexity is sometimes a reason to not start with one of these solutions.

Unstructured Data

Not all data should go into a SQL database or even a structured data source. Data that is heavily comprised of text and markup is not easy to search within the confines of a transactional database, even with features such as SQL Server's Full-Text Search enabled.

When the data being worked with is dollars, time, or metrics, there is great flexibility in where that data can effectively be stored, but large text and files make more sense to be stored in an unstructured data repository, such as a data lake underpinned by Hadoop, Hive, or a similar technology offered by a given software vendor.

If a data storage solution is needed and the source data is large and text based, consider destinations outside of the confines of a transactional database. While this book is not intended to explore these solutions, knowing when they should be considered is helpful to avoid architecting around the wrong technology for that data.

Third-Party Analytics Software

There are many analytic software solutions available for use both on premises and in the cloud. Even creating a list of these solutions would take hours, consume many pages, and likely still be incomplete.

Like with a data warehouse solution, the primary benefit of a third-party analytic solution is that it is built for this purpose and can be used with a relatively minimal amount of effort. Unlike a data warehouse solution, analytics software varies greatly in its structure, interface, and usage. An organization's data analytic needs will dictate the type of solution needed, and some analytics software will meet those needs while some will not.

The downsides of using a third-party vendor are cost and vendor lock-in. Costs typically increase as data volume and/or usage increases. Therefore, an analytics project may begin inexpensively, but end up being quite costly when the data is ten or a hundred (or a million?!) times larger than its initial size. When architecting any data solution, be certain to determine cost based on current and future needs. This ensures that there are no surprises when data and its usage inevitably grow by orders of magnitude from where they begin.

Vendor lock-in may also pose a challenge. Moving data into an analytics solution is easy, but is there a well-documented and convenient way to extract that data in the future? If not, then moving away from that solution may become costly and time-consuming. If those costs exceed the costs of remaining on that platform, then an organization may have to begrudgingly choose to maintain its data there indefinitely. For those that are comfortable and familiar with a given data analytics solution, this is likely not an issue, though.

OLAP Data in an OLTP Table in a Transactional Database

Storing analytic data in OLTP tables is likely a trap. OLTP tables are intended for workloads in which small ranges of rows are frequently written and read. In these scenarios, many columns are typically requested from those rows. These tables are designed to manage concurrency based on the idea that a given transaction will involve few rows.

OLTP tables are counter to analytic data, which often involves queries against many rows in aggregate, but usually not as many columns.

For small tables (less than a few million rows), an OLTP table is adequate for analytic data. For larger tables that contain millions or billions of rows, these tables will have difficulty in serving up data across large ranges. They will likely consume more space and drive slower queries against their data than any other analytic solutions discussed here. This is because they are optimized for small range lookups (few rows, many columns) and are not architected to service the vast row counts and aggregates required for analytics.

Reserve OLTP tables for small analytic data sets where scanning most (or all) of a table is not prohibitively expensive. Alternatively, they can be used for lookup tables or other small dimensions. For a previous example in Listing 1-3, the *LogSource* table used a SMALLINT to number its rows. With a primary key that can contain no more than 65,535 values (-32,767 through 32,767), this table is destined to be relatively small. It is compact enough that indexing the text column would not be prohibitively expensive, if needed.

OLAP Data in an Analytic Table in a Transactional Database

The final option for storing analytic data is an OLAP table within a transactional database. This is the focus of the remainder of this book and will provide an alternative to the solutions presented thus far.

An OLAP table is a table structure that is designed specifically to service queries that typically access a large volume of rows in aggregate, but also do not require returning all of the columns at any one given time. An OLAP table is expected to grow to be millions or billions of rows and can easily service queries that crunch millions of rows at a time with ease.

There are many benefits to storing analytic data in an OLAP table within SQL Server, including the following:

- Can use existing technology and licenses to maintain analytic data.

- Far smaller learning curve to implement and use.

- Data is maintained completely by its owners.

- Data can be stored in close proximity to its transactional data source.

These are not trivial considerations and can make the effort to implement an analytic solution fast, inexpensive, and easy to revise, if needed. In addition, performance can be measured and optimized as needed to ensure that the end users of analytic data enjoy acceptable access speeds. In addition, the processes that load data into analytic tables can be fine-tuned to be exceptionally fast.

Given their simplicity and ease of implementation, it is worthwhile to take the time and resources to create a proof of concept for storing analytic data in SQL Server, specifically using columnstore indexes.

Analytic data can be large, consume immense resources, and be challenging to move when change is needed. Choosing the correct target data structure for analytic data and making the best possible initial decision is critical to the long-term success of an analytics project.

This book will explore in detail the nature of analytic workloads and why columnstore indexes in SQL Server can provide a cost-effective and performant solution.

CHAPTER 2

Transactional vs. Analytic Workloads

Transactional and analytic data are fundamentally different in terms of how they are written, read, stored, and managed. To achieve optimal performance of either type of data requires architecting data structures and software that cater to each of these paradigms.

Choosing the optimal data structure is critical in large, busy production systems as the cost to rebuild an existing system is significantly higher than to architect it effectively from the start. This chapter explores the differences in these workloads and will allow for the effective introduction of columnstore indexes as the optimal solution for a wide variety of analytic data storage needs.

Transactional Data

The data that is readily created, altered, deleted, and read by applications is transactional data. This data may not always be stored in structured databases or adhere to the mantra of ACID transactions (**A**tomic, **C**onsistent, **I**solated, **D**urable), but for this discussion, it will all be considered transactional data.

Consider an order system that handles product orders from a website and a popular mobile app. This is decidedly a transactional system. Many people access the site regularly and create orders, check their status, and await the arrival of what they've ordered. The *WideWorldImporters* sample database contains an *Orders* table that is representative of what would be seen in a typical order system, as seen in Figure 2-1.

E. Pollack, *Analytics Optimization with Columnstore Indexes in Microsoft SQL Server*,
https://doi.org/10.1007/978-1-4842-8048-5_2

	OrderID	CustomerID	SalespersonPersonID	PickedByPersonID	ContactPersonID	BackorderOrderID	OrderDate	ExpectedDeliveryDate	CustomerPurchaseOrderNumber	IsUndersupplyBackordered	Comments
1	1	832	2	NULL	3032	45	2013-01-01	2013-01-02	12126	1	NULL
2	2	803	8	NULL	3003	46	2013-01-01	2013-01-02	15342	1	NULL
3	3	105	7	NULL	1209	47	2013-01-01	2013-01-02	12211	1	NULL
4	4	57	16	3	1113	NULL	2013-01-01	2013-01-02	17129	1	NULL
5	5	905	3	NULL	3105	48	2013-01-01	2013-01-02	10369	1	NULL
6	6	976	13	3	3176	NULL	2013-01-01	2013-01-02	13383	1	NULL
7	7	575	8	NULL	2349	49	2013-01-01	2013-01-02	17913	1	NULL
8	8	964	7	NULL	3164	50	2013-01-01	2013-01-02	14518	1	NULL
9	9	77	7	NULL	1153	51	2013-01-01	2013-01-02	17577	1	NULL
10	10	191	20	NULL	1381	52	2013-01-01	2013-01-02	18030	1	NULL

Figure 2-1. *Example of an order table used by a busy order processing system*

Note that there are many columns, each of which represents a detail of an order, such as the salesperson, customer, contact, order date, and purchase order number. Regardless of how large this table became over time, the average user would usually not want to view more than a handful of rows at a time. The quantity of data accessed is typically small as users will rarely view more than current or recent orders. If they do, pre-existing filters and links would be built to ensure that data can be served up quickly.

Oftentimes, many columns are returned to the application at one time. When viewing an order, it is far faster and efficient to return any column that may be needed rather than be forced to return to the table multiple times to retrieve more columns.

Because users are interacting directly with an application, there is an expectation that performance will be as fast as possible. Waiting a second or two for an order to process would be seen as acceptable, whereas waiting 1 or 2 minutes would result in immediate complaints and lost business. Similarly, because many users are accessing the site at one time, contention is expected to be high. Since many people will be accessing their orders at one time, the tables storing that data need to be capable of fast reads and writes, even when thousands (or millions) of orders are being accessed at one time.

In general, transactional queries tend to be simple. For example, a user that is retrieving information on a current order may do so via the following query:

```
SELECT
        Orders.OrderID,
        Customers.CustomerName,
        Orders.OrderDate,
        Orders.ExpectedDeliveryDate,
        Orders.CustomerPurchaseOrderNumber,
        OrderLines.*
```

```
FROM Sales.Orders
INNER JOIN Sales.Customers
ON Customers.CustomerID = Orders.CustomerID
INNER JOIN Sales.OrderLines
ON OrderLines.OrderID = Orders.OrderID
WHERE Customers.CustomerID = 10
AND Orders.OrderDate >= '5/20/2016'
AND Orders.OrderDate < '5/27/2016';
```

This is a relatively simple query that pulls 5 specific columns, as well as all 12 columns of line-item detail from 3 tables. Figure 2-2 shows the results of this query.

	OrderID	CustomerName	OrderDate	ExpectedDeliveryDate	CustomerPurchaseOrderNumber	OrderLineID	OrderID	StockItemID	Description
1	73045	Tailspin Toys (Wimbledon, ND)	2016-05-24	2016-05-25	15204	229708	73045	54	IT joke mug - that
2	73045	Tailspin Toys (Wimbledon, ND)	2016-05-24	2016-05-25	15204	229709	73045	152	Pack of 12 action

Figure 2-2. *Results of a sample transactional order query*

Note that only two rows are returned via a filter on both customer and date. It would be unusual for a user of this system to request data on hundreds or thousands of orders at once. Viewing so much data at one time would be challenging, and it is unlikely that the user interface is built to allow so much data to be retrieved at one time anyway.

Any data that is served up by a transactional system needs to be accurate at runtime. Someone checking their bank balance needs to get an accurate number without exception. This means that data integrity needs to be enforced at runtime either by the database, the application, or a combination of both. Inaccurate data in a transactional system could have disastrous results if the application in question, for example, belongs to a hospital, the military, or meteorologists.

Similarly, if a transactional operation fails, that failure needs to be addressed immediately so that that user's data is not left in an uncertain state. If a user renews their passport online, but the payment never correctly processes, their application may not be handled as it should be. Worse, there may not be an easy way for the user to fix it. Therefore, the ability of that system to properly handle each step of that process together as a unit is very important. The use of ACID for transactional data is heavily dependent on the data and its use. A bank cannot afford an inconsistent transaction, but a social media site probably can. Similarly, data that is eventually consistent will be perfectly acceptable in some organizational models, whereas it would be destructive in others.

OLTP data is often normalized to assist in ensuring relational integrity and the ability to generate lists of lookup values efficiently. Normalization can save space and memory in transactional applications as more verbose text columns are replaced with numeric lookups. It also allows for easy lookups within the application by querying the normalized table directly.

In summary, transactional data generally shares these characteristics:

- Often the target of INSERT, UPDATE, and DELETE operations.

- Many columns are returned at one time, for use by the application.

- Volume of data accessed by a single user at one time is typically small.

- Transaction speed is paramount.

- High levels of contention are expected.

- Data must be accurate at runtime, when needed, without exception.

- Accessed by application end users.

- Often normalized.

While these characteristics are generally true of transactional data, analytic data is quite different and is worth exploring further in detail.

Analytic Data

While transactional data is found in live/busy systems processing orders or bank operations, analytic data is found further downstream. This data is most often associated with reporting, visualization, and analytics. It is what powers business intelligence, data science, and the decision making that drives organizations worldwide.

OLAP systems are fundamentally different from transactional systems. To ensure optimal speed and reliability, each needs to be architected, implemented, and managed in distinctly different ways.

Analytics typically require queries that access large batches of data at one time, but will need far fewer columns to perform the calculations needed to drive results. For example, a common financial request may be to compare revenue for the current quarter with revenue from the previous quarter. The calculations needed to drive this request would need to access all revenue data for each quarter or have that data pre-crunched in a convenient location.

The following query is an example of an analytic data request that seeks to understand order counts and totals over time:

```
SELECT
        Date.[Calendar Year] AS Order_Year,
        Date.[Calendar Month Number] AS Order_Month,
        COUNT(*) AS Order_Count,
        SUM(Quantity) AS Quantity_Total,
        SUM([Total Excluding Tax]) AS [Total Excluding Tax]
FROM Fact.[Order]
INNER JOIN Dimension.Date
ON Date.Date = [Order].[Order Date Key]
WHERE [Order].[Order Date Key] >= '1/1/2016'
AND [Order].[Order Date Key] < '1/1/2017'
GROUP BY Date.[Calendar Year], Date.[Calendar Month Number]
ORDER BY Date.[Calendar Year], Date.[Calendar Month Number];
```

Note that only a handful of columns are requested, but that almost 30k orders were queried to return the results shown in Figure 2-3.

	Order_Year	Order_Month	Order_Count	Quantity_Total	Total Excluding Tax
1	2016	1	6017	261688	4612140.45
2	2016	2	5247	222689	4099480.35
3	2016	3	6159	261119	4807110.70
4	2016	4	6022	263172	4739058.60
5	2016	5	6457	282360	5138002.65

Figure 2-3. *Results of a sample analytic query*

A larger OLAP system could easily process millions of rows as a part of a single request with similar-looking results. An effective analytic data store needs to be able to scale to support millions (or billions) of rows in any given table without consuming excessive system resources or queries taking too long to execute.

Unlike transactional systems where data is written in small batches from many sources, analytic data is typically created in larger bulk operations from a limited set of organized data load processes. Inserting thousands (or millions) of rows at one time needs to be fast and efficient as that will be the norm. The diagram in Figure 2-4 illustrates the differences between how data is written in each type of system.

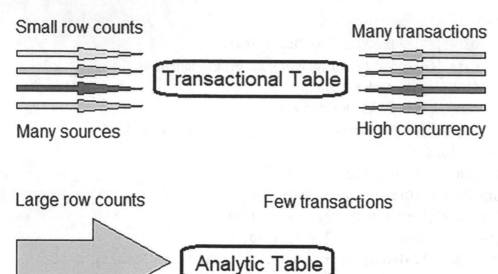

Figure 2-4. *Summary of OLAP vs. OLTP data access patterns*

It is important to note that not all OLTP and OLAP systems behave precisely like this, but will generally follow these usage patterns.

Because analytic data is typically used for reporting, analytics, and data science, the need for real-time results is less important. Many analytic processes are asynchronous and not directly monitored by the user that will consume the resulting data. Because OLAP data changes less often, complex data processing can occur prior to data usage, ensuring that there is no need to wait too long for results, if the need for interactive reporting is important.

Similarly, because the number of data sources, users, and apps accessing the data is smaller, contention is far less of a challenge. A query may require reading millions of rows from a table to return its results, but the quantity of queries accessing that table will be orders of magnitude less than a busy transactional table.

Because OLAP data is updated infrequently, the need to maintain relational integrity via constraints is lower. The set of new data that is loaded can be independently validated and confirmed to be accurate prior to its insertion into an analytic table. Foreign keys and constraints may be still used as conveniences for joining or reporting, but their use will depend on their impact on load speeds. The decision on how to validate analytic data depends on each use case, the nature of its source transactional data, and the amount of change that can occur in the OLAP data outside of organized data load processes.

Similarly, architects of OLAP data load processes can take liberties with how they handle failures. In transactional applications, failures need to be immediately retried or rolled back. There can be no middle ground that could result in bad or inconsistent data. A failed analytic load process can be resolved with a more brute-force approach such as this:

1.   Troubleshoot and fix the broken load process.

2.   Identify and remove all newly loaded data.

3.   Rerun the load process.

There is likely no need to preserve any of the partially loaded data, nor is the removal of partially loaded data complex, as it is typically time-stamped. Many OLAP data load processes will include steps that automatically remove any data previously loaded for the same time period. This allows a failed process to be rerun without the prerequisite cleanup step.

The consumers of analytic data are also quite different from those that use transactional applications. Whereas an OLTP application may have a wide range of end users that regularly interact directly with the software, analytic data consumers tend to be analysts, domain experts, and business leaders. Domain experts are people that are close enough to the data to understand its meaning and usage. For example, a network administrator would be a domain expert for network traffic data, whereas a chief financial officer would be a domain expert for quarterly earnings data. Domain experts may have a clear understanding of data meaning, but they are less likely to be familiar with how that data is stored and processed.

Unlike OLTP data, analytic data is often denormalized. Lookup tables may be maintained for reporting purposes, but not used exclusively as lookups to fact tables. Normalization does not always save significant storage or memory resources in OLAP tables. Equally important, joining lookup tables during data load processes can greatly increase their latency, resulting in longer delays before new analytic data becomes available. Most compression algorithms used in mainstream analytic data structures utilize dictionary lookups to "normalize" data when it is physically stored. This means that repeated values take up far less space than in a transactional table, regardless of the column's specific width. Despite that, dictionaries are limited in size and wider data types will pose compression challenges, which will be tackled in Chapter 5.

Analytic data can be summarized as follows:

- **Written by large, infrequent, and controlled data load processes.**

- **Rows are read in large batches for use in analytics.**

- **Less columns are typically read in each operation.**

- **Low levels of contention are expected.**

- **Data integrity can be enforced via validation, rather than constraints.**

- **Accessed by business leaders, analysts, and domain experts.**

- **Often denormalized.**

The characteristics of analytic data are quite different from those of transactional data. These different characteristics tend to lead toward using different systems to store each.

The Need for Two Systems

Because the workloads of transactional and analytic systems are so vastly different, the need for unique data structures to maintain them becomes more apparent the larger their data gets.

While a thousand rows of data can be quickly accessed in any structure, a billion rows would be cumbersome unless its data structure was built to accommodate the types of workloads it is expected to service.

Many applications attempt to mix analytic and transactional workloads to maintain convenience and avoid the creation of new systems. This works until the various differences between these types of data begin to clash with each other. For example, a common pitfall in mixing OLAP and OLTP workloads occurs when large, slow analytic queries cause locking and blocking against objects that application users are trying to write to. If a salesperson running an annual report is blocking the users trying to purchase new products, then the result will be lost sales and disgruntled users.

Similarly, those large reports may consume vast amounts of memory, forcing common transactional data out of the buffer pool in favor of reporting data. This will further exacerbate slowness for application users.

In general, mixing analytic and transactional workloads may not always be avoidable, but considering the ramifications of this architectural decision up front can help in predicting (and planning for) problems before they become costly.

Many other considerations will vary between OLTP and OLAP systems, such as

- Maintenance

- High availability

- Disaster recovery

- SQL Server licensing

- Hardware resources

The architect of an application will need to ensure that each of these topics is visited separately for both transactional and analytic workloads. While it is possible that similar systems can be used when data sizes are small, it is unlikely that those same systems will scale indefinitely. Eventually, data becomes large enough that unique solutions are required to differentiate each type of workload.

The nuance of these decisions can travel deeper. For example, a small analytic database would likely be architected differently than a large data repository. Therefore, it's important to consider size, scale, data growth, and workload together when architecting new data structures or when revisiting existing database objects.

Building Better Analytic Data Structures

The discussion thus far makes it clear that the tables and structures used to support analytic data need to be distinct from what is used for transactional workloads. In this chapter, many details were outlined that differentiate OLTP and OLAP applications, how they read and write data, and their typical usage patterns.

Taking this information into account allows for a vision to be created of where analytic data should be stored. The remainder of this book will focus on how columnstore indexes in SQL Server can be used to effectively meet the needs of large analytic tables and workloads. This technology is mature and can be used to effectively manage a wide variety of analytic use cases, ensuring that it provides an ideal solution to many of the analytics challenges that architects and administrators face on a regular basis.

CHAPTER 3

What Are Columnstore Indexes?

Thus far, a compelling case has been presented to separate OLTP and OLAP workloads into unique data structures and optimize each for their respective use cases. Columnstore indexes are a SQL Server feature that provides native support for large analytic data. This chapter will dive into what they are and why they are an effective solution to analytic data challenges.

The Limits of Transactional Data Storage

Tables that contain millions or billions of rows of analytic data do not scale well when implemented as classic transactional tables. To fully understand why this is the case, it is helpful to compare how data is stored in both transactional and analytic tables. The following example table contains five columns. Figure 3-1 shows how data is stored in an OLTP (rowstore) version of this table.

Row 1-1	Row 1-2	Row 1-3	Row 1-4	Row 1-5	Row 2-1	Row 2-2	Row 2-3	Row 2-4
Row 2-5	Row 3-1	Row 3-2	Row 3-3	Row 3-4	Row 3-5	Row 4-1	Row 4-2	Row 4-3
Row 4-4	Row 4-5	Row 5-1	Row 5-2	Row 5-3	Row 5-4	Row 5-5	Row 6-1	Row 6-2
Row 6-3	Row 6-4	Row 6-5	Row 7-1	Row 7-2	Row 7-3	Row 7-4	Row 7-5	Row 8-1
Row 8-2	Row 8-3	Row 8-4	Row 8-5	Row 9-1	Row 9-2	Row 9-3	Row 9-4	Row 9-5

Figure 3-1. *Illustration of data storage in a clustered rowstore index*

In a clustered rowstore index, each row is stored on pages sequentially, one row after another in the order prescribed by the clustered index. If many columns from a single row or small subset of rows are required by a query, then this is an exceptionally efficient

© Edward Pollack 2022
E. Pollack, *Analytics Optimization with Columnstore Indexes in Microsoft SQL Server*,
https://doi.org/10.1007/978-1-4842-8048-5_3

storage structure. For example, retrieving all columns from row 1 through row -5 would require low effort as the data is contiguous and ordered. Figure 3-2 highlights the data needed to satisfy this query.

Row 1-1	Row 1-2	Row 1-3	Row 1-4	Row 1-5	Row 2-1	Row 2-2	Row 2-3	Row 2-4
Row 2-5	Row 3-1	Row 3-2	Row 3-3	Row 3-4	Row 3-5	Row 4-1	Row 4-2	Row 4-3
Row 4-4	Row 4-5	Row 5-1	Row 5-2	Row 5-3	Row 5-4	Row 5-5	Row 6-1	Row 6-2
Row 6-3	Row 6-4	Row 6-5	Row 7-1	Row 7-2	Row 7-3	Row 7-4	Row 7-5	Row 8-1
Row 8-2	Row 8-3	Row 8-4	Row 8-5	Row 9-1	Row 9-2	Row 9-3	Row 9-4	Row 9-5

Figure 3-2. *How an OLTP query retrieving five rows would read a sample table*

A table with sequential columns models how typical transactional queries operate for a query such as this:

```
SELECT
      OrderID, --  An identity/primary key column
      CustomerID,
      SalespersonPersonID,
      ContactPersonID,
      OrderDate
FROM Sales.Orders
WHERE OrderId = 289;
```

Transactional queries write single rows or small ranges of rows that often correlate to a lookup on a single index. Here, a numeric identity is used to filter out five rows of interest from a larger table.

The basic unit of SQL Server storage is the page. A page is comprised of 8 kilobytes of data. Pages contain all data and index storage for a given table. If a single row is required for a query, then the entire page it is stored on will be read into memory, even if the remaining data on the page is not needed. Therefore, transactional queries rely on clustered or nonclustered indexes to ensure that index seeks can return data in an ordered fashion, such as the example in Figure 3-2. In this scenario, reading those five rows will not require much more effort, even if the table grows to be significantly larger.

Analytic queries, though, are quite different. They often aggregate a select few columns, but do so across many rows. Consider a typical OLAP query against the example table where a single column is aggregated across a large portion of the table that happens to include all of the rows shown here. Figure 3-3 shows how this would look.

Row 1-1	Row 1-2	Row 1-3	Row 1-4	Row 1-5	Row 2-1	Row 2-2	Row 2-3	Row 2-4
Row 2-5	Row 3-1	Row 3-2	Row 3-3	Row 3-4	Row 3-5	Row 4-1	Row 4-2	Row 4-3
Row 4-4	Row 4-5	Row 5-1	Row 5-2	Row 5-3	Row 5-4	Row 5-5	Row 6-1	Row 6-2
Row 6-3	Row 6-4	Row 6-5	Row 7-1	Row 7-2	Row 7-3	Row 7-4	Row 7-5	Row 8-1
Row 8-2	Row 8-3	Row 8-4	Row 8-5	Row 9-1	Row 9-2	Row 9-3	Row 9-4	Row 9-5

Figure 3-3. *An analytic query aggregating a single column from a sample table*

The physical layout of rows shows that a query requiring only column 2 needs to also read the adjacent columns, even if not needed. The following is an example of a query that accesses a large amount of data in a table, but only aggregates a single column.

```
SELECT
        SUM(Quantity) AS Total_Quantity
FROM Sales.OrderLines
WHERE OrderID >= 1
AND OrderID < 10000;
```

Even though only a single column was summed, any page that contains values for that column will need to be read into memory. Even a covering nonclustered index would still necessitate reading data for each row, though the number of pages read can be reduced in that fashion.

Now consider a larger table with 50 million rows that is stored on 250,000 pages using a clustered rowstore index. The transactional query demonstrated in Figure 3-2 would still only read 5 rows that are stored consecutively and could therefore ignore most of the remaining 249,995 rows and the pages they are stored on. Additional rows would be read that happened to be stored on the same page(s) as those five rows, but the added burden of that data is measured in kilobytes and is comparatively insignificant.

The analytic query presented in Figure 3-3 aggregates only a single column, but does so across many rows. If the requested order data spans one-fourth of the table, then processing this query in the transactional table would force SQL Server to read about one-fourth of the pages in the table, since the values for column 2 are dispersed within each row throughout the table. Regardless of the filter used that reduces the row count needed for the query, every page in the range specified by the filter would need to be read.

As an analytic table continues to grow and spans billions of rows and/or terabytes of storage (or more), the ability to read large swaths of its data becomes too slow and resource intensive to be realistic. A better solution is needed that allows analytic queries to read column data without the rest of the underlying columns being brought along for the ride.

Introducing Columnstore Indexes

The technology needed to solve this problem has existed in some form for a long time. Applications such as SQL Server Analysis Services and PowerPivot have used columnar data storage formats for years, but their implementation was hidden from view of the user.

Columnstore indexes allow for data to be stored in tables in an optimal analytic format that provides many valuable benefits, such as

- Ability to scale to any table size

- Increase query speeds by 10–100 times

- Exceptional compression ratios, saving storage and memory

- Natively supported by SQL Server

- Can take advantage of bulk loading for fast write speeds

While this may sound like a sales pitch, there are no exaggerations here. Comparing a large analytic data set stored in a classic rowstore clustered index vs. a columnstore indexed table yields vast differences in storage and performance that will be demonstrated and quantified throughout the remainder of this book.

Note that all demonstrations of columnstore indexes in this book are tested on SQL Server 2019. Those running an earlier version should test thoroughly before implementing any suggestions in this book as the features available may be different.

Figure 3-4 illustrates how data stored in a columnstore index is stored using the same table from Figure 3-1.

Row 1-1	Row 2-1	Row 3-1	Row 4-1	Row 5-1	Row 6-1	Row 7-1	Row 8-1	Row 9-1
Row 1-2	Row 2-2	Row 3-2	Row 4-2	Row 5-2	Row 6-2	Row 7-2	Row 8-2	Row 9-2
Row 1-3	Row 2-3	Row 3-3	Row 4-3	Row 5-3	Row 6-3	Row 7-3	Row 8-3	Row 9-3
Row 1-4	Row 2-4	Row 3-4	Row 4-4	Row 5-4	Row 6-4	Row 7-4	Row 8-4	Row 9-4
Row 1-5	Row 2-5	Row 3-5	Row 4-5	Row 5-5	Row 6-5	Row 7-5	Row 8-5	Row 9-5

Figure 3-4. Illustration of data storage in a clustered columnstore index

Note the critical difference: Data is ordered by column rather than by row. Each value for column 1 is stored together in a single structure, whereas each other column is stored in its own sets of pages. In the rowstore table shown in Figure 3-3, a single column was aggregated, but every page had to be read in order to return data for that one column.

Figure 3-5 shows the same query against an analytic columnstore indexed table.

Row 1-1	Row 2-1	Row 3-1	Row 4-1	Row 5-1	Row 6-1	Row 7-1	Row 8-1	Row 9-1
Row 1-2	Row 2-2	Row 3-2	Row 4-2	Row 5-2	Row 6-2	Row 7-2	Row 8-2	Row 9-2
Row 1-3	Row 2-3	Row 3-3	Row 4-3	Row 5-3	Row 6-3	Row 7-3	Row 8-3	Row 9-3
Row 1-4	Row 2-4	Row 3-4	Row 4-4	Row 5-4	Row 6-4	Row 7-4	Row 8-4	Row 9-4
Row 1-5	Row 2-5	Row 3-5	Row 4-5	Row 5-5	Row 6-5	Row 7-5	Row 8-5	Row 9-5

Figure 3-5. *Aggregating a single column against a columnstore index*

Because data is grouped physically by column, it is no longer necessary to read the entire table to return a single aggregated column. The other four columns can be ignored. This greatly reduces reads against storage systems and reduces memory usage as less pages need to be read into memory. For each new row that is inserted into this table, only a single additional value for the second column needs to be read.

A significant benefit of this data structure is that compression becomes more effective. A set of values for a single column will tend to have more repeated values that will more easily compress, whereas values from different columns are less likely to overlap and compress well. Better compression means more data can fit on pages, saving additional storage and memory.

An important clarification on columnstore indexes is that they are not "just another index." They are not comparable to nonclustered rowstore indexes, XML indexes, spatial indexes, memory-optimized indexes, or other types of indexing included in SQL Server. They comprise a unique architecture that provides benefits well beyond what a typical index can deliver.

Note that throughout this book, when not otherwise specified, all demonstrations and discussion will reference clustered columnstore indexes. Chapter 11 will delve into non-clustered columnstore indexes in more detail.

Benefits of Columnstore Indexes in SQL Server

There are many reasons why columnstore indexes can be an ideal solution for storing large analytic data. They cross a variety of areas from cost to convenience to speed and illustrate how a seemingly simple feature can provide exceptional value with a low time and resource cost to implement. This is not a complete list of the benefits of columnstore indexes, but highlights the keys to performance and efficiency that make them attractive for use with analytic data. The remainder of this book will dive into greater detail about the benefits and optimal use cases for columnstore indexes.

Native Analytic Data in SQL Server

One of the greatest benefits of columnstore indexes is that they store analytic data directly in SQL Server without any added licensing or configuration changes. Similarly, no hardware or software changes are required to begin testing or implementing columnstore indexes.

A rowstore table containing analytic data could be converted to use a columnstore index, with the entire process taking place on the same SQL Server database instance or even as an in-place index swap. This can allow for easy testing, validation, and implementation, when ready.

Because columnstore indexes are a feature that is core to analytic data storage in SQL Server, it is updated with each new version. Each update provides new functionality and ways in which reading or writing columnstore indexes can become faster and more efficient. The following document from Microsoft outlines in detail the columnstore index features available in each version of SQL Server since their inception:

```
https://docs.microsoft.com/en-us/sql/relational-databases/indexes/
columnstore-indexes-what-s-new
```

The list is quite extensive and shows how columnstore indexes have evolved from an inflexible read-only structure into one rich in features and optimizations.

Storing data natively in SQL Server means there is no need for third-party products, no costly migrations, and no need to configure new hardware and software. The time required to implement them is less guided by technology and more by typical development and quality assurance needs. When building a project plan for the storage

and maintenance of analytic data, factoring in these resource costs can help in making an accurate,
fact-based decision. The following is a summary of these considerations:

- Need to purchase/license new hardware to support analytic data

- Cost of software licenses for analytics software and any supporting software

- Cost of computing resources, whether on premises or in the cloud

- Time required to architect, develop test, and implement analytic data solution

- Resources needed to educate people on how to use the new solution

Quantifying each of these factors can assist in comparing and contrasting different solutions and will generally provide favorable results for an organization that already uses SQL Server for its transactional data storage.

Scalability

Given the rapid rate in which analytic data can grow, any data structures used to store it must be capable of efficiently servicing OLAP workloads, even when data depth or width increases unexpectedly fast over time.

The ability for an analytic data storage solution to scale has many important benefits, including

- Ensure high performance, even during periods of rapid data growth

- Avoid costly migrations to new technologies

- Avoid disruptions to reporting/analytic services

- Reduce maintenance and downtime

- Reduce the need for hardware upgrades

For an OLAP solution to be effective, it needs to be fast and efficient with one thousand rows, one million rows, one billion rows, or more. If a system is destined to become inefficient when it gets large, then it is also destined to fail.

The growth of analytic data is a metric worthy of measuring and revisiting periodically to fully understand its long-term resource requirements. OLAP data rarely gets smaller, and its growth rate rarely decreases. This growth is ultimately tied to two measurements for any given organization:

- Growth

- Complexity

As an organization grows and serves more customers, those customers will generate more data. Similarly, organizational growth almost always leads to both technical and nontechnical processes becoming more complex. This complexity may manifest itself in increased software features, more processes that require tracking, or requests for more types of data to maintain and crunch over time.

The rate of growth of data can be summarized as follows:

$$1.00 * N * G * C$$

In this representation, the letters denote the following:

- **N = Natural Growth:** This is the growth of data that occurs currently. If nothing else changes and no external influences adjust the data growth rate, then this would be the only factor needed to predict future data growth. This can be measured in rows per unit time and also as an increase in physical data size as average bytes per row times rows per unit time.

- **G = Data Growth:** Natural growth provides a baseline of how much data will be added to a table or database over time. This growth is rarely linear, though. New customers, increased sample frequency, and other factors will account for additional growth above and beyond the current baseline. This can also be measured in rows per unit time or as physical data usage per unit time.

- **C = Increased Complexity:** This accounts for more columns being added to tables as well as new tables being created and populated. This also increases the amount of data that needs to flow (via more entities) from transactional systems into the target analytic system. This is challenging to measure, but can be estimated as a measure of new metrics over time. That is, on average how many new metrics per unit time will be added to an analytic data source. This can be approximated in storage units as soon as the data types for new metrics are known.

Each of these factors is defined here as linear in nature, but may not be linear in actuality. Therefore, they should be revisited regularly to ensure that unexpected changes in growth are accounted for when predicting future data size. Linear approximations per unit time can be used to approximate nonlinear growth so long as those approximations remain updated with current and future trends.

To provide a sample of the preceding formula, consider an analytic table that contains 100,000,000 rows, currently grows by 250,000 rows per day, and is expected to see its growth accelerate by an additional 25% per year, but not see any new dimensions added in the foreseeable future. The estimated row count in 1 year would be given by

$$1.00 * N * G * C * Row\ Count = 1.00 * 1.9125 * 1.25 * 1.00 * 100,000,000 = 239,062,500\ rows\ for\ the\ upcoming\ year.$$

$$1.00 * N * G * C * Row\ Count = 1.00 * 1.9125 * 1.25 * 1.00 * 239,062,500 = 571,508,789\ rows\ for\ the\ 2nd\ year.$$

$$1.00 * N * G * C * Row\ Count = 1.00 * 1.9125 * 1.25 * 1.00 * 571,508,789 = 1,366,263,198\ rows\ for\ the\ 3rd\ year.$$

Note how quickly the added acceleration grew this data – from 100 million rows to over 1.3 billion rows in 3 years! 1.9125 was calculated as the annual growth factor by multiplying 250,000 rows per day by 365 days per year.

To summarize, any technology that manages analytic data needs to be capable of efficient data access given that typical data growth can cause data sizes to balloon far faster than conventional wisdom might suggest. The architecture of columnstore indexes will be discussed in detail in Chapter 4 and will lay the foundation for explaining why they can scale so effectively for rapidly growing data.

Exceptional Compression

Any analytic data store needs to take full advantage of compression to make its data as compact as possible. Columnstore indexes use multiple compression algorithms to achieve impressively high compression ratios. This can result in data that is 10–100 times smaller than it would be in an uncompressed table.

Compressing data by column rather than row is inherently more efficient for a number of reasons:

- A single column contains values of the same data type, improving the chances of values being repeated.

- Dimensions often have many repeated values and will compress exceptionally well.

- Data is typically created sequentially, ordered by time. Rows that are in close proximity to other rows from similar time periods will tend to contain more similar data and compress better than with data from much earlier or later in time.

Chapter 5 dives into more detail on columnstore index compression and demonstrates how effective these compression algorithms are and why they are crucial to optimal analytic query performance.

Faster Analytic Reads

First and foremost, columnstore indexes are built to provide highly performant analytic query speeds. Whether accessing data from structured stored procedures and code or from ad hoc analytics and visualization, the compact and segmented columnstore index structure allows for the requested data to be returned quickly and efficiently. This is true even when large row counts are scanned.

Faster Data Loads

When data is written millions of rows at a time, processes need to exist that allow for that data to be written as quickly as possible. A fully logged process optimized for transactional data will not perform adequately for data of this size.

Columnstore indexes can make full use of the SQL Server bulk load API and can achieve write speeds far faster than other processes available in SQL Server, and in many other products. Data loads can execute faster, improving OLAP availability and allowing new data to appear more quickly. In addition, the impact of data loads on system resources such as the transaction log and on backups is minimized, ensuring that large volumes of data can be written in short spans of time without the pitfalls of doing so on a fully logged OLTP table.

Chapter 8 will fully explore how data is written to columnstore indexes, including performance measurements, resource consumption details, and best practices for loading data as efficiently as possible.

Analytic data requires a versatile, scalable, and performant solution. Columnstore indexes provide an ideal data structure to create and analyze analytic data, and that can manage data growth over time with ease.

The remainder of this book will discuss columnstore indexes in exhaustive detail, providing architectural details, demonstrations, best practices, and tools that can improve their use.

CHAPTER 4

Columnstore Index Architecture

A solid understanding of the architecture of columnstore indexes is necessary to make optimal use of them. Best practices, query patterns, maintenance, and troubleshooting are all based on the internal structure of columnstore indexes. This chapter will focus on these architectural components, providing the foundation for the rest of this book.

Sample Data

To demonstrate the topics presented throughout this book, a sample data set will be created based on the *Fact.Sale* table in the *WideWorldImportersDW* database.

The data set can be generated using the query in Listing 4-1.

Listing 4-1. Query Used to Generate a Data Set for Use in Columnstore Index Testing

```
SELECT
    Sale.[Sale Key], Sale.[City Key], Sale.[Customer Key], Sale.[Bill
    To Customer Key], Sale.[Stock Item Key], Sale.[Invoice Date Key],
    Sale.[Delivery Date Key],Sale.[Salesperson Key], Sale.[WWI
    Invoice ID], Sale.Description, Sale.Package, Sale.Quantity,
    Sale.[Unit Price], Sale.[Tax Rate],
    Sale.[Total Excluding Tax], Sale.[Tax Amount], Sale.Profit,
    Sale.[Total Including Tax], Sale.[Total Dry Items],
    Sale.[Total Chiller Items], Sale.[Lineage Key]
```

© Edward Pollack 2022

E. Pollack, *Analytics Optimization with Columnstore Indexes in Microsoft SQL Server*,
https://doi.org/10.1007/978-1-4842-8048-5_4

```
FROM Fact.Sale
CROSS JOIN
Dimension.City
WHERE City.[City Key] >= 1 AND City.[City Key] <= 110;
```

This generates 25,109,150 rows of data spanning invoice date ranges of 1/1/2013 through 5/31/2016. While this data is not massive, it is large enough for suitable demonstrations without being cumbersome to those that wish to replicate it at home. This data set will be reused in future chapters, being placed into a number of test tables to illustrate a wide variety of topics related to columnstore indexes, OLAP performance, and database architecture.

For this chapter, the data will be loaded into a table without any indexes, and a columnstore index added at the end, as seen in Listing 4-2.

Listing 4-2. Script That Creates and Populates a Columnstore Index Test Table

```
CREATE TABLE Fact.Sale_CCI
(       [Sale Key] [bigint] NOT NULL,
        [City Key] [int] NOT NULL,
        [Customer Key] [int] NOT NULL,
        [Bill To Customer Key] [int] NOT NULL,
        [Stock Item Key] [int] NOT NULL,
        [Invoice Date Key] [date] NOT NULL,
        [Delivery Date Key] [date] NULL,
        [Salesperson Key] [int] NOT NULL,
        [WWI Invoice ID] [int] NOT NULL,
        [Description] [nvarchar](100) NOT NULL,
        [Package] [nvarchar](50) NOT NULL,
        [Quantity] [int] NOT NULL,
        [Unit Price] [decimal](18, 2) NOT NULL,
        [Tax Rate] [decimal](18, 3) NOT NULL,
        [Total Excluding Tax] [decimal](18, 2) NOT NULL,
        [Tax Amount] [decimal](18, 2) NOT NULL,
        [Profit] [decimal](18, 2) NOT NULL,
        [Total Including Tax] [decimal](18, 2) NOT NULL,
```

```
        [Total Dry Items] [int] NOT NULL,
        [Total Chiller Items] [int] NOT NULL,
        [Lineage Key] [int] NOT NULL);

INSERT INTO Fact.Sale_CCI
        ([Sale Key], [City Key], [Customer Key], [Bill To Customer Key],
        [Stock Item Key], [Invoice Date Key], [Delivery Date Key],
         [Salesperson Key], [WWI Invoice ID], Description, Package, Quantity,
         [Unit Price], [Tax Rate], [Total Excluding Tax], [Tax Amount],
         Profit, [Total Including Tax], [Total Dry Items],
         [Total Chiller Items], [Lineage Key])
SELECT
        Sale.[Sale Key], Sale.[City Key], Sale.[Customer Key], Sale.[Bill To
        Customer Key], Sale.[Stock Item Key], Sale.[Invoice Date Key],
        Sale.[Delivery Date Key], Sale.[Salesperson Key], Sale.[WWI
        Invoice ID], Sale.Description, Sale.Package, Sale.Quantity,
        Sale.[Unit Price], Sale.[Tax Rate],
        Sale.[Total Excluding Tax], Sale.[Tax Amount], Sale.Profit,
        Sale.[Total Including Tax], Sale.[Total Dry Items],
        Sale.[Total Chiller Items], Sale.[Lineage Key]
FROM fact.Sale
CROSS JOIN
Dimension.City
WHERE City.[City Key] >= 1 AND City.[City Key] <= 110;

-- Create a columnstore index on the table.
CREATE CLUSTERED COLUMNSTORE INDEX CCI_fact_sale_CCI ON fact.Sale_CCI;
```

The size and shape of this data can be confirmed with a simple query:

```
SELECT
        COUNT(*),
        MIN([Invoice Date Key]),
        MAX([Invoice Date Key])
FROM fact.Sale_CCI;
```

The results are shown in Figure 4-1.

▦ Results	▤ Messages	
	(No column name)	(No column name)	(No column name)
1	25109150	2013-01-01	2016-05-31

Figure 4-1. *Query results showing the size and date range for a set of test data*

Rowgroups and Segments

Analytic data cannot be stored in one large contiguous structure. While each column is compressed and stored separately, the data within those columns needs to be grouped and compressed separately. Each compressed unit is what is read into memory. If that unit is too small, then the storage and management of a multitude of compressed structures would be expensive, and its compression poor. Conversely, if the number of rows in each unit is too large, then the amount of data that needs to be read into memory to satisfy queries would also become too large.

Columnstore indexes group rows into units of 2^{20} (1,048,576) rows that are called *rowgroups*. Each column within that rowgroup is individually compressed into the fundamental unit of a columnstore index called a *segment*. This structure can be visualized using the representation in Figure 4-2.

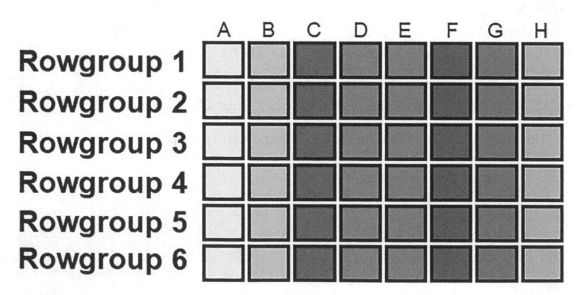

Figure 4-2. *Rowgroups and segments within a columnstore index*

Note that columnstore indexes are not built on binary tree structures like clustered and nonclustered rowstore indexes are. Instead, each rowgroup contains a set of compressed segments, one per column in a table. The example in Figure 4-2 is for a table with eight columns and up to $6*2^{20}$ rows, containing a total of 48 segments (one segment per column per rowgroup). The only significant architectural convention shared between rowstore and columnstore indexes are their use of 8KB pages to store their data.

Rowgroups are created and managed automatically as data is created in a columnstore index. There is no cap on the number of rowgroups that can exist, nor are there limits on the count of segments within the index. Because a rowgroup contains up to 2^{20} rows, a table should have many more rows than this to make optimal use of a columnstore index. If a table has 500k rows, then it is likely to all be stored in a single rowgroup. As a result, any query requiring data from the table would need to read segments that contain data for all rows in the table. For a table to make effective use of a columnstore index, it should have at least 5 million or 10 million rows so that it can be broken into separate rowgroups of which not all need to be read each time a query is issued against it.

The rowgroups within a columnstore index may be viewed using the dynamic management view *sys.column_store_row_groups*. The query in Listing 4-3 returns rowgroup metadata for the columnstore index created earlier in this chapter.

Listing 4-3. Script to Return Basic Rowgroup Metadata for a Columnstore Index

```
SELECT
        tables.name AS table_name,
        indexes.name AS index_name,
        column_store_row_groups.partition_number,
        column_store_row_groups.row_group_id,
        column_store_row_groups.state_description,
                column_store_row_groups.total_rows,
        column_store_row_groups.deleted_rows,
        column_store_row_groups.size_in_bytes
FROM sys.column_store_row_groups
INNER JOIN sys.indexes
ON indexes.index_id = column_store_row_groups.index_id
AND indexes.object_id = column_store_row_groups.object_id
INNER JOIN sys.tables
```

```
ON tables.object_id = indexes.object_id
WHERE tables.name = 'Sale_CCI'
ORDER BY tables.object_id, indexes.index_id,
column_store_row_groups.row_group_id;
```

The results of this query can be found in Figure 4-3.

	table_name	index_name	partition_number	row_group_id	state_description	total_rows	deleted_rows	size_in_bytes
1	Sale_CCI	CCI_fact_sale_CCI	1	0	COMPRESSED	1048576	0	12982576
2	Sale_CCI	CCI_fact_sale_CCI	1	1	COMPRESSED	1048576	0	13036096
3	Sale_CCI	CCI_fact_sale_CCI	1	2	COMPRESSED	1048576	0	13010760
4	Sale_CCI	CCI_fact_sale_CCI	1	3	COMPRESSED	1048576	0	13169120
5	Sale_CCI	CCI_fact_sale_CCI	1	4	COMPRESSED	1048576	0	13270896
6	Sale_CCI	CCI_fact_sale_CCI	1	5	COMPRESSED	1048576	0	12961528
7	Sale_CCI	CCI_fact_sale_CCI	1	6	COMPRESSED	1048576	0	13265848
8	Sale_CCI	CCI_fact_sale_CCI	1	7	COMPRESSED	1048576	0	13026080

Figure 4-3. *Rowgroup metadata for fact.Sale_CCI*

By joining in other system views, such as *sys.indexes* and *sys.tables*, it is possible to return additional information about the table that the columnstore index resides on. *sys.column_store_row_groups* contains some additional columns of interest, such as the compression status of the rowgroup, the row count, and its size. Note that the selection of eight rowgroups in Figure 4-3 all contain the maximum number of rows allowed in a rowgroup, 2^{20}.

Using rowgroup metadata allows the user to quickly measure the size of a columnstore index and gain a basic understanding of its structure.

Within each rowgroup are segments for each column in the table. A dynamic management view also exists that provides details about compressed segments: *sys.column_store_segments*. Listing 4-4 provides a query that returns information from this view, including joins back to the parent table and column for each segment.

Listing 4-4. Script to Return Basic Segment Metadata for a Columnstore Index

```
SELECT
        tables.name AS table_name,
        indexes.name AS index_name,
        columns.name AS column_name,
        partitions.partition_number,
```

```
        column_store_segments.row_count,
        column_store_segments.has_nulls,
        column_store_segments.min_data_id,
        column_store_segments.max_data_id,
        column_store_segments.on_disk_size
FROM sys.column_store_segments
INNER JOIN sys.partitions
ON column_store_segments.hobt_id = partitions.hobt_id
INNER JOIN sys.indexes
ON indexes.index_id = partitions.index_id
AND indexes.object_id = partitions.object_id
INNER JOIN sys.tables
ON tables.object_id = indexes.object_id
INNER JOIN sys.columns
ON tables.object_id = columns.object_id
AND column_store_segments.column_id = columns.column_id
WHERE tables.name = 'Sale_CCI'
ORDER BY columns.name, column_store_segments.segment_id;
```

Figure 4-4 contains a sample of the results.

	table_name	index_name	column_name	partition_number	row_count	has_nulls	min_data_id	max_data_id	on_disk_size
22	Sale_CCI	CCI_fact_sale_CCI	Bill To Customer Key	1	1048576	0	0	202	2920
23	Sale_CCI	CCI_fact_sale_CCI	Bill To Customer Key	1	1048576	0	0	202	2744
24	Sale_CCI	CCI_fact_sale_CCI	Bill To Customer Key	1	16228	0	1	202	1704
25	Sale_CCI	CCI_fact_sale_CCI	Bill To Customer Key	1	975674	0	0	202	3424
26	Sale_CCI	CCI_fact_sale_CCI	City Key	1	1048576	0	37955	115719	1678312
27	Sale_CCI	CCI_fact_sale_CCI	City Key	1	1048576	0	37955	115719	1678312
28	Sale_CCI	CCI_fact_sale_CCI	City Key	1	1048576	0	37955	115719	1678312

Figure 4-4. *Segment metadata for fact.Sale_CCI*

The row count returned by the query is equal to the total number of segments in the index, which is subsequently equal to the count of rowgroups multiplied by the number of columns in the table. In addition to the row count contained in each segment and its size on disk, there are details given as to whether the segment has NULLs in it, and *min_data_id*/*max_data_id*, which provide dictionary lookups for values contained in the segment. Details about dictionaries and how they work will be provided alongside the discussion of compression in Chapter 5.

The Delta Store

Writing data to highly compressed segments is a resource-intensive process. The resources required to decompress a set of segments, write additional data to them, compress them, and update metadata is not trivial. The effort to write a million rows to one rowgroup is comprised of the effort needed to decompress, write, and compress all segments in the rowgroup. The effort to write a million rows one at a time to that rowgroup would be comparable to the same process being executed one million times.

Because of this, processes that frequently write small numbers of rows need a way to manage those writes so that a columnstore index is not consuming all of a server's resources decompressing, writing, and re-creating segments. The delta store is a set of clustered rowstore indexes that temporarily store small writes alongside the columnstore index. Each delta rowgroup is one of these clustered indexes. Changes accumulate in the delta store until its row count reaches a threshold (2^{20} rows per delta rowgroup) and is pushed all at once into the columnstore index.

The delta store is maintained automatically by SQL Server. An asynchronous background process called the tuple mover manages the movement of data from delta store into columnstore index. While operators can run maintenance scripts to influence the behavior of the delta store, doing so is not necessary for using columnstore indexes. More information on columnstore maintenance can be found in Chapter 14.

When queries are executed against a columnstore index, the contents of the delta store are read alongside the compressed segments that are needed. While the delta store is comprised of classic rowstore indexes, its size is generally very small compared to the compressed portion of the columnstore index; therefore, reading it is generally not detrimental to performance. The benefit of the delta store is that it greatly reduces the computing resources needed to write smaller batches of data to a columnstore index and ensures that frequent smaller writes do not become unscalable bottlenecks during a data load, maintenance, or software release process.

The basic flow of data can be shown in Figure 4-5.

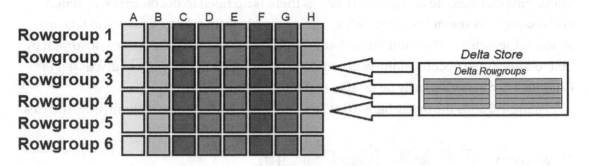

Figure 4-5. *Flow of data from the delta store into a columnstore index*

Note that the delta store is not used to manage all INSERT operations against a columnstore index. Chapter 8 discusses in detail how bulk load processes are used to greatly speed up larger INSERT operations.

The Delete Bitmap

Deletion of data from a columnstore index poses similar challenges to those solved for inserts by the delta store. Deleting a single row would require a compressed segment per column to be decompressed, modified, and recompressed. This is inherently expensive and becomes prohibitively costly when the number of rowgroups affected increases.

SQL Server needs to be able to delete data from a columnstore index quickly and without having a prolonged negative impact on server performance. To accomplish this, data is not physically deleted from a columnstore index when a DELETE statement is executed. Instead, the deleted status of the affected rows is written to a structure called the delete bitmap.

Only one delete bitmap can exist per partition within a columnstore index, and its purpose is to track which rows are deleted (if any). When rows are deleted from a columnstore index, the delete bitmap is updated to indicate the deletion. The corresponding rows within the columnstore index are not modified in any way. These soft deletes allow DELETE operations to execute quickly and not become burdensome to data loads or maintenance processes.

When a query reads data from a columnstore index, the contents of the delete bitmap are also read and any rows that are flagged as deleted will be omitted from the results. The delete bitmap is also a clustered rowstore index that exists side by side with the columnstore index. The biggest upside of having a delete bitmap is that DELETE operations can execute exceptionally fast as there is no need to decompress, update, and recompress segments in the index. The downside is that deleted rows still take up space in the index and are not immediately removed. Over time, the space consumed by deleted rows may become nontrivial, at which point index maintenance (discussed in Chapter 14) can periodically be used to reclaim this space.

Figure 4-6 adds the delete bitmap into the architecture diagram of columnstore indexes.

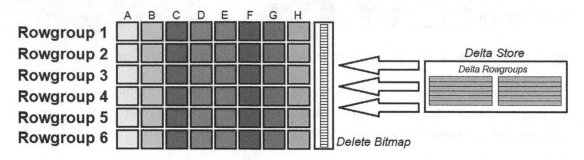

Figure 4-6. *Adding the delete bitmap into the columnstore index architecture*

Both the delete bitmap and the delta store are components of a columnstore index that only exist when needed. If no deleted rows exist, then there will be no delete bitmap to overlay onto the compressed rowgroups. Similarly, an empty delta store will not need to be checked when queries are executed against the columnstore index. These components exist when necessary, but otherwise will have no impact on performance when not needed.

Nonclustered Columnstore Index Architecture

The architecture of nonclustered columnstore indexes is quite similar to that of clustered indexes. Instead of being the primary storage mechanism for a table, the nonclustered columnstore index is an additional index structure that exists alongside a clustered rowstore index.

An important difference is that a column list may be specified on the nonclustered columnstore index, allowing for more targeted optimization projects. Additionally, filters may be applied to nonclustered columnstore indexes, allowing for data to be targeted based on whether it is hot, warm, or cold, thus decreasing index size and the cost to write to the index.

Note the following brief definitions for the usage of hot/warm/cold data:

- **Hot Data:** Real time and actively used by a system with regular reads, writes, and high concurrency. Availability is expected to be high and latency should be very low.

- **Warm Data:** Represents data that is used less frequently. Availability is still expected to be high, but there is a tolerance for more latency when retrieving it.

- **Cold Data:** Represents infrequently accessed data that is old, archived, or maintained for posterity. Availability is more flexible for cold data and high latency is tolerable. Concurrency is very low for cold data.

Organizations will label data in a range from hot to cold, and the specifics will vary depending on how their data is used. Figure 4-7 shows the interaction between a clustered rowstore index and a filtered nonclustered columnstore index.

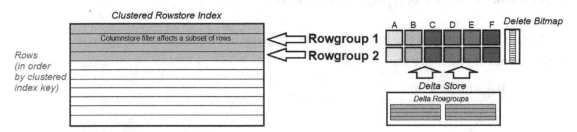

Figure 4-7. *A clustered rowstore index with a filtered nonclustered columnstore index*

Note that the purpose of a nonclustered columnstore index is to provide real-time analytics against a transactional table, which requires careful consideration prior to implementing. Chapter 12 will dive into more detail with regard to nonclustered columnstore indexes including options, demonstrations, and optimal use cases.

Physical Data on Pages

Thus far, the discussion of architecture has occurred at a logical level. That is, rowgroups, segments, delta store, and the delete bitmap have been presented as generic containers for columns of data. The physical storage of columnstore indexes on pages helps in fully appreciating how they can efficiently service analytic queries.

All data in SQL Server that is not stored in memory-optimized structures is stored on 8 kilobyte pages. These pages reside on physical storage and are read into memory when needed as-is. If a page is compressed, it remains compressed until its data is needed. Whether a page is in a rowstore or columnstore index, it is read into memory in the same fashion. The delete bitmap and delta store are also maintained on pages and read into memory as needed.

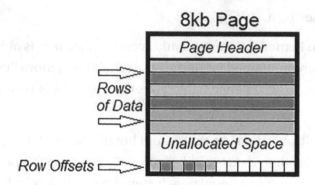

Figure 4-8. *Structure of a page in SQL Server*

Figure 4-8 illustrates the basic structure of a page in SQL Server. The primary components of pages are the

- Page header

- Data

- Row offsets

The page header contains basic information about the page such as the object that owns it, the type of data stored in it, and the amount of unallocated space available for additional data to be written.

The data rows are the actual data stored on the page. This may be the physical data in a table (the clustered index or heap), index entries, or a variety of other contents that are available under a variety of circumstances. For this discussion of columnstore and rowstore indexes, the data and index data are all that is of immediate concern.

Row offsets store the position that each row starts, allowing SQL Server to locate the data for any given row once a page is read into memory.

When data is stored in clustered indexes on a rowstore table, data is written to pages row by row. That is, each column is written sequentially on the page for each row one after another, as seen in Figure 4-9.

SQL Server Page: Row Data

Row1Col1	Row1Col2	Row1Col3	Row1Col4	Row1Col5
Row1Col6	Row2Col1	Row2Col2	Row2Col3	Row2Col4
Row2Col5	Row2Col6	Row3Col1	Row3Col2	Row3Col3
Row3Col4	Row3Col5	Row3Col6	Row4Col1	Row4Col2
Row4Col3	Row4Col4	Row4Col5	Row4Col6	Row5Col1
Row5Col2	Row5Col3	Row5Col4	Row5Col5	Row5Col6
Row6Col1	Row6Col2	Row6Col3	Row6Col4	Row6Col5
Row6Col6	Row7Col1	Row7Col2	Row7Col3	Row7Col4

Figure 4-9. *Storage of rowstore data on a page in SQL Server*

This table has six columns, and they are written sequentially for each row, one after another. SQL Server will continue to write rows sequentially for this table to the same page until it runs out of space, at which point a new page will be allocated to the table and the data will continue there.

This structure is optimized for reading or writing small range lookups that consist of a set of sequential rows. For example, a query that returned some (or all) of columns from rows two through five would only need to read the single page shown in Figure 4-9. If additional rows were required that were on other pages, then those pages would also be read into memory to satisfy the query.

A clustered or nonclustered rowstore index writes its binary tree structure to pages as a sequence of pointers. The root level is written first, followed by intermediate levels that ultimately point to the underlying data at the leaf level of the index. Each level of the index includes the clustered index keys, which are used to organize and link between levels of the index. This structure is also optimized for seeking single or small contiguous ranges of rows. For queries like this, less intermediate levels of an index need to be read, reducing the number of pages needed to satisfy a query. Figure 4-10 shows a visualization of a clustered rowstore (binary tree) index.

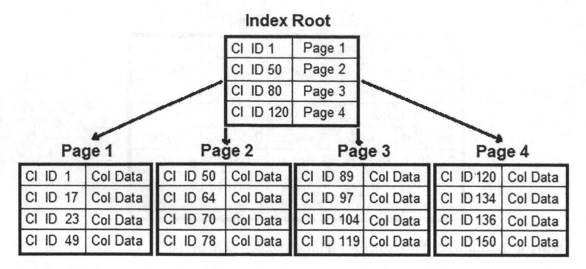

Figure 4-10. *Structure of a clustered rowstore index*

Because this is the clustered index, the leaf levels contain the column data for each row that is referenced by the clustered index. In a nonclustered index, the lowest level of the index would contain pointers to the target data, to be used for key lookups. Similarly, the leaf level of a nonclustered index would also contain any included columns that are defined on the index.

A query that needed to read clustered index ID values between 25 and 75 could do so by reading the index root page first and then pages 1 and 2. A query reading only clustered index ID value 136 would read the index root and page 4.

In a columnstore index, there is no binary tree structure. A clustered columnstore index is written as a sequence of compressed segments on as many pages as is needed to support them. Figure 4-11 illustrates how this would look for a single page of a columnstore index.

SQL Server Page: Column Data

Row1Col1	Row2Col1	Row3Col1	Row4Col1	Row5Col1
Row6Col1	Row7Col1	Row8Col1	Row9Col1	Row10Col1
Row11Col1	Row12Col1	Row13Col1	Row14Col1	Row15Col1
Row16Col1	Row17Col1	Row18Col1	Row19Col1	Row20Col1
Row21Col1	Row22Col1	Row23Col1	Row24Col1	Row25Col1
Row26Col1	Row27Col1	Row28Col1	Row29Col1	Row30Col1
Row31Col1	Row32Col1	Row33Col1	Row34Col1	Row35Col1
Row36Col1	Row37Col1	Row38Col1	Row39Col1	Row40Col1

Figure 4-11. *Storage of columnstore data on a page in SQL Server*

Note that this data, a subset of a compressed segment, contains sequential values for the same column. This sequence would continue until the end of the rowgroup, at which point a new segment would begin, or if it were the last of the rowgroups, the next column would begin.

A query that aggregated values for the first 40 rows of column 1 could retrieve data very efficiently and do so by simply reading this single page. In a rowstore index for the same table, it would be necessary to scan data for all columns in those 40 rows and read those pages into memory. For a table with 20 columns, that would require 20 times the effort.

Summarizing Differences

The key to understanding the difference between the architecture of rowstore indexes and columnstore indexes is to consider the logical storage of data vs. the physical storage of data.

Rowstore indexes store data physically in order by row and then column. Data is logically accessible as it is ordered by row. Therefore, this architecture is optimized for queries that seek a sequence or limited subset of rows. Binary tree indexes provide a speedy way to search for that data based on other columns that the clustered index does not order the data by.

Columnstore indexes store data physically grouped by column, but ordered by row. This convention allows for filters to limit the number of rows returned and column groupings to reduce the pages read as the number of columns needed for a query decreases. This allows queries to read significantly more rows, but maintain excellent performance when the column list is limited. Chapter 10 explores how the order of data within a columnstore index can be controlled to add an additional dimension of filtering so that data can be sliced both horizontally and vertically.

CHAPTER 5

Columnstore Compression

There are many features that allow columnstore indexes to perform exceptionally well for analytic workloads. Of those features, compression is the most significant driver in both performance and resource consumption. Understanding how SQL Server implements compression in columnstore indexes and how different algorithms are used to shrink the size of this data allows for optimal architecture and implementation of analytic data storage in SQL Server.

Basics of Columnstore Compression

Data written to segments within a columnstore index is heavily compressed prior to storage. The delta store helps buffer incoming writes to a columnstore index, ensuring that the frequency that segments need to be written is not high enough to negatively impact server performance.

Without any additional optimizations, data stored by columns rather than rows will be quite efficient to compress. This is because the values within a given column will usually repeat often and therefore can be more easily compressed that data that repeats less often. Typical analytic tables will contain many rows, but generally repetitive columns, such as

- Entity types
- Money
- Dates
- Counts
- Repetitive dimensions

49

© Edward Pollack 2022
E. Pollack, *Analytics Optimization with Columnstore Indexes in Microsoft SQL Server*,
https://doi.org/10.1007/978-1-4842-8048-5_5

Consider the three columns illustrated in Figure 5-1.

Date: 9/1/2021, 9/1/2021, 9/1/2021, 9/1/2021, 9/1/2021, 9/2/2021, 9/2/2021, 9/2/2021, 9/2/2021, 9/3/2021, 9/3/2021
Status: New, New, In Progress, In Progress, Complete, New, Complete, In Progress, Cancelled, New, In Progress
Hours: 10.00, 15.25, 5.00, 10.00, 12.50, 20.00, 10.00, 5.00, 37.75, 20.00, 5.00

Figure 5-1. *Example of repeated values within a representative data set*

Eleven rows are represented, of which each column contains repeated values. The *Date* column contains only three distinct values, whereas *Status* contains four and *Hours* contains six. This repetition tends to scale well. If this were the data from a rowgroup containing one million rows, it would be reasonable to expect a column like *Status* to only contain a small number of values that are repeated frequently throughout the data set. The more repetitive the data is, the more effectively it will compress.

As is expected, more values are repeated within the values present in a single column than across different columns. This is true for two primary reasons:

- Different data types will have vastly different values. For example, the contents of a string column are not easily comparable to that of a money column.

- Columns representing different dimensions will have different ranges of values that correspond to their typical usage. For example, a decimal column containing the tax rates charged on new cars would contain a very different set of common values than a decimal column containing the cost of those cars.

Columnstore indexes align perfectly with these conventions, whereas rowstore indexes struggle because row and page compression are forced to take into account all columns in a row or page, which will comprise a wide variety of data types and dimensions.

Note that the delta store is not columnstore compressed. This data structure needs to be written to as quickly as possible at runtime, and therefore forgoing expensive compression removes the time and overhead required to process writes against it. This will mean that the delta store takes up more space than it may have if columnstore compression were used. Since the delta store tends to be small in comparison to the compressed columnstore index contents and contain a predictable count of rows, the effort needed to maintain it is constant and does not grow over time. Depending on SQL Server version, delta rowgroups may use row or page compression to limit their storage and memory footprint.

Columnstore Compression Algorithms

Columnstore indexes do not repeatedly store strings, decimals, or dates as is in segments. Instead, SQL Server makes use of a dictionary encoding and value encoding to shrink and compress data, even if the raw values are large.

Compression may be summarized in the following sequential steps:

1. Encode all values prior to compression.

2. Calculate optimal row order (aka Vertipaq optimization).

3. Individually compress each segment.

Encoding is an important step in the compression process. The following are details that explain different encoding algorithms, how they are used, and how they impact overall compression effectiveness.

Value Encoding

This process seeks to reduce the footprint of numeric columns by adjusting their storage to be able to use smaller sized objects. For integer data, which consists of TINYINT, SMALLINT, INT, and BIGINT, values are compressed by a variety of mathematical transformations that can divide all values by a common divisor or subtract all values with a common subtrahend. Consider a column that is a 4-bit integer data type and contains the values shown in Table 5-1.

Table 5-1. Sample Integer Column Data to Be Compressed

Values	Minimum Size in Bits
60	6
150	8
90	7
9000	13
630	10
300000	19

Columnstore compression seeks to find common divisors and immediately notes that each number is divisible by 10. For this example, the base is 10 and each value will be referenced using the maximum common negative exponent of that base that it is divisible by, as seen in Table 5-2.

Table 5-2. Integer Data Compressed Using a Negative Exponent

Values	Value *10^{-1}	Minimum Size in Bits
60	6	3
150	15	4
90	9	4
9000	900	10
630	63	6
300000	30000	15

The next compression step is to take the smallest value in the list as the base, zero it out, and reference other values by subtracting that base from them, as seen in Table 5-3.

Table 5-3. Integer Data Compressed by Rebasing

Values	Value *10^{-1}	Value *10^{-1} - 6	Minimum Size in Bits
60	6	0	0
150	15	9	4
90	9	3	2
9000	900	894	10
630	63	57	6
300000	30000	29994	15

Reviewing the minimum space required to store the values, the original size was 63 bits. After the first transformation, the size is reduced to 42 bits, and after the last transformation, it is reduced to 37 bits. Overall, the reduction in size for this set of values was 38%. The level of value compression seen will vary based on the set of values and can be significantly higher or lower. For example, a set of values that are all the same will compress into a single zeroed-out reference, as seen in Table 5-4.

Table 5-4. Identical Integer Data Compressed by Rebasing

Values	Value - 1700000	Original Size in Bits	Reduced Size in Bits
1700000	0	22	0
1700000	0	22	0
1700000	0	22	0
1700000	0	22	0
1700000	0	22	0

While this example may seem extreme, it is not that unusual as dimensions often contain repeated values that fall into limited ranges.

Note that real-world transformations of data that occur in columnstore indexes are more complex than this, but the process to determine their details is essentially the same.

Decimals are converted into integers prior to compression, at which point they follow the same value encoding rules as integers would. For example, Table 5-5 shows the compression process for a set of tax rates that are stored in decimal format.

Table 5-5. Value Compression for Decimals

Values	Value * 100	Value / 5	Value / 5 - 70	Original Size in Bits	Reduced Size in Bits
15.2	1520	304	234	40	8
8.8	880	176	106	40	7
4.3	430	86	16	40	5
3.5	350	70	0	40	0
6.25	625	125	55	40	6

The original data is stored as DECIMAL(4,2), which consumes 5 bytes (40 bits) per value. By converting to integers prior to compression, multiple transformations are applied that reduce storage from 200 bits to 26 bits. Decimals may not seem the most likely candidates for effective compression, but once they are converted into integer values, they can take advantage of any of the transformations that can be applied to integers.

Dictionary Encoding

String data is stored more efficiently using dictionary encoding. In this algorithm, each distinct string value in a segment is inserted into a dictionary and indexed using an integer pointer to the dictionary. This provides significant space savings for string columns that contain repeated values. Consider a segment that contains foods of the data type VARCHAR(50), as seen in Table 5-6.

Table 5-6. Sample Data Set Containing VARCHAR(50) String Data

Values	Original Size in Bytes
Taco	4
Hamburger	9
Fish Fry	8
Taco	4
Hamburger	9
Taco	4
Triple-Layer Chocolate Cake	27
Triple-Layer Chocolate Cake	27
Triple-Layer Chocolate Cake	27
Cup of Coffee	13

The first step to compressing this data is to create an indexed dictionary, as seen in Table 5-7.

Table 5-7. Example of a Dictionary That Is Generated from VARCHAR Data

Index ID	VARCHAR Value
0	**Fish Fry**
1	**Hamburger**
2	**Taco**
3	**Triple-Layer Chocolate Cake**
4	**Cup of Coffee**

Since the segment contains five distinct values, the index ID for the dictionary will consume 3 bits. The resulting mapping in Figure 5-2 shows the resulting dictionary compression of this data.

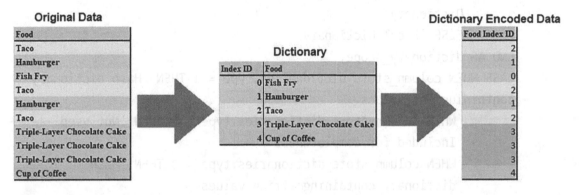

Figure 5-2. *Sample dictionary compression of a set of ten strings*

The original data required 132 bytes in storage, whereas the encoded data required only 30 bits (3 bits per value), plus the space required to store the lookup values in the dictionary. The dictionary itself consumes space for each distinct value in the segment data, but as a bonus, a dictionary may be shared by multiple rowgroups. Therefore, a table with 100 rowgroups may reuse dictionaries for each column across all of those rowgroups.

The key to dictionary compression is cardinality. The less distinct values present in the column, the more efficiently the data will compress. A CHAR(100) column with 5 distinct values will compress significantly better than a CHAR(10) column with 1000 distinct values. The dictionary size can be roughly estimated as the product of distinct values and their initial size. Lower cardinality means that there are less string values to store in the dictionary and the index used to reference the dictionary will be smaller. Since the dictionary index IDs are repeated throughout rows in the table, a smaller size can greatly improve compression.

Dictionaries can be viewed in SQL Server using the view *sys.column_store_ dictionaries*. The query in Listing 5-1 returns information about the dictionaries used in the *fact.Sale_CCI* table created in Chapter 4.

Listing 5-1. Query to Return Dictionary Metadata

```
SELECT
        partitions.partition_number,
        objects.name AS table_name,
        columns.name AS column_name,
        CASE
                WHEN column_store_dictionaries.dictionary_id = 0 THEN 'Global
                Dictionary'
                ELSE 'Local Dictionary'
        END AS dictionary_scope,
        CASE WHEN column_store_dictionaries.type = 1 THEN 'Hash dictionary
        containing int values'
                WHEN column_store_dictionaries.type = 2 THEN 'Not used' --
                Included for completeness
                WHEN column_store_dictionaries.type = 3 THEN 'Hash
                dictionary containing string values'
                WHEN column_store_dictionaries.type = 4 THEN 'Hash
                dictionary containing float values'
        END AS dictionary_type,
        column_store_dictionaries.entry_count,
        column_store_dictionaries.on_disk_size
FROM sys.column_store_dictionaries
INNER JOIN sys.partitions
ON column_store_dictionaries.hobt_id = partitions.hobt_id
INNER JOIN sys.objects
ON objects.object_id = partitions.object_id
INNER JOIN sys.columns
```

```
ON columns.column_id = column_store_dictionaries.column_id
AND columns.object_id = objects.object_id
WHERE objects.name = 'Sale_CCI';
```

The results of this query are shown in Figure 5-3.

	partition_number	table_name	column_name	dictionary_scope	dictionary_type	entry_count	on_disk_size
1	1	Sale_CCI	City Key	Global Dictionary	Hash dictionary containing int values	1240	5016
2	1	Sale_CCI	Customer Key	Global Dictionary	Hash dictionary containing int values	403	1668
3	1	Sale_CCI	Bill To Customer Key	Global Dictionary	Hash dictionary containing int values	3	68
4	1	Sale_CCI	Stock Item Key	Global Dictionary	Hash dictionary containing int values	227	964
5	1	Sale_CCI	Invoice Date Key	Global Dictionary	Hash dictionary containing int values	1069	4332
6	1	Sale_CCI	Delivery Date Key	Global Dictionary	Hash dictionary containing int values	1068	4328
7	1	Sale_CCI	Salesperson Key	Global Dictionary	Hash dictionary containing int values	101	460
8	1	Sale_CCI	Description	Global Dictionary	Hash dictionary containing string values	227	10596
9	1	Sale_CCI	Package	Global Dictionary	Hash dictionary containing string values	4	178

Figure 5-3. *Dictionary metadata results for the table fact.Sale_CCI*

This view provides the cardinality of the column in *entry_count*, as well as the size of the dictionary and its type. There are a number of noteworthy takeaways from this data:

- Dictionaries may be global or local. A local dictionary only applies to a single rowgroup (or on rare occasions, rowgroups compressed via the same process as that one). A global dictionary is shared across many or all segments for a given column.

- Dictionaries may be created for numeric columns if SQL Server believes that will provide better compression than value compression. As a result, numeric columns can appear in this metadata, but some will not. Typically, numeric columns with a low cardinality will tend to use dictionary compression, whereas numeric columns that have a high cardinality will use value compression. In the preceding example, *Sale Key*, the primary key on the underlying data, is value compressed, whereas *Bill To Customer Key* (containing only three unique values) is dictionary compressed.

- Additional metadata may be gleaned from *sys.columns*, if needed, such as the data type of the underlying data, its length, precision, and scale.

This metadata provides detail about each dictionary in the columnstore index, but does not directly relate segments to dictionaries. The query in Listing 5-2 links *sys.column_store_segments* to *sys.column_store_dictionaries* to provide this added information.

Listing 5-2. Query to Return More Detailed Dictionary Metadata

```
SELECT
        column_store_segments.segment_id,
        types.name AS data_type,
        types.max_length,
        types.precision,
        types.scale,
        CASE
                WHEN PRIMARY_DICTIONARY.dictionary_id IS NOT NULL THEN 1
                ELSE 0
        END AS does_global_dictionary_exist,
        PRIMARY_DICTIONARY.entry_count AS global_dictionary_entry_count,
        PRIMARY_DICTIONARY.on_disk_size AS global_dictionary_on_disk_size,
        CASE
                WHEN SECONDARY_DICTIONARY.dictionary_id IS NOT NULL THEN 1
                ELSE 0
        END AS does_local_dictionary_exist,
        SECONDARY_DICTIONARY.entry_count AS local_dictionary_entry_count,
        SECONDARY_DICTIONARY.on_disk_size AS local_dictionary_on_disk_size
FROM sys.column_store_segments
INNER JOIN sys.partitions
ON column_store_segments.hobt_id = partitions.hobt_id
INNER JOIN sys.objects
ON objects.object_id = partitions.object_id
INNER JOIN sys.columns
ON columns.object_id = objects.object_id
AND column_store_segments.column_id = columns.column_id
INNER JOIN sys.types
ON types.user_type_id = columns.user_type_id
LEFT JOIN sys.column_store_dictionaries PRIMARY_DICTIONARY
```

```
ON column_store_segments.primary_dictionary_id =
PRIMARY_DICTIONARY.dictionary_id
AND column_store_segments.primary_dictionary_id <> -1
AND PRIMARY_DICTIONARY.column_id = columns.column_id
AND PRIMARY_DICTIONARY.hobt_id = partitions.hobt_id
LEFT JOIN sys.column_store_dictionaries SECONDARY_DICTIONARY
ON column_store_segments.secondary_dictionary_id =
SECONDARY_DICTIONARY.dictionary_id
AND column_store_segments.secondary_dictionary_id <> -1
AND SECONDARY_DICTIONARY.column_id = columns.column_id
AND SECONDARY_DICTIONARY.hobt_id = partitions.hobt_id
WHERE objects.name = 'Sale_CCI'
AND columns.name = 'Bill To Customer Key';
```

Note that if a table is partitioned or has many columns, the result set could become quite large, so this query is filtered by both table and column to focus on a single set of segments, for demonstration purposes. The results help to fill in the blanks for dictionary metadata, as seen in Figure 5-4.

	data_type	max_length	precision	scale	does_global_dictionary_exist	global_dictionary_entry_count	global_dictionary_on_disk_size	does_local_dictionary_exist	local_dictionary_entry_count	local_dictionary_on_disk_size
1	int	4	10	0	1	3	68	0	NULL	NULL
2	int	4	10	0	1	3	68	0	NULL	NULL
3	int	4	10	0	1	3	68	0	NULL	NULL
4	int	4	10	0	1	3	68	0	NULL	NULL
5	int	4	10	0	1	3	68	0	NULL	NULL
6	int	4	10	0	1	3	68	0	NULL	NULL
7	int	4	10	0	1	3	68	0	NULL	NULL
8	int	4	10	0	1	3	68	0	NULL	NULL
9	int	4	10	0	1	3	68	0	NULL	NULL

Figure 5-4. *Dictionary metadata detail for Sale_CCI. [Bill To Customer Key]*

This detail differentiates between local and global dictionaries, as well as adds in some column-level detail. Based on the results, the integer column *[Bill To Customer Key]* compresses quite well as it contains only three distinct values in its dictionary. Sixty-eight bytes for a dictionary is tiny and will provide immense savings for a column that was previously 4 bytes per row across 25 million rows. Each value is reduced from 4 bytes to 2 bits, allowing it to be compressed at a ratio of 16:1!

It is important to note that a dictionary is limited in size to 16 megabytes. Since a segment may only have one global and one local dictionary assigned to it, if a dictionary reaches the 16MB threshold, then a rowgroup will be split into smaller rowgroups to allow for each to possess dictionaries that are below this limit. If inserting new rows into a table would cause any of its dictionaries to exceed the dictionary size cap, then a new rowgroup will be created to accommodate new rows. There are two key takeaways from this information:

1. Very long columns may force dictionary splits and result in undersized rowgroups. This will reduce compression efficiency and increase the number of dictionaries required to service the table.

2. Columns with very high cardinality may also approach this limit and result in dictionary splits that lead to the creation of undersized rowgroups.

Numeric columns with high cardinality will typically use value compression to avoid this problem, whereas string columns that are long and/or have a high cardinality may not be able to avoid this issue. Sixteen megabytes may sound small when compared to massive OLAP tables, but dictionaries themselves are compressed and typical analytic data will not approach the dictionary size limit. Testing should always be used to confirm either of these scenarios, rather than assuming they will or will not happen.

Should String Data Be Normalized?

Before advancing to a discussion of the remainder of the compression process, a question that arises from the efficiency of dictionary compression is whether or not normalization of dimensions is necessary or useful for columnstore compressed data that uses dictionary compression.

In the world of transactional data, dimensions are often normalized. This saves space and memory and allows for relational integrity, uniqueness, and other constraints to be implemented at runtime. In analytic data, though, data validation is often implemented via validation, rather than the use of triggers, keys, or check constraints. As a result, normalization was often used more to save resources or provide convenient lookup tables for use by visualization or analytics applications.

This question can be tested by creating a new version of *Fact.Sale_CCI* where the Description column is normalized into a lookup table and referenced by a SMALLINT key. Listing 5-3 provides definitions for this new table and its corresponding lookup table.

Listing 5-3. Table Structure for Fact.Sale_CCI with a Normalized Description

```
CREATE TABLE Dimension.Sale_Description
(       Description_Key SMALLINT NOT NULL IDENTITY(1,1) PRIMARY KEY
        CLUSTERED, [Description] NVARCHAR(100) NOT NULL);
CREATE TABLE Fact.Sale_CCI_Normalized
(       [Sale Key] [bigint] NOT NULL,
        [City Key] [int] NOT NULL,
        [Customer Key] [int] NOT NULL,
        [Bill To Customer Key] [int] NOT NULL,
        [Stock Item Key] [int] NOT NULL,
        [Invoice Date Key] [date] NOT NULL,
        [Delivery Date Key] [date] NULL,
        [Salesperson Key] [int] NOT NULL,
        [WWI Invoice ID] [int] NOT NULL,
        [Description Key] SMALLINT NOT NULL,
        [Package] [nvarchar](50) NOT NULL,
        [Quantity] [int] NOT NULL,
        [Unit Price] [decimal](18, 2) NOT NULL,
        [Tax Rate] [decimal](18, 3) NOT NULL,
        [Total Excluding Tax] [decimal](18, 2) NOT NULL,
        [Tax Amount] [decimal](18, 2) NOT NULL,
        [Profit] [decimal](18, 2) NOT NULL,
        [Total Including Tax] [decimal](18, 2) NOT NULL,
        [Total Dry Items] [int] NOT NULL,
        [Total Chiller Items] [int] NOT NULL,
        [Lineage Key] [int] NOT NULL);
```

When populated with data, the *Dimension.Sale_Description* table is loaded first with
any new distinct *Description* values, and then *Fact.Sale_CCI_Normalized* is loaded with
data that joins the dimension table to retrieve values for *Description_Key*. Figure 5-5
shows the side-by-side comparison of the storage of these tables.

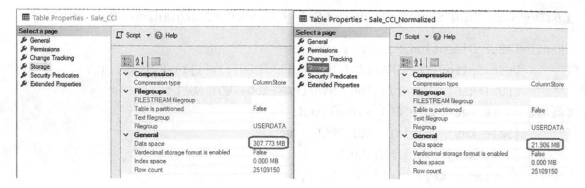

Figure 5-5. *Storage comparison between normalized and denormalized columns*

The table on the left is the original table, whereas the table on the right has the *Description* column normalized into a SMALLINT. In this specific example, normalization allowed for a significant space savings, about 15:1 compression savings from the original table!

Generally speaking, normalization will help most when the number of distinct values is low and the length of the columns is high, as dictionary encoding for a SMALLINT column will produce superior compression than dictionary encoding for a large VARCHAR column.

The downside to normalization is that data load processes will take longer. Joining additional dimension columns at runtime to load data requires time and resources. The decision as to whether to normalize or not should be carefully considered and testing conducted to determine if sufficient gains are realized to justify the change.

Ultimately, business logic and organizational needs will drive this decision at a high level, whereas technical considerations will allow for further tuning as needed. There is no right or wrong answer to this question; therefore, consider either approach valid until hands-on testing proves otherwise.

Row Order (Vertipaq) Optimization

Because a columnstore index is organized by column, rather than by row, it is possible for SQL Server to rearrange the order of rows within each rowgroup at the time each segment is compressed. This optimization is used whenever possible and attempts to arrange rows such that like values are adjacent to each other.

Columnstore compression is highly sensitive to repeated sequences of values; therefore, this optimization can provide exceptional compression and performance improvements. Vertipaq optimization is the algorithm that seeks to rearrange rows in the order that results in the most effective compression of the underlying data. This algorithm is used in other Microsoft storage technologies, such as SQL Server Analysis Services, PowerPivot, and PowerBI.

Vertipaq optimization is an expensive process, and the more columns a columnstore index has, the longer it takes to find the optimal row order. Therefore, SQL Server will limit the search time to ensure that building the index doesn't take an excessive amount of time. As a result, Vertipaq optimization will be somewhat less effective on wider tables. This fact should not affect database architecture decisions, but can be a useful troubleshooting step if a columnstore index on a wide table begins to experience suboptimal compression as more columns continue to be added.

A critically important key to this optimization is that some architectural decisions can prevent it from being used. There are two scenarios in which Vertipaq optimization will not be used:

1. When the tuple mover merges rows from the delta store into a clustered columnstore index that has at least one nonclustered rowstore index

2. For columnstore indexes that are built on memory-optimized tables

This does not mean that nonclustered rowstore indexes should never be used on clustered columnstore indexes. Nor should memory-optimized columnstore indexes be avoided. Instead, the fact that Vertipaq compression will not operate on these structures should be an additional input into architectural decision-making process. If a nonclustered rowstore index is required to service a specific set of critical queries, then it should be used. If its use is optional, then consider the negative impact it may have on compression.

While the details of how the algorithm works for a given columnstore index are not exposed through any convenient views, it is possible to check whether or not a rowgroup has Vertipaq optimization with the query in Listing 5-4.

Listing 5-4. Query That Returns Whether or Not Vertipaq Optimization Is Used

```
SELECT
        objects.name,
        partitions.partition_number,
        dm_db_column_store_row_group_physical_stats.row_group_id,
        dm_db_column_store_row_group_physical_stats.has_vertipaq_
optimization
FROM sys.dm_db_column_store_row_group_physical_stats
INNER JOIN sys.objects
ON objects.object_id =
dm_db_column_store_row_group_physical_stats.object_id
INNER JOIN sys.partitions
ON partitions.object_id = objects.object_id
AND partitions.partition_number =
dm_db_column_store_row_group_physical_stats.partition_number
WHERE objects.name = 'Sale_CCI'
ORDER BY dm_db_column_store_row_group_physical_stats.row_group_id;
```

The column *has_vertipaq_optimization* in *sys.dm_db_column_store_row_group_physical_stats* indicates if that rowgroup was compressed using the Vertipaq optimization or not. In general, expect to see this column return a value of 1, unless the columnstore index is either on a memory-optimized table or is used in conjunction with nonclustered rowstore indexes. If *has_vertipaq_optimization* is unexpectedly zero, further research is warranted to understand why that is the case and determine what changes were made that prevented this optimization from being used. Figure 5-6 shows a sample of the results of the previous query.

	name	partition_number	row_group_id	has_vertipaq_optimization
1	Sale_CCI	1	0	1
2	Sale_CCI	1	1	1
3	Sale_CCI	1	2	1
4	Sale_CCI	1	3	1
5	Sale_CCI	1	4	1
6	Sale_CCI	1	5	1
7	Sale_CCI	1	6	1
8	Sale_CCI	1	7	1
9	Sale_CCI	1	8	1

Figure 5-6. *Results of query to validate if Vertipaq optimization was used*

In this scenario, Vertipaq optimization is in use for all rowgroups in this columnstore index.

Other Compression Algorithms

After segments have been encoded and rowgroups have been reordered, the final step in columnstore compression is to apply any remaining compression algorithms to the resulting data. At this point, it is possible that no further compression gains are possible for a given segment. This will be most often true with values that do not repeat. The details of how columnstore indexes compress data are provided here to assist in more advanced optimization of compression and performance, when possible.

One form of compression used by columnstore indexes is ***run-length encoding***, which seeks to group together like values and a count, rather than listing repetitive values in a segment. Vertipaq optimization is a prerequisite to this step, and without it, run-length encoding will be significantly less effective.

Consider the example of foods provided earlier in Figure 5-2. The encoded data has five different values that have been dictionary encoded to 3-bit numeric values. Vertipaq optimization would take the resulting data set and order it, as shown in Figure 5-7.

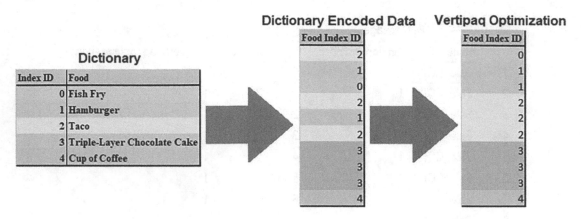

Figure 5-7. *Vertipaq optimization of a set of encoded values*

Note that the encoded values are now reordered so that each value is grouped next to the same value. Run-length encoding groups together each like value logically to reduce the overall amount of storage required for the segment. Logically, the resulting structure can be illustrated as shown in Figure 5-8.

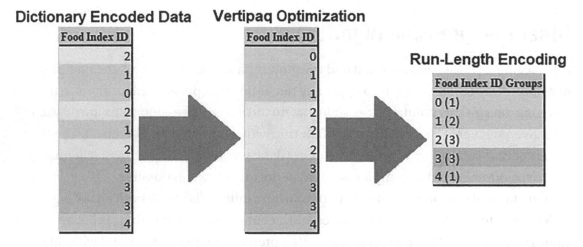

Figure 5-8. *Run-length encoding applied to a numeric data set*

Each value has been provided with a count, shown in parenthesis after it. There is a single instance of the value 0, followed by two instances of 1, three instances of 2, three instances of 3, and one instance of 4. This algorithm thrives on data that is repetitive and works exceptionally well in conjunction with dictionary encoding and Vertipaq compression.

Bit array compression is used when a segment contains a small number of distinct values and the data cannot benefit significantly from Vertipaq compression and run-length encoding. A bit array is an array in which each distinct value is assigned a column and each row is mapped to that column using bits. Figure 5-9 illustrates how this compression would look when used on an unencoded and unsorted data set.

Unencoded Data

Food
Taco
Hamburger
Fish Fry
Taco
Hamburger
Taco
Triple-Layer Chocolate Cake
Triple-Layer Chocolate Cake
Triple-Layer Chocolate Cake
Cup of Coffee

Bit Array Compression

Fish Fry	Hamburger	Taco	Triple-Layer Chocolate Cake	Cup of Coffee
0	0	1	0	0
0	1	0	0	0
1	0	0	0	0
0	0	1	0	0
0	1	0	0	0
0	0	1	0	0
0	0	0	1	0
0	0	0	1	0
0	0	0	1	0
0	0	0	0	1

Figure 5-9. *Bit array compression applied to an unencoded data set*

While this may seem like a complicated transformation, the resulting ones and zeros are quite compact and provide a structure that can be quickly decompressed.

There are a handful of other more complex compression algorithms that may be used to progressively shrink the size of each segment of data. The algorithms used can vary by segment and may be used often, sometimes, or not at all. When this process is complete, the final level of compression is applied by SQL Server, which utilized its xVelocity compression algorithm.

Columnstore segments are stored as Large Objects (LOB) in SQL Server. The details of xVelocity compression are not public, and therefore we cannot delve further into how they work. While the transformations used to convert the structures discussed thus far in this chapter into their final form are not fully known, we can infer their effectiveness by turning on STATISTICS IO and viewing the reads against a columnstore index when a query is issued. Consider the simple analytic query in Listing 5-5.

Listing 5-5. Simple Analytic Query to Demonstrate Columnstore IO

```
SELECT
      SUM(Quantity)
FROM fact.Sale_CCI
WHERE [Invoice Date Key] >= '1/1/2016'
AND [Invoice Date Key] < '2/1/2016'
```

The result of this query is shown in Figure 5-10.

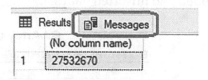

Figure 5-10. *Sample query output*

Clicking the *Messages* tab as shown in the results provides additional information on the reads and writes performed by the query, as seen in Figure 5-11.

```
Table 'Sale_CCI'. Scan count 2, logical reads 0, physical reads 0, page server reads 0,
read-ahead reads 0, page server read-ahead reads 0, lob logical reads 9521, lob physical
reads 4, lob page server reads 0, lob read-ahead reads 1800, lob page server read-ahead
reads 0.
Table 'Sale_CCI'. Segment reads 24, segment skipped 1.
Table 'Worktable'. Scan count 0, logical reads 0, physical reads 0, page server reads 0,
read-ahead reads 0, page server read-ahead reads 0, lob logical reads 0, lob physical
reads 0, lob page server reads 0, lob read-ahead reads 0, lob page server read-ahead
reads 0.
```

Figure 5-11. *Statistics IO output for a sample query*

There is quite a bit of information returned, but for the moment, the *LOB logical reads* circled in red provide an indication of the reads required to satisfy this query. Columnstore indexes will not report reads as *logical reads*, but instead as *LOB logical reads*, which indicates that their segments are stored as Large Objects and not as traditional SQL Server data structures. If this number of reads seems high, that is because it is! Later chapters in this book will provide additional optimizations that will reduce storage and memory footprint, as well as greatly improve query performance.

Columnstore Archive Compression

SQL Server provides an additional level of compression that can be used to further shrink the footprint of columnstore index data. While archive compression can provide a higher compression ratio than standard columnstore compression, it costs more computing resources to read and write the data. As a result, this option should be reserved for data that is not frequently used, such as

- Cold or warm storage
- Data that is rarely accessed
- Data used for applications where performance is not critical

Columnstore archive compression uses the Microsoft Xpress compression algorithm. While this algorithm is complex, it is publicly documented and is not a Microsoft trade secret. This algorithm relies on compressing data with repeated byte sequences and combines the LZ77 and Huffman compression algorithms to further shrink the size of columnstore data. The details of these compression algorithms are too extensive for the pages of this book, but are publicly available to anyone interested.

The type of compression used in a columnstore index may be specified on a partition-by-partition basis, allowing older/less used data to effectively use archive compression, whereas newer data can use standard columnstore compression. Chapter 11 delves into how partitioning can be combined with columnstore indexes to improve data storage, maintenance, and performance.

To demonstrate the effectiveness of columnstore archive compression, a new version of the Sale_CCI table will be created, as seen in Listing 5-6.

Listing 5-6. Table Created with Columnstore Archive Compression

```
CREATE TABLE Fact.Sale_CCI_Archive
(     [Sale Key] [bigint] NOT NULL,
      [City Key] [int] NOT NULL,
      [Customer Key] [int] NOT NULL,
      [Bill To Customer Key] [int] NOT NULL,
      [Stock Item Key] [int] NOT NULL,
      [Invoice Date Key] [date] NOT NULL,
      [Delivery Date Key] [date] NULL,
      [Salesperson Key] [int] NOT NULL,
      [WWI Invoice ID] [int] NOT NULL,
      [Description] NVARCHAR(100) NOT NULL,
      [Package] [nvarchar](50) NOT NULL,
      [Quantity] [int] NOT NULL,
      [Unit Price] [decimal](18, 2) NOT NULL,
```

```
    [Tax Rate] [decimal](18, 3) NOT NULL,
    [Total Excluding Tax] [decimal](18, 2) NOT NULL,
    [Tax Amount] [decimal](18, 2) NOT NULL,
    [Profit] [decimal](18, 2) NOT NULL,
    [Total Including Tax] [decimal](18, 2) NOT NULL,
    [Total Dry Items] [int] NOT NULL,
    [Total Chiller Items] [int] NOT NULL,
    [Lineage Key] [int] NOT NULL);
CREATE CLUSTERED COLUMNSTORE INDEX CCI_Sale_CCI_Archive ON
fact.Sale_CCI_Archive WITH (DATA_COMPRESSION=COLUMNSTORE_ARCHIVE);
```

Once populated with data, this table can be compared to the previous version that used standard columnstore compression, as seen in Figure 5-12.

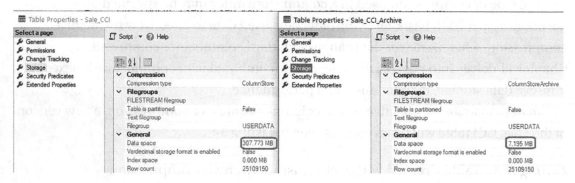

Figure 5-12. *Comparison of columnstore and columnstore archive compression*

Columnstore archive compression provided an immense space savings when compared to standard columnstore compression. This may seem absurdly impressive, but some of this savings can be achieved by optimizing data order, which will be discussed in detail in Chapter 10.

In practice with typical production data loads, archive compression will deliver an additional 15–30% savings over standard columnstore compression. For a large analytic table, this can equate to a significant reduction in its data footprint! In general, only consider archive compression for data that will not be written to or read often, as the cost to compress and decompress it is nontrivial. For data that is rarely accessed, it is an easy way to save on both storage and memory resources.

The Compression Life Cycle

A key to all compression within SQL Server is that compressed pages remain compressed until needed by a query. Therefore, pages are compressed on storage and remain compressed there for the lifetime of an index. When pages are read into memory, they remain compressed. Therefore, any storage space saved by the use of compression will equate into memory savings when the data is needed.

This fact is critical to the efficiency of columnstore indexes. Compressed segments remain compressed on disk as well as in memory and are not decompressed until a query requires their data. Any optimizations that further decrease the size of compressed segments will translate directly into memory savings. The remainder of this book will focus on optimizations, best practices, and features that allow columnstore indexes to be used as efficiently as possible, thus making the most of their compression and ensuring they can scale for any data, regardless of how big it gets.

CHAPTER 6

Columnstore Metadata

Each compressed segment within a columnstore index not only stores analytic data, but through metadata can describe its contents with more precision than rowstore tables can.

This metadata resides in system views and allows SQL Server to make intelligent query processing decisions at runtime. This chapter dives into this metadata in detail, how SQL Server uses it, and how it can be used to improve the performance of columnstore indexes.

Available Columnstore Metadata

Metadata is available through a handful of system views that provide overview-level data about segments and rowgroups, as well as detail data that describes physical properties, dictionaries, and operational metrics. The following is a brief review of each view and its contents.

Rowgroup Metadata

Each compressed rowgroup contains up to 2^{20} rows whose contents are typically static outside of the influence of index maintenance. Because of this, the row counts, deleted row counts, size, and other details are accurate and can be used to understand the size and shape of the underlying data.

The query in Listing 6-1 returns the table and index name, as well as all columns from the view *sys.column_store_row_groups*.

© Edward Pollack 2022
E. Pollack, *Analytics Optimization with Columnstore Indexes in Microsoft SQL Server*,
https://doi.org/10.1007/978-1-4842-8048-5_6

Listing 6-1. Query to Return Metadata for All Rowgroups in a Columnstore Index

```
SELECT
        tables.name AS table_name,
        indexes.name AS index_name,
        column_store_row_groups.*
FROM sys.column_store_row_groups
INNER JOIN sys.indexes
ON indexes.index_id = column_store_row_groups.index_id
AND indexes.object_id = column_store_row_groups.object_id
INNER JOIN sys.tables
ON tables.object_id = indexes.object_id
WHERE tables.name = 'Sale_CCI'
ORDER BY tables.object_id, indexes.index_id,
column_store_row_groups.row_group_id;
```

Figure 6-1 contains a subset of the rowgroup metadata returned.

	table_name	index_name	object_id	index_id	partition_number	row_group_id	delta_store_hobt_id	state	state_description	total_rows	deleted_rows	size_in_bytes
1	Sale_CCI	CCI_fact_sale_CCI	1394104007	1	1	0	NULL	3	COMPRESSED	1048576	0	12982576
2	Sale_CCI	CCI_fact_sale_CCI	1394104007	1	1	1	NULL	3	COMPRESSED	1048576	0	13036096
3	Sale_CCI	CCI_fact_sale_CCI	1394104007	1	1	2	NULL	3	COMPRESSED	1048576	0	13010760
4	Sale_CCI	CCI_fact_sale_CCI	1394104007	1	1	3	NULL	3	COMPRESSED	1048576	0	13169120
5	Sale_CCI	CCI_fact_sale_CCI	1394104007	1	1	4	NULL	3	COMPRESSED	1048576	0	13270896
6	Sale_CCI	CCI_fact_sale_CCI	1394104007	1	1	5	NULL	3	COMPRESSED	1048576	0	12961528
7	Sale_CCI	CCI_fact_sale_CCI	1394104007	1	1	6	NULL	3	COMPRESSED	1048576	0	13265848
8	Sale_CCI	CCI_fact_sale_CCI	1394104007	1	1	7	NULL	3	COMPRESSED	1048576	0	13026080
9	Sale_CCI	CCI_fact_sale_CCI	1394104007	1	1	8	NULL	3	COMPRESSED	1048576	0	12986432

Figure 6-1. *Rowgroup metadata for the columnstore index on Sale_CCI*

Each row returned by *sys.column_store_row_groups* represents the set of rows contained within a rowgroup, regardless of how many columns are in the table. A table with ten columns will contain ten segments per rowgroup. Similarly, a table with 30 columns will contain 30 segments per rowgroup. The following is a brief overview of each column in the view.

Partition_number

A rowgroup cannot span multiple partitions; therefore, a partitioned table will have separate sets of rowgroups in each partition, without overlap between them. This column provides the partition that a given rowgroup resides on.

Delta_store_hobt_id

For open rowgroups in the delta store, an ID is provided here that links to *sys.internal_partitions* and represents the delta rowgroup data it contains. A standard compressed rowgroup will contain NULL for this column.

State and State_Description

This describes the current status of the rowgroup, whether it is OPEN and accepting new rows, CLOSED, but not yet compressed by the tuple mover, COMPRESSED, or INVISIBLE (a rowgroup in the process of being created).

Total_rows

This provides the row count for the rowgroup. Summing this value across all rowgroups allows for an accurate row count to be collected for the table without querying it directly. If many rowgroups have low row counts, it is indicative of a process problem worthy of investigation.

Deleted_rows

If any rows are flagged as deleted in the delete bitmap for this rowgroup, the count of deleted rows is provided here.

Size_in_bytes

The total size of the rowgroup, which is the sum space used by all segments residing in that rowgroup. This can be used to quickly determine the size of all or part of a columnstore index.

Segment Metadata

The basic unit of storage in a columnstore index is the segment. Each segment represents a single column and its contents for the set of rows contained in each rowgroup. The number of segments that comprise a columnstore index is the product of the number of rowgroups in the index and columns in the table.

Sys.column_store_segments provides extensive detail on the contents of each segment. This data is accurate and updated whenever data within the segment changes, unlike SQL Server statistics which require periodic updating to ensure a reasonable approximation of reality.

The data in this view is more than a reference for curious administrators. It is also used by the query optimizer to make intelligent decisions about what data to read at runtime when a columnstore index is queried. This allows segments to be skipped when the metadata indicates they are not needed to satisfy a query. This can significantly reduce reads and improve query performance in ways that are unavailable to rowstore tables in SQL Server.

The query in Listing 6-2 returns a variety of useful columns from this view.

Listing 6-2. Query That Returns Columnstore Segment Metadata

```
SELECT
        tables.name AS table_name,
        indexes.name AS index_name,
        columns.name AS column_name,
        partitions.partition_number,
        column_store_segments.encoding_type,
        column_store_segments.row_count,
        column_store_segments.has_nulls,
        column_store_segments.base_id,
        column_store_segments.magnitude,
        column_store_segments.min_data_id,
        column_store_segments.max_data_id,
        column_store_segments.null_value,
        column_store_segments.on_disk_size
FROM sys.column_store_segments
INNER JOIN sys.partitions
ON column_store_segments.hobt_id = partitions.hobt_id
INNER JOIN sys.indexes
ON indexes.index_id = partitions.index_id
AND indexes.object_id = partitions.object_id
INNER JOIN sys.tables
ON tables.object_id = indexes.object_id
INNER JOIN sys.columns
```

```
ON tables.object_id = columns.object_id
AND column_store_segments.column_id = columns.column_id
WHERE tables.name = 'Sale_CCI'
ORDER BY columns.name, column_store_segments.segment_id;
```

The segment metadata returned can be seen in Figure 6-2.

	table_name	index_name	column_name	partition_number	encoding_type	row_count	has_nulls	base_id	magnitude	min_data_id	max_data_id	null_value	on_disk_size
74	Sale_CCI	CCI_fact_sale_CCI	Customer Key	1	2	16228	0	-1	-1	1	402	-1	19632
75	Sale_CCI	CCI_fact_sale_CCI	Customer Key	1	2	975674	0	-1	-1	0	402	-1	707304
76	Sale_CCI	CCI_fact_sale_CCI	Delivery Date Key	1	2	1048576	1	-1	-1	734869	736114	2	1678312
77	Sale_CCI	CCI_fact_sale_CCI	Delivery Date Key	1	2	1048576	1	-1	-1	734869	736114	2	1678312
78	Sale_CCI	CCI_fact_sale_CCI	Delivery Date Key	1	2	1048576	1	-1	-1	734869	736114	2	1678312
79	Sale_CCI	CCI_fact_sale_CCI	Delivery Date Key	1	2	1048576	1	-1	-1	734869	736114	2	1678312
80	Sale_CCI	CCI_fact_sale_CCI	Delivery Date Key	1	2	1048576	1	-1	-1	734869	736114	2	1678312
81	Sale_CCI	CCI_fact_sale_CCI	Delivery Date Key	1	2	1048576	1	-1	-1	734869	736114	2	1678312

Figure 6-2. *Segment metadata for the columnstore index on Sale_CCI*

Details about columnstore segments delve into how they are compressed and stored, which can provide valuable clues to the efficiency of columnstore compression for each column within a columnstore index. The following is detail about some of the key columns in this view.

Encoding_type

This indicates if this segment is encoded using a dictionary and the type of data stored in it, as follows:

- 1: Nonstring/nonbinary data with no dictionary. The values in this segment are transformed using base/magnitude encoding.

- 2: Nonstring/nonbinary data with a dictionary.

- 3: String or binary data with a dictionary.

- 4: Nonstring/nonbinary data with no dictionary. The values in this segment are stored as is, with no additional transformations.

- 5: String or binary data with no dictionary.

Typically, segments with many distinct values (aka high cardinality) will tend to use value-based encoding and not implement a dictionary lookup, whereas segments with low cardinality will more often use a dictionary to reduce the storage of repeated values. This decision is made internally by SQL Server to improve compression and reduce the space consumed by a segment.

77

Row_Count

This row count matches the row count of the corresponding rowgroup and represents the number of values (repeated or distinct) contained within a columnstore segment.

Has_nulls

If a segment contains at least one NULL, then this is set to 1; otherwise, it is 0. Note that this column does not indicate if a column allows NULL, but instead reports on whether a segment happens to have NULL within its set of values. Therefore, different segments for the same column can have different values for this bit.

Base_id and Magnitude

These columns report directly on value-based encoding. If values were modified using a base and exponent to reduce their storage size, that detail is represented here. The base and magnitude can vary segment to segment and do not need to be the same for each segment for any one column.

Min_data_id and Max_data_id

This incredibly useful pair of columns provides the minimum and maximum values for a segment, or the dictionary lookup values, if a dictionary is used. If transformations have been made for value-based encoding, then the values provided by these columns will include those modifications.

The minimum and maximum values for a segment are used by the query optimizer to skip unnecessary rowgroups when reading a columnstore index. For example, if a segment contains a minimum value of 1 and a maximum value of 400, then queries that filter for values outside of this range can skip this rowgroup altogether. This optimization is known as segment elimination and is key to the performance of large columnstore indexes. Chapter 10 discusses segment elimination in detail and provides the conventions needed to take full advantage of this feature.

Null_value

If a segment contains NULLs, then the value provided by this column is the numeric representation for NULL within the encoding of the column.

On_disk_size

The space consumed by the columnstore segment is provided by the column *on_disk_size*, allowing for the space consumed by a columnstore index to be easily broken down into granular details. If one segment out of many has an unusually large size, there can be value in exploring why and determining if further optimizations can be made to improve data compression.

This granular detail also allows for the space consumed by each column to be calculated, as well as space consumed per column per partition. If a columnstore index is growing large unusually quickly, this metadata allows for the source of growth to be isolated to a column and set of segments to determine the source of that growth.

Rowgroup Physical Metadata

SQL Server provides the view *sys.dm_db_column_store_row_group_physical_stats* as a reference to each rowgroup. Included are details regarding their current state and how rowgroups were created. This information is invaluable when troubleshooting unexpected performance challenges or when trying to understand why a columnstore index rowgroups were built in a particular way.

The query in Listing 6-3 returns key information from this view, as well as some associated metadata.

Listing 6-3. Query That Returns Columnstore Rowgroup Physical Details

```
SELECT
        objects.name AS table_name,
        indexes.name AS index_name,
        dm_db_column_store_row_group_physical_stats.partition_number,
        dm_db_column_store_row_group_physical_stats.row_group_id,
        dm_db_column_store_row_group_physical_stats.state_desc,
        dm_db_column_store_row_group_physical_stats.total_rows,
        dm_db_column_store_row_group_physical_stats.deleted_rows,
        dm_db_column_store_row_group_physical_stats.size_in_bytes,
        dm_db_column_store_row_group_physical_stats.trim_reason_desc,
        dm_db_column_store_row_group_physical_stats.transition_to_
        compressed_state_desc,
```

```
            dm_db_column_store_row_group_physical_stats.has_vertipaq_
            optimization,
            dm_db_column_store_row_group_physical_stats.created_time
FROM sys.dm_db_column_store_row_group_physical_stats
INNER JOIN sys.objects
ON objects.object_id = dm_db_column_store_row_group_physical_stats
.object_id
INNER JOIN sys.indexes
ON indexes.object_id = dm_db_column_store_row_group_physical_stats
.object_id
AND indexes.index_id = dm_db_column_store_row_group_physical_stats.index_id
WHERE objects.name = 'Sale_CCI';
```

The results provide additional information about rowgroups, as seen in Figure 6-3.

	table_name	index_name	partition_number	row_group_id	state_desc	total_rows	deleted_rows	size_in_bytes	trim_reason_desc	transition_to_compressed_state_desc	has_vertipaq_optimization	created_time
1	Sale_CCI	CCI_fact_sale_CCI	1	24	COMPRESSED	975674	0	12175912	RESIDUAL_ROW_GROUP	INDEX_BUILD	1	2021-09-20 17:44:06.003
2	Sale_CCI	CCI_fact_sale_CCI	1	23	COMPRESSED	16228	0	299776	RESIDUAL_ROW_GROUP	INDEX_BUILD	1	2021-09-20 17:44:04.487
3	Sale_CCI	CCI_fact_sale_CCI	1	22	COMPRESSED	1048576	0	13008872	NO_TRIM	INDEX_BUILD	1	2021-09-20 17:44:04.430
4	Sale_CCI	CCI_fact_sale_CCI	1	21	COMPRESSED	1048576	0	13027608	NO_TRIM	INDEX_BUILD	1	2021-09-20 17:44:02.170
5	Sale_CCI	CCI_fact_sale_CCI	1	20	COMPRESSED	1048576	0	12987832	NO_TRIM	INDEX_BUILD	1	2021-09-20 17:44:00.190
6	Sale_CCI	CCI_fact_sale_CCI	1	19	COMPRESSED	1048576	0	13083816	NO_TRIM	INDEX_BUILD	1	2021-09-20 17:43:57.907
7	Sale_CCI	CCI_fact_sale_CCI	1	0	COMPRESSED	1048576	0	12982576	NO_TRIM	INDEX_BUILD	1	2021-09-20 17:43:04.470
8	Sale_CCI	CCI_fact_sale_CCI	1	6	COMPRESSED	1048576	0	13265848	NO_TRIM	INDEX_BUILD	1	2021-09-20 17:43:22.680

Figure 6-3. *Rowgroup physical stats for the columnstore index on Sale_CCI*

This information provides clues as to how and when rowgroups were built. The following are descriptions of the key columns presented in Figure 6-3.

State_desc

This is the current state of the rowgroup, which is identical to the value found in *sys.column_store_row_groups*. A rowgroup with a state of TOMBSTONE indicates that it previously was part of a delta store and has been transitioned into compressed rowgroups, but has yet to be cleaned up. This cleanup occurs asynchronously and automatically, without the need for operator intervention.

Total_rows, Deleted_rows, Size_in_bytes

These are the same as their corresponding values in *sys.column_store_row_groups* and are provided in this view for convenience.

Trim_reason_desc

A rowgroup may contain up to 2^{20} rows. There are many reasons why a rowgroup is created and compressed with less than its full complement of rows. If this column shows "NO_TRIM" for a rowgroup, then that indicates that it is a full rowgroup with 1,048,576 rows. If the rowgroup contains less than its maximum possible size in rows, then the trim reason will explain why.

Typically, a columnstore index should mostly contain rowgroups with row counts near 1,048,576. In the event that this is not the case, and a majority of rowgroups are undersized, then understanding why is key to improving columnstore storage and performance. There is no firm threshold for defining what "undersized" is, but typically an undersized rowgroup contains less than 900,000 rows, or less than about 10% of its maximum size.

Common reasons for a rowgroup to be trimmed include

- **BULKLOAD:** A bulk load process limited the resulting row count to less than its maximum size. This is normal and rarely a cause for concern.

- **REORG:** An index reorganize process was used to force compression of a rowgroup. Since this is a manual process, it is easy to control, if needed.

- **DICTIONARY_SIZE:** A dictionary is limited to 16 megabytes of space. If a dictionary exceeds that size, then the rowgroup it corresponds to will be split into another rowgroup. If this happens often and if the resulting row counts are low, it indicates that dictionary compression is harming compression performance. Normalizing a large dimension into a lookup table is an effective way to resolve this problem.

- **MEMORY_LIMITATION:** This indicates that SQL Server ran low on memory while compressing the rowgroup and could not include all rows. This is indicative of memory pressure, and research should be conducted to determine why memory was low and if additional memory should be added to the SQL Server to resolve this problem. It is likely that memory pressure of this nature would affect other processes on the server as well and alleviating it would be beneficial to them, in addition to the columnstore index build process.

- **RESIDUAL_ROW_GROUP:** When an index build operation completes, leftover rows will be compressed into rowgroups using this trim reason. This is normal and does not require investigation.

- **AUTO_MERGE:** This results when the tuple mover runs and merges multiple rowgroups together. This is a good thing as it contributes to larger rowgroups and the removal of undersized ones.

Transition_to_compressed_state_desc

This column describes how a rowgroup was moved from the delta store into a set of compressed segments within a columnstore index. It provides additional information for how the rowgroup was created and can be used in conjunction with the trim reason to understand how all rowgroups were created, whether trimmed or not. The possible values for the transition to compressed state description include

- **NOT_APPLICABLE:** This is found either in delta store rowgroups or for rowgroups compressed prior to SQL Server 2016, when this history was not maintained.

- **INDEX_BUILD:** This rowgroup was compressed via an index build process.

- **TUPLE_MOVER:** This rowgroup was compressed by the tuple mover after it inserted data into it from the delta store.

- **REORG_NORMAL:** An index reorganize process was executed that moved a closed rowgroup from the delta store into the columnstore index. This occurred after it was closed with its full number of rows but before it was moved asynchronously via the tuple mover.

- **REORG_FORCED:** An index reorganize process was executed that moved an open rowgroup from the delta store into the columnstore index. This occurred before it had its full number of rows and would normally be moved asynchronously via the tuple mover.

- **BULKLOAD:** A minimally logged bulk load process created the rowgroup without using the delta store.

- **MERGE:** The tuple mover merged multiple rowgroups together into this compressed rowgroup.

Note that with the exception of the two transition reasons related to index reorganize operations, the remaining reasons indicate the creation of compressed rowgroups through automatic processes in SQL Server. These reasons should be seen as part of normal operations and only investigated if an unsolved performance problem is encountered.

Has_vertipaq_optimization

This indicates that the rows within a rowgroup could be reordered via Vertipaq optimization to improve the compression ratio for this rowgroup.

If zero is indicated by this column, it is worth investigation. The space savings associated with Vertipaq optimization is nontrivial and will result in faster queries and less memory and storage consumption by a columnstore index. As discussed in the previous chapter, the two reasons why Vertipaq optimization may not occur are as follows:

1. The columnstore index resides on a memory-optimized table.

2. The columnstore index contains nonclustered rowstore indexes.

Note that if a nonclustered rowstore index is removed from a clustered columnstore index, the Vertipaq optimization status will not change until an index rebuild is executed.

Consider the benefits and drawbacks of architectural decisions that lead to Vertipaq optimization not being used, as there are valid reasons to have a columnstore index in memory, or to include nonclustered rowstore indexes.

One solution for a columnstore index that requires a supporting nonclustered rowstore index is to implement a nonclustered index on the partitions with the data relevant to the queries requiring the index. Vertipaq optimization will only be impacted on rowgroups on partitions that contain the nonclustered index. Typically, data can be separated into hot, warm, and cold data, depending on common workloads. Secondary indexes can be split across partitions to target those different workloads effectively.

Similarly, filtered nonclustered rowstore indexes may be used to further limit the size of the index and reduce its scope and impact on compression and storage.

Created_time

This indicates the time that a rowgroup was created. This can help in understanding how many rowgroups are created over time and the number of rows being added to the columnstore index per unit time. In addition, *created_time* can be correlated to *size_in_bytes*, allowing the increase in size of the columnstore index to be measured over time in bytes.

Rowgroup Operational Statistics

SQL Server maintains cumulative details on the usage of columnstore indexes and provides those details at the rowgroup level. This allows for an understanding of which rowgroups within a columnstore index constitute hot, warm, or cold data and for granular detail as to how each rowgroup is used.

The query in Listing 6-4 returns operational data for a single columnstore index.

Listing 6-4. Query That Returns Columnstore Rowgroup Operational Statistics

```
SELECT
        objects.name AS table_name,
        indexes.name AS index_name,
        dm_db_column_store_row_group_operational_stats.row_group_id,
        dm_db_column_store_row_group_operational_stats.index_scan_count,
        dm_db_column_store_row_group_operational_stats.scan_count,
        dm_db_column_store_row_group_operational_stats.delete_buffer_
        scan_count,
        dm_db_column_store_row_group_operational_stats.row_group_lock_count,
        dm_db_column_store_row_group_operational_stats.row_group_lock_
        wait_count,
        dm_db_column_store_row_group_operational_stats.row_group_lock_
        wait_in_ms,
        dm_db_column_store_row_group_operational_stats.returned_row_count
FROM sys.dm_db_column_store_row_group_operational_stats
INNER JOIN sys.objects
ON objects.object_id = dm_db_column_store_row_group_operational_stats
.object_id
```

```
INNER JOIN sys.indexes
ON indexes.object_id = dm_db_column_store_row_group_operational_stats
.object_id
AND indexes.index_id = dm_db_column_store_row_group_operational_stats
.index_id
WHERE objects.name = 'Sale_CCI';
```

The results in Figure 6-4 show individualized operational data for each rowgroup.

	table_name	index_name	row_group_id	index_scan_count	scan_count	delete_buffer_scan_count	row_group_lock_count	row_group_lock_wait_count	row_group_lock_wait_in_ms	returned_row_count
1	Sale_CCI	CCI_fact_sale_CCI	24	13	12	0	11	0	0	1041296
2	Sale_CCI	CCI_fact_sale_CCI	23	13	5	0	3	0	0	17340
3	Sale_CCI	CCI_fact_sale_CCI	22	13	10	0	8	0	0	1119008
4	Sale_CCI	CCI_fact_sale_CCI	21	13	10	0	8	0	0	1119006
5	Sale_CCI	CCI_fact_sale_CCI	20	13	10	0	8	0	0	1119006
6	Sale_CCI	CCI_fact_sale_CCI	19	13	10	0	8	0	0	1119006
7	Sale_CCI	CCI_fact_sale_CCI	18	13	10	0	8	0	0	1119004
8	Sale_CCI	CCI_fact_sale_CCI	17	13	10	0	8	0	0	1119006

Figure 6-4. *Rowgroup operational stats for the columnstore index on Sale_CCI*

All metrics in this view are cumulative since the last restart of the SQL Server service. Therefore, to meaningfully use this data, it must be captured periodically to calculate the difference in measurements from one sample to the next.

The following is a subset of columns that can be used to track detailed columnstore rowgroup usage.

Index_scan_count

This counts the number of times the columnstore index was scanned, regardless of which rowgroups were requested. This value will be identical for all rowgroups in a given partition.

Scan_count

This only counts the number of times this rowgroup was scanned. Comparing this to *index_scan_count* allows for an understanding of how often a particular rowgroup is needed to satisfy queries against the columnstore index.

In typical OLAP data, older data will be required less often than newer data, and therefore rowgroups containing older data will see less scans than newer rowgroups. The scan count columns in this view can provide the necessary data to support storage changes for cold or warm data. If older data is needed for posterity but rarely queried, it can likely be off-loaded to slower and cheaper storage. Similarly, if there is a portion of data that is newer and critically important, it may benefit from faster storage.

Delete_buffer_scan_count

This counts the number of times that the delete bitmap was consulted in order to complete a query against this rowgroup. The delete buffer refers to both the delete bitmap as it is stored alongside the columnstore index as a b-tree, as well as the in-memory hash-table representation of that index.

Typically, deleted rows in a columnstore index are not problematic until their quantity become large when compared to the size of the index. If *delete_buffer_scan_count* is a larger number that is close in value to scan_count, then an index rebuild may be worthwhile to remove the deleted rows from the index. Check the value for *deleted_rows* in *dm_db_column_store_row_group_physical_stats* first to validate that the number of deleted rows is indeed large before proceeding with index maintenance. While an index rebuild can be executed as an online operation, it is still computationally expensive and can be time-consuming for a large columnstore index.

Row_group_lock_count, Row_group_lock_wait_count, and Row_group_lock_wait_in_ms

These provide the count (and details) of lock requests against this rowgroup. These are typically the result of columnstore index writes colliding with reads. Rowgroup locks are most frequent against rowgroups that are actively being written, whereas locks against older rowgroups are uncommon.

Rowgroup locking is not inherently a bad thing, but if severe contention is occurring between data loads and analytic processes, then understanding which rowgroups are causing contention can assist in troubleshooting that situation.

Update operations will be the most likely to cause contention as they require writing both to the delete bitmap and to the delta store. While updating a single row would impact two rowgroups (one for the delete bitmap and one for the delta store), a larger update might impact many rowgroups. In these scenarios, the locking caused by the update can be quite disruptive.

Similarly, if data is trickled into a columnstore index throughout the day, there is more opportunity for contention than if it is managed via a single centralized process less frequently and during a nonpeak time for analytics.

As is the case for many performance challenges, investigate contention when needed. If *row_group_lock_count* appears high, but analytics speeds (and end-user happiness) are good, then that fact is best saved for posterity, but not acted on yet. Always cross-reference *Row_group_lock_wait_count* and *Row_group_lock_wait_in_ms* to determine if locking resulted in waits or not. If the count of waits or the wait time is not high, then further action is likely not needed. If unsure of whether or not the aggregate wait time is high or not, consider the lock wait time per lock incident, as given by the query in Listing 6-5.

Listing 6-5. Formula That Calculates the Lock Time per Lock Incidence

```
SELECT
      objects.name AS table_name,
      indexes.name AS index_name,
      dm_db_column_store_row_group_operational_stats.row_group_id,
      dm_db_column_store_row_group_operational_stats.scan_count,
      dm_db_column_store_row_group_operational_stats.row_group_lock_
      wait_count,
      dm_db_column_store_row_group_operational_stats.row_group_lock_
      wait_in_ms,
      CASE
            WHEN dm_db_column_store_row_group_operational_stats.row_
            group_lock_wait_count = 0 THEN 0
            ELSE CAST(CAST(dm_db_column_store_row_group_operational_
            stats.row_group_lock_wait_in_ms AS DECIMAL(16,2)) /
                  CAST(dm_db_column_store_row_group_operational_stats
                  .row_group_lock_wait_count AS DECIMAL(16,2))
                  AS DECIMAL(16,2))
      END AS lock_wait_ms_per_wait_incidence
FROM sys.dm_db_column_store_row_group_operational_stats
INNER JOIN sys.objects
ON objects.object_id = dm_db_column_store_row_group_operational_stats
.object_id
```

```
INNER JOIN sys.indexes
ON indexes.object_id = dm_db_column_store_row_group_operational_stats
.object_id
AND indexes.index_id = dm_db_column_store_row_group_operational_stats
.index_id
WHERE objects.name = 'Sale_CCI';
```

The details returned provide an understanding of

- How many of the operations against a rowgroup resulted in locking/waits?

- How long were waits due to locking when they occurred?

- How does wait time compare to overall rowgroup performance?

If contention is a problem within a columnstore index, consider streamlining data load processes. Break update operations into sequences of deletes and inserts. This reduces transaction size during data loads, speeds up update operations, and reduces the opportunity for contention to be significant. Utilize bulk load processes via large insert batches when possible as they will be faster, generate less contention, and reduce transaction log size. Lastly, ensure that writes against the columnstore index are reduced and centralized as much as possible. If intermediary write operations can be made against a temporary table prior to modifying columnstore index data, then the result will be less contention on the data used for analytics and faster data load speeds. Best practices such as these are discussed in more detail in Chapter 15.

Returned_row_count

One additional metric provided that can assist in quantifying utilization is the overall count of rows returned. This provides an additional dimension as to how much data is read from this rowgroup over a period of time and can be compared to other rowgroups in the index. Note that a lower row count may be the result of the rowgroup having less rows and not simply less usage.

Columnstore Index Memory Usage

The system view *sys.dm_column_store_object_pool* provides details about the memory allocated to columnstore indexes. This can assist in troubleshooting memory pressure, as well as capacity planning when creating a columnstore index table. This is a shared view across an entire server; therefore, filtering on the database name is useful when viewing metadata solely for a single database.

The query in Listing 6-6 returns details about memory usage for one specific columnstore index.

Listing 6-6. Columnstore Memory Usage by the Sale_CCI Table

```
SELECT
        databases.name,
        objects.name,
        indexes.name,
        columns.name,
        dm_column_store_object_pool.row_group_id,
        dm_column_store_object_pool.object_type_desc,
        dm_column_store_object_pool.access_count,
        dm_column_store_object_pool.memory_used_in_bytes,
        dm_column_store_object_pool.object_load_time
FROM sys.dm_column_store_object_pool
INNER JOIN sys.objects
ON objects.object_id = dm_column_store_object_pool.object_id
INNER JOIN sys.indexes
ON indexes.object_id = dm_column_store_object_pool.object_id
AND indexes.index_id = dm_column_store_object_pool.index_id
INNER JOIN sys.databases
ON databases.database_id = dm_column_store_object_pool.database_id
LEFT JOIN sys.columns
ON columns.column_id = dm_column_store_object_pool.column_id
AND columns.object_id = dm_column_store_object_pool.object_id
WHERE objects.name = 'Sale_CCI'
AND databases.name = DB_NAME()
ORDER BY dm_column_store_object_pool.row_group_id, columns.name;
```

The results are shown in Figure 6-5.

	name	name	name	name	row_group_id	object_type_desc	access_count	memory_used_in_bytes	object_load_time
1	WideWorldImportersDW	Sale_CCI	CCI_fact_sale_CCI	NULL	0	DELETE_BITMAP	4874	131072	2021-10-06 08:59:46.9670000
2	WideWorldImportersDW	Sale_CCI	CCI_fact_sale_CCI	Invoice Date Key	0	PRIMARY_DICTIONARY	24	16384	2021-10-07 13:28:54.4660000
3	WideWorldImportersDW	Sale_CCI	CCI_fact_sale_CCI	Invoice Date Key	0	COLUMN_SEGMENT	89	1687552	2021-10-07 13:28:54.4920000
4	WideWorldImportersDW	Sale_CCI	CCI_fact_sale_CCI	Quantity	0	COLUMN_SEGMENT	19	57344	2021-10-07 13:28:54.4920000
5	WideWorldImportersDW	Sale_CCI	CCI_fact_sale_CCI	Quantity	0	PRIMARY_DICTIONARY	22	8192	2021-10-07 13:28:54.4650000
6	WideWorldImportersDW	Sale_CCI	CCI_fact_sale_CCI	NULL	1	DELETE_BITMAP	4874	131072	2021-10-06 08:20:23.0930000
7	WideWorldImportersDW	Sale_CCI	CCI_fact_sale_CCI	Invoice Date Key	1	COLUMN_SEGMENT	89	1687552	2021-10-07 13:28:54.4920000
8	WideWorldImportersDW	Sale_CCI	CCI_fact_sale_CCI	Quantity	1	COLUMN_SEGMENT	76	57344	2021-10-07 13:28:54.4920000

Figure 6-5. *Sample of memory consumption by a columnstore index*

Note the level of detail returned by *sys.dm_column_store_object_pool*. The results indicate a query was recently run that targeted *Invoice Date Key*, as well as *Quantity*. Because a columnstore index stores each column separately in their own segments, it is only necessary to read segments into memory for the requested columns. This differs from rowstore indexes, where pages contain all columns in the index and must be read together.

In addition to column segments, memory is consumed by delete bitmaps and dictionaries, allowing for a granular view of the memory consumed by each object within a columnstore index. The following is a description of each new column returned in Figure 6-5.

Object_type_desc

This is the type of columnstore object residing in memory. It will be one of the following values:

- **COLUMN_SEGMENT:** Each row with this type represents a single columnstore segment. These entries will contain a value for *column_id*, allowing for further detail to be returned regarding the column that the segment belongs to.

- **PRIMARY_DICTIONARY, SECONDARY_DICTIONARY, and BULKINSERT_DICTIONARY:** These represent dictionaries used for segments that are encoded with dictionary-based encoding. Typically, the space consumed by dictionaries and their corresponding column segments will be less than if the column were stored using value-based encoding.

- **DELETE_BITMAP:** This represents memory consumed by delete bitmap objects. There will always be one delete bitmap per partition that spans all rowgroups in a columnstore index on that partition. The entries for each rowgroup indicate the granular details for the part of the delete bitmap associated with that particular rowgroup. These objects are present as containers, even if there are no rows indicated as deleted within them.

Access_count

This is a count of all read and write operations to this object in memory. This provides a rough measure of how much use the object has gotten and which objects in memory are used often vs. those that are used rarely.

Because this view examines objects residing in memory, the data is transient and maintains history only for as long as an object is in memory. Therefore, access counts are only cumulative since the time given by *object_load_time*.

Object_load_time

This is the time that this object was read into the object pool in memory. Combined with *access_count*, the number of read or write operations per unit time can be calculated, which may be useful in gauging how much usage particular objects are getting in memory.

The data provided in *dm_column_store_object_pool* can also be aggregated so that overall memory consumption by a given rowgroup, column, index, or object type can be measured. For example, the query in Listing 6-7 quantifies how much memory is consumed by each rowgroup.

Listing 6-7. Columnstore Memory Consumption by Rowgroup

```
SELECT
    databases.name,
    objects.name,
    indexes.name,
    dm_column_store_object_pool.row_group_id,
    SUM(dm_column_store_object_pool.access_count) AS access_count,
    SUM(dm_column_store_object_pool.memory_used_in_bytes) AS
    memory_used_in_bytes
```

```
FROM sys.dm_column_store_object_pool
INNER JOIN sys.objects
ON objects.object_id = dm_column_store_object_pool.object_id
INNER JOIN sys.indexes
ON indexes.object_id = dm_column_store_object_pool.object_id
AND indexes.index_id = dm_column_store_object_pool.index_id
INNER JOIN sys.databases
ON databases.database_id = dm_column_store_object_pool.database_id
LEFT JOIN sys.columns
ON columns.column_id = dm_column_store_object_pool.column_id
AND columns.object_id = dm_column_store_object_pool.object_id
WHERE objects.name = 'Sale_CCI'
AND databases.name = DB_NAME()
GROUP BY databases.name, objects.name, indexes.name,
dm_column_store_object_pool.row_group_id
ORDER BY dm_column_store_object_pool.row_group_id;
```

Figure 6-6 shows the results.

	name	name	name	row_group_id	access_count	memory_used_in_bytes
1	WideWorldImportersDW	Sale_CCI	CCI_fact_sale_CCI	0	5043	1900544
2	WideWorldImportersDW	Sale_CCI	CCI_fact_sale_CCI	1	5054	1875968
3	WideWorldImportersDW	Sale_CCI	CCI_fact_sale_CCI	2	4892	1875968
4	WideWorldImportersDW	Sale_CCI	CCI_fact_sale_CCI	3	4892	1884160
5	WideWorldImportersDW	Sale_CCI	CCI_fact_sale_CCI	4	4892	1892352
6	WideWorldImportersDW	Sale_CCI	CCI_fact_sale_CCI	5	4892	1875968
7	WideWorldImportersDW	Sale_CCI	CCI_fact_sale_CCI	6	4892	1884160
8	WideWorldImportersDW	Sale_CCI	CCI_fact_sale_CCI	7	4892	1875968

Figure 6-6. *Memory consumption grouped by rowgroup*

Depending on the index, its metadata, and its usage, some rowgroups may use significantly more memory than others. In the example results in Figure 6-6, memory is used relatively equally per rowgroup, indicating that queries are reading data evenly from each rowgroup.

Internal Columnstore Index Objects

There is one additional view that provides internal details about the structure of a columnstore index, *sys.internal_partitions*. The query in Listing 6-8 returns details about any internal partitions associated with the rowgroups in a columnstore index.

Listing 6-8. Internal Partitions Associated with a Columnstore Index

```
SELECT
        tables.name AS table_name,
        indexes.name AS index_name,
        partitions.partition_number,
        column_store_row_groups.row_group_id,
        column_store_row_groups.state_description,
        column_store_row_groups.total_rows,
        column_store_row_groups.size_in_bytes,
        column_store_row_groups.deleted_rows,
        internal_partitions.internal_object_type_desc,
                internal_partitions.rows,
        internal_partitions.data_compression_desc
FROM sys.column_store_row_groups
INNER JOIN sys.indexes
ON indexes.index_id = column_store_row_groups.index_id
AND indexes.object_id = column_store_row_groups.object_id
INNER JOIN sys.tables
ON tables.object_id = indexes.object_id
INNER JOIN sys.partitions
ON partitions.partition_number = column_store_row_groups.partition_number
AND partitions.index_id = indexes.index_id
AND partitions.object_id = tables.object_id
LEFT JOIN sys.internal_partitions
ON internal_partitions.object_id = tables.object_id
WHERE tables.name = 'Sale_CCI'
ORDER BY indexes.index_id, column_store_row_groups.row_group_id;
```

The results of this query provide at least one row per rowgroup per partition, depending on the contents. Figure 6-7 contains a sample of this output.

	table_name	index_name	partition_number	row_group_id	state_description	total_rows	size_in_bytes	deleted_rows	internal_object_type_desc	rows	data_compression_desc
1	Sale_CCI	CCI_fact_sale_CCI	1	0	COMPRESSED	1048576	13072456	47333	COLUMN_STORE_DELETE_BITMAP	1210440	PAGE
2	Sale_CCI	CCI_fact_sale_CCI	1	0	COMPRESSED	1048576	13072456	47333	COLUMN_STORE_DELTA_STORE	161864	NONE
3	Sale_CCI	CCI_fact_sale_CCI	1	1	COMPRESSED	1048576	12886472	35479	COLUMN_STORE_DELETE_BITMAP	1210440	PAGE
4	Sale_CCI	CCI_fact_sale_CCI	1	1	COMPRESSED	1048576	12886472	35479	COLUMN_STORE_DELTA_STORE	161864	NONE
5	Sale_CCI	CCI_fact_sale_CCI	1	2	COMPRESSED	1048576	12810240	80474	COLUMN_STORE_DELETE_BITMAP	1210440	PAGE
6	Sale_CCI	CCI_fact_sale_CCI	1	2	COMPRESSED	1048576	12810240	80474	COLUMN_STORE_DELTA_STORE	161864	NONE
7	Sale_CCI	CCI_fact_sale_CCI	1	3	COMPRESSED	1048576	12975384	36388	COLUMN_STORE_DELETE_BITMAP	1210440	PAGE
8	Sale_CCI	CCI_fact_sale_CCI	1	3	COMPRESSED	1048576	12975384	36388	COLUMN_STORE_DELTA_STORE	161864	NONE

Figure 6-7. *Sample of internal columnstore index objects*

The internal columnstore objects shown illustrate the presence of both deleted rows and delta store contents. The *deleted_rows* column contains an individual count for each rowgroup, whereas the *rows* column contains aggregate details.

The following are short descriptions of each new column in the result set and how it can be used to track the growth and usage of a columnstore index.

Internal_object_type_desc

This indicates what type of internal object is referenced, and may be one of the following values:

- **COLUMN_STORE_DELETE_BITMAP:** This is the portion of the delete bitmap associated with each rowgroup in the columnstore index. The value in the *rows* column indicates how many deleted rows are accounted for in this portion of the delete bitmap, if any. Delete bitmaps are stored in rowstore b-tree structures. Each rowgroup will have a delete bitmap associated with it, even if the row count indicated as deleted is zero.

- **COLUMN_STORE_DELTA_STORE:** This represents delta rowgroups that are not yet in compressed segments within the columnstore index. These entries in the view will not exist unless a delta rowgroup exists for that rowgroup. Delta rowgroups within the delta store are stored in rowstore b-tree structures.

- **COLUMN_STORE_DELETE_BUFFER:** This object is exclusive to nonclustered columnstore indexes and buffers deleted rows from the clustered rowstore index into the nonclustered columnstore delete bitmap. The movement of deleted row data from the buffer into the delete bitmap is managed via the tuple mover and can be forced via an index reorganize command. This buffer helps improve delete speeds on OLTP tables where update and delete operations may be frequent, therefore helping to improve write speeds to the nonclustered columnstore index. When data is read from the nonclustered columnstore index, both the delete buffer and delete bitmap are read in tandem to produce a complete picture of deleted rows in the index. This internal object will not exist in *sys.internal_partitions* unless a nonclustered columnstore index exists on a table.

- **COLUMN_STORE_MAPPING_INDEX:** This is used when a clustered columnstore index also has a nonclustered rowstore index present on it. This mapping index is used to link nonclustered index key columns back to the correct rows within each rowgroup in the clustered columnstore index. The mapping index is only used when rows move between rowgroups, such as when a delta store rowgroup is moved into a compressed rowgroup or when the tuple mover merges rowgroups together. This internal object will not display in *sys.internal_partitions* unless these conditions are met and rows are present in the object.

CHAPTER 7

Batch Execution

Processing of rows in SQL Server is traditionally managed one row at a time. For transactional workloads, this is a sensible convention, as row counts for read and write operations are typically small.

Analytic queries that routinely operate on thousands or millions of rows do not benefit from reading rows in this fashion. Batch mode execution is a SQL Server execution mode that allows groups of rows to be read and passed between execution plan operators, ultimately improving performance.

As a query is executed and each operator is processed, rows are passed between those operators in quantities determined by the execution mode. In row mode, each row is passed from operator to operator sequentially. In batch mode, groups of rows are passed between operators. The result of this convention is that in batch mode, control is passed between operators less often as rows can be handed off in fewer batches.

Row Mode Execution

Queries with a low estimated cardinality will typically use row mode execution. In row mode execution, rows are read one by one as they are passed through each operator in an execution plan. This sounds inefficient, but it is important to note that processing rows in batches incurs overhead to do so. Therefore, SQL Server will make decisions at runtime to determine if a query would be more efficiently processed in row mode or batch mode.

Consider the query in Listing 7-1.

Listing 7-1. Transactional Query Returning a Single Row

```
SELECT
      Employee,
      [WWI Employee ID],
```

© Edward Pollack 2022
E. Pollack, *Analytics Optimization with Columnstore Indexes in Microsoft SQL Server*,
https://doi.org/10.1007/978-1-4842-8048-5_7

```
        [Preferred Name],
        [Is Salesperson]
FROM Dimension.Employee
WHERE [Employee Key] = 17;
```

The result of this query is a single row, as it seeks a single ID value by the primary key in the table. Turning on the actual execution plan, the details for the clustered index seek can be viewed, as seen in Figure 7-1.

	Clustered Index Seek (Clustered)	
11 FROM Dimension.Emplo	Scanning a particular range of rows from a clustered index.	
12 WHERE [Employee Key]		
13	**Physical Operation**	Clustered Index Seek
14 ⊟SELECT	**Logical Operation**	Clustered Index Seek
15 COUNT(*),	**Actual Execution Mode**	Row
16 MIN([Invoice Dat	**Estimated Execution Mode**	Row
17 MAX([Invoice Dat	Storage	RowStore
	Number of Rows Read	1
146 %	Actual Number of Rows for All Executions	1
	Actual Number of Batches	0
⊞ Results ⊟ Messages Execution plan	**Estimated Operator Cost**	0.0032831 (100%)
Query 1: Query cost (relative to the	Estimated I/O Cost	0.003125
SELECT [Employee],[WWI Employee ID],[	Estimated Subtree Cost	0.0032831
	Estimated CPU Cost	0.0001581
	Estimated Number of Executions	1
	Number of Executions	1
Clustered Index Seek (Cluste	**Estimated Number of Rows for All Executions**	1
[Employee].[PK_Dimension_Empl	Estimated Number of Rows to be Read	1
SELECT Cost: 100 %	Estimated Number of Rows Per Execution	1
Cost: 0 % 0.000s	**Estimated Row Size**	118 B
1 of	Actual Rebinds	0
1 (100%)	Actual Rewinds	0
	Ordered	True
	Node ID	0

Figure 7-1. Execution plan with details displayed

Note the execution modes provided in the query operator details. Row mode is indicated for both the estimated and actual execution modes. Given that the underlying table is a rowstore table and that the query only returns a single row, execution via row mode is expected for this operation.

While columnstore indexes are optimized for analytic queries that operate against large row counts and will usually take advantage of batch mode processing, row mode can be chosen as the execution mode if the optimizer believes that is the most efficient option.

The query in Listing 7-2 shows a narrow query executed against a columnstore indexed table that also happens to have a nonclustered rowstore primary key.

98

Listing 7-2. Query That Uses Row Mode Execution Against a Columnstore Index

```
SELECT
      *
FROM fact.Sale
WHERE [Invoice Date Key] = '1/1/2016'
AND [Sale Key] = 198840;
```

This query returns a single row against a clustered columnstore index in which row mode was used, as shown in Figure 7-2.

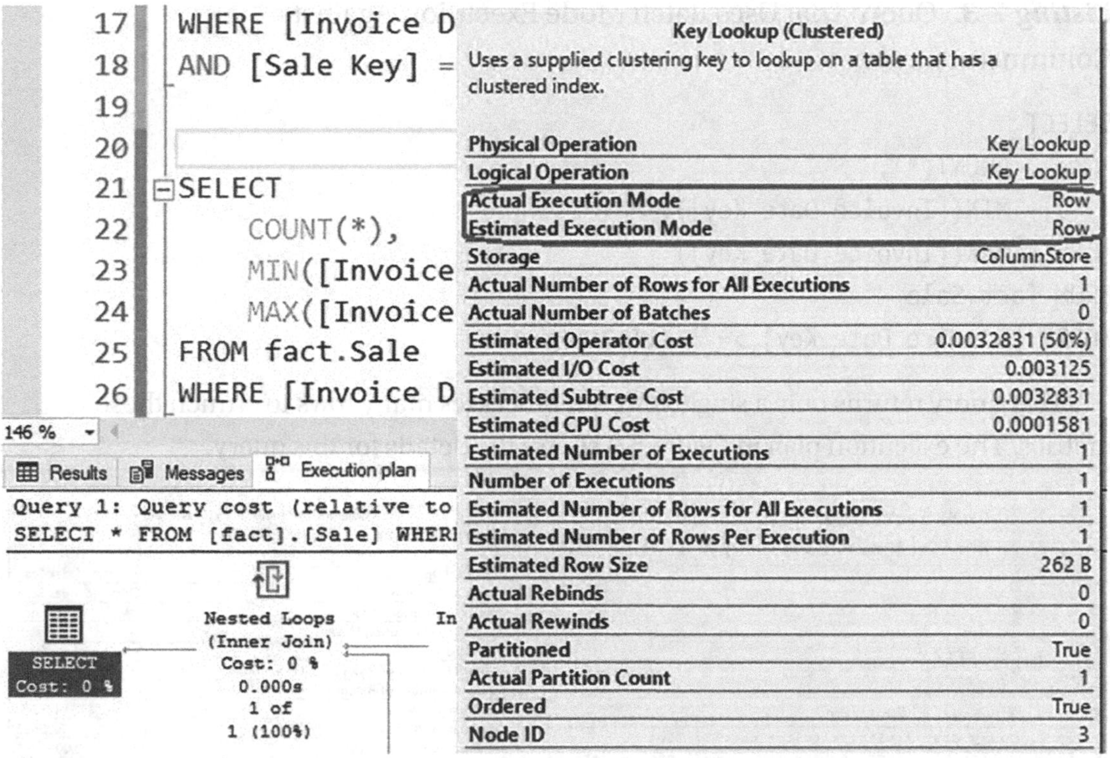

17	WHERE [Invoice D	Key Lookup (Clustered)	
18	AND [Sale Key] =	Uses a supplied clustering key to lookup on a table that has a clustered index.	
19			
20		Physical Operation	Key Lookup
21	⊟SELECT	Logical Operation	Key Lookup
22	COUNT(*),	Actual Execution Mode	Row
23	MIN([Invoice	Estimated Execution Mode	Row
24	MAX([Invoice	Storage	ColumnStore
25	FROM fact.Sale	Actual Number of Rows for All Executions	1
26	WHERE [Invoice D	Actual Number of Batches	0
		Estimated Operator Cost	0.0032831 (50%)
		Estimated I/O Cost	0.003125
		Estimated Subtree Cost	0.0032831
		Estimated CPU Cost	0.0001581
		Estimated Number of Executions	1
		Number of Executions	1
		Estimated Number of Rows for All Executions	1
		Estimated Number of Rows Per Execution	1
		Estimated Row Size	262 B
		Actual Rebinds	0
		Actual Rewinds	0
		Partitioned	True
		Actual Partition Count	1
		Ordered	True
		Node ID	3

146 %

Results   Messages   Execution plan

Query 1: Query cost (relative to
SELECT * FROM [fact].[Sale] WHER

SELECT
Cost: 0 %

Nested Loops
(Inner Join)
Cost: 0 %
0.000s
1 of
1 (100%)

In

Figure 7-2. *Execution plan with row mode execution against a columnstore index*

While the execution plan operator indicates it is using columnstore storage, the optimizer chooses row mode as the execution mode. This should not be seen as unusual or suboptimal. Because the query only returns a single row, the use of row mode is optimized for that expected outcome, even if the table is stored in a clustered columnstore index.

Batch Mode Execution

Queries that have a high cardinality can benefit from batch mode execution. In this execution mode, rows are divided into batches and processed in those batches for each operator in an execution plan where batch mode is chosen. In columnstore indexes, this will be the expected execution mode. For a large analytic query to not use batch mode would be considered an outlier. If that outlier was identified as a poorly performing query, then further investigation as to why batch mode was not used would be worthwhile.

Consider the query in Listing 7-3.

Listing 7-3. Query That Uses Batch Mode Execution Against a Columnstore Index

```
SELECT
        COUNT(*),
        MIN([Invoice Date Key]),
        MAX([Invoice Date Key])
FROM fact.Sale
WHERE [Invoice Date Key] >= '1/1/2016';
```

This query returns only a single row, but processes many rows to crunch these metrics. The execution plan in Figure 7-3 shows the details for this query.

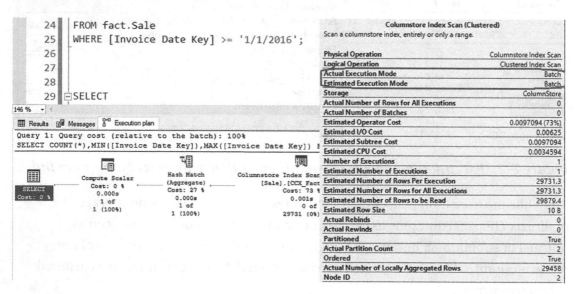

Figure 7-3. *Execution plan with batch mode execution on a columnstore index*

Batch is the expected execution mode and is what SQL Server chose for this query. Note that the plan details indicate that the "Actual Number of Locally Aggregated Rows" is 29,458. This is the number of rows required by SQL Server to satisfy the query, which is confirmed in the results shown in Figure 7-4.

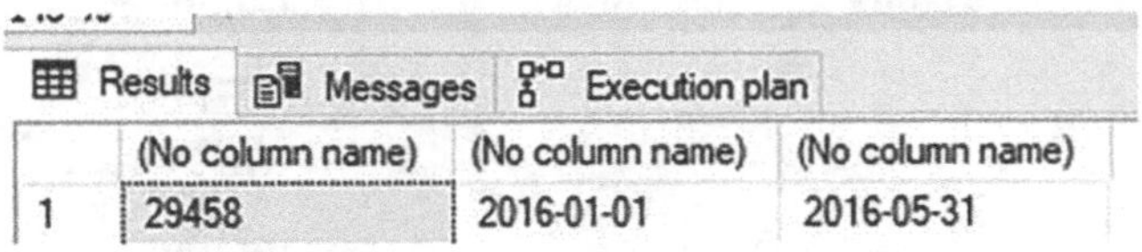

	(No column name)	(No column name)	(No column name)
1	29458	2016-01-01	2016-05-31

Figure 7-4. *Results of a simple columnstore aggregation query*

Whether batch mode is chosen by the query optimizer for a given plan operator depends on the number of rows processed by that operator and not on the number of rows returned by a query.

Execution modes are not all-or-nothing choices for a query. The query optimizer can choose batch mode for some operators and row mode for others and will do so based on whatever mode it determines is most efficient for each.

A common analytic query pattern is to aggregate data from a large columnstore index and join into dimension tables to provide lookup values where needed. The query in Listing 7-4 illustrates a classic scenario in which both dimension and fact tables are queried together.

Listing 7-4. Query That Joins a Large Analytic Table with a Small Lookup Table

```
SELECT
      City.City,
      City.[State Province],
      City.Country,
      COUNT(*)
FROM Fact.Sale
INNER JOIN Dimension.City
ON City.[City Key] = Sale.[City Key]
WHERE [Invoice Date Key] >= '1/1/2016'
AND [Invoice Date Key] < '2/1/2016'
GROUP BY City.City, City.[State Province], City.Country;
```

The execution plan for this query is found in Figure 7-5.

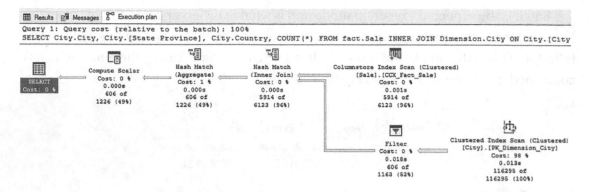

Figure 7-5. *Execution plan for a query against fact and dimension tables*

In the execution plan is a columnstore index scan on *fact.Sale*, as well as a scan against the *Dimension.City* lookup table. Figure 7-6 shows the properties for each table access operator, with the columnstore scan on the left and the rowstore scan on the right.

Columnstore Index Scan (Clustered) Scan a columnstore index, entirely or only a range.		Clustered Index Scan (Clustered) Scanning a clustered index, entirely or only a range.	
Physical Operation	Columnstore Index Scan	Physical Operation	Clustered Index Scan
Logical Operation	Clustered Index Scan	Logical Operation	Clustered Index Scan
Actual Execution Mode	Batch	Actual Execution Mode	Row
Estimated Execution Mode	Batch	Estimated Execution Mode	Row
Storage	ColumnStore	Storage	RowStore
Actual Number of Rows for All Executions	5914	Number of Rows Read	116295
Actual Number of Batches	19	Actual Number of Rows for All Executions	116295
Estimated Operator Cost	0.0077229 (0%)	Actual Number of Batches	0
Estimated I/O Cost	0.0044205	Estimated I/O Cost	2.57127
Estimated Subtree Cost	0.0077229	Estimated Operator Cost	2.69935 (98%)
Estimated CPU Cost	0.0033024	Estimated CPU Cost	0.128081
Number of Executions	1	Estimated Subtree Cost	2.69935
Estimated Number of Executions	1	Number of Executions	1
Estimated Number of Rows Per Execution	6122.63	Estimated Number of Executions	1
Estimated Number of Rows for All Executions	6122.63	Estimated Number of Rows for All Executions	116295
Estimated Number of Rows to be Read	29879.4	Estimated Number of Rows Per Execution	116295
Estimated Row Size	14 B	Estimated Number of Rows to be Read	116295
Actual Rebinds	0	Estimated Row Size	78 B
Actual Rewinds	0	Actual Rebinds	0
Partitioned	True	Actual Rewinds	0
Actual Partition Count	1	Ordered	False
Ordered	True	Node ID	5
Node ID	3		

Figure 7-6. *Operator properties for columnstore and rowstore index scans*

The columnstore index scan operates in batch mode, whereas the rowstore index scan operates in row mode. This query was executed against a database with SQL Server 2016 compatibility level (130). To test the effects of batch mode on rowstore usage, the compatibility level is adjusted to 150 (SQL Server 2019), as shown by the query in Listing 7-5.

Listing 7-5. Query to Alter the Database Compatibility Level to SQL Server 2019

```
ALTER DATABASE WideWorldImportersDW SET COMPATIBILITY_LEVEL = 150;
```

After this change, the query in Listing 7-4 is executed again, with the execution plan shown in Figure 7-7.

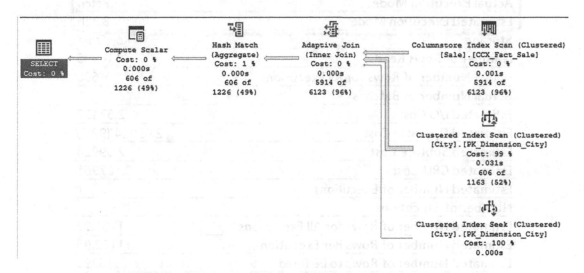

Figure 7-7. *Execution plan for a query in compatibility level 150*

When the compatibility level is switched to 150, multiple new features in SQL Server 2019 are enabled. The execution plan shows the use of adaptive joins, where the join to *Dimension.City* is given the option of either a clustered index scan or a clustered index seek. The actual row counts for each operator confirm that SQL Server chose to use the clustered index scan, due to the large number of rows returned. Figure 7-8 shows the operator properties for the clustered index scan against *Dimension.City*.

Clustered Index Scan (Clustered)

Scanning a clustered index, entirely or only a range.

Physical Operation	Clustered Index Scan
Logical Operation	Clustered Index Scan
Actual Execution Mode	Batch
Estimated Execution Mode	Batch
Storage	RowStore
Number of Rows Read	116295
Actual Number of Rows for All Executions	606
Actual Number of Batches	1
Estimated I/O Cost	2.57127
Estimated Operator Cost	2.69924 (99%)
Estimated Subtree Cost	2.69924
Estimated CPU Cost	0.127965
Estimated Number of Executions	1
Number of Executions	1
Estimated Number of Rows for All Executions	1162.95
Estimated Number of Rows Per Execution	1162.95
Estimated Number of Rows to be Read	116295
Estimated Row Size	78 B
Actual Rebinds	0
Actual Rewinds	0
Ordered	False
Node ID	6

Figure 7-8. *Operator properties for the rowstore clustered index scan*

With SQL Server 2019 features available, batch mode is chosen as the execution mode for the rowstore clustered index scan. For a query scanning many rows, this makes perfect sense.

Starting in SQL Server 2019, batch mode can be used by SQL Server against rowstore tables, but will be limited to scenarios when row counts are higher and using batch mode is expected to improve performance. Prior to SQL Server 2019, batch mode was only available for columnstore indexes. This is a significant improvement as it can greatly improve analytic query performance against rowstore tables.

This leads to an immediate question: If batch mode on rowstore tables can improve analytic performance, are columnstore indexes still useful? If batch mode were the only feature that made columnstore indexes highly performant, then that would be a valid question. Batch mode on rowstore tables does not provide the other benefits

104

of columnstore indexes, such as columnstore compression, segment elimination, or actionable metadata. For tables that service primarily analytic workloads, clustered columnstore indexes will be the correct solution. For tables that service mixed OLAP and OLTP workloads, batch mode on rowstore will improve performance and potentially remove the need to create nonclustered columnstore indexes, assuming OLAP queries are isolated and do not scan too many rows at once. Ultimately, testing is required to determine the optimal indexing solution for a given application, but batch mode on rowstore is a helpful tool that will aid in this decision-making process. For more information on mixing rowstore and columnstore indexes, see Chapters 12 and 13.

How Does Batch Mode Work?

The goal of batch mode processing is to improve the throughput of data from its storage location to a SQL Server's CPUs. To accomplish this, SQL Server fundamentally changes how data flows through execution plans from start to finish.

A query execution plan can contain one or many operators that retrieve, join, or transform data before results can be returned. In row mode processing, rows are passed between each of those operators one at a time. The basic unit of work in query execution when using row mode is the row. Consider the execution plan shown in Figure 7-9.

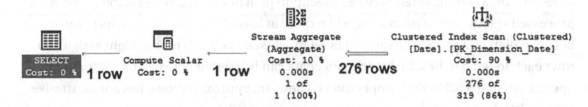

Figure 7-9. *Sample row mode execution plan with row counts*

In the execution plan, a clustered index scan is retrieving 276 rows that are passed into an aggregation that results in a single row that is in turn returned by the query. In row mode, each of the 276 rows is individually transferred from the clustered index scan operator to the stream aggregate operator.

When used, batch mode processes multiple rows together, storing the resulting data structure as a set of vectors in memory. This results in a completely new way of data being passed from operator to operator in an execution plan. Each batch can consume up to 64 kilobytes and contain between 64 and 900 rows. The row batch can be visualized in Figure 7-10.

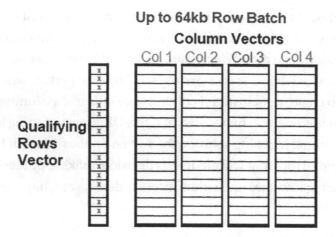

Figure 7-10. *Basic structure of a row batch*

A row batch looks somewhat similar to the structure of a columnstore index and provides similar benefits in memory as a query is executed. The qualifying rows vector performs a similar function to the columnstore index's delete bitmap in that it flags rows that are no longer logically needed by the batch. For example, if a filter is applied to a data set, it can be processed solely by updating the qualifying rows vector for the rows that are to be filtered out.

Batch mode processing reduces CPU consumption by decreasing the number of times that data is transferred between execution plan operators. For example, 5000 rows processed via row mode processing will require at least 5000 CPU operations to move it between plan operators. The same data set processed via batch mode might assign 500 rows each to ten batches. In this scenario, data can be passed between execution plan operators using 5000/500 = 10 operations. These are approximations, but are illustrative for how batch mode and row mode processing affect CPU consumption.

Another boon to batch mode processing is the ease in which it can take advantage of parallelism. Batches can be processed in parallel, allowing a multicore CPU architecture with available CPU capacity to process query plan operators more efficiently. Parallelism is a process that requires some CPU overhead to utilize. Therefore, the amount of rows involved in parallelism needs to be significant enough that the benefits of breaking a workload into smaller chunks outweigh the cost to do so. Row mode does not as easily benefit from parallelism in this regard as the effort to split single row operations into separate parallel operations and then combine them back together is far greater than the trivial savings afforded by that process.

While batch mode may not always be chosen for rowstore tables, it will be the default choice for columnstore indexes. Since a rowgroup will contain up to 2^{20} rows, the volume of data that needs to be processed by a columnstore index scan will be large enough to ensure that SQL Server chooses batch mode as the likely candidate to provide the best performance for queries against that data.

Batch Mode vs. Row Mode Performance

While columnstore indexes will most often default to using batch mode processing, rowstore tables will have a choice as to which mode to utilize. That decision will be based on the cardinality of the query, the amount of data that needs to be read, and the version of SQL Server involved.

There is value in directly comparing the performance of a query when it uses row mode vs. using batch mode and measuring the performance gains provided by batch mode.

The following query performs a simple analytic operation against a columnstore index twice: once using compatibility level 120 (SQL Server 2014) and once using compatibility level 130 (SQL Server 2016). Listing 7-6 provides the code to perform this comparison.

Listing 7-6. Analytic Query Executed in Two Compatibility Levels

```
ALTER DATABASE WideWorldImportersDW SET COMPATIBILITY_LEVEL = 120;
GO

SELECT
      Sale.[City Key],
      COUNT(*)
FROM fact.Sale
GROUP BY Sale.[City Key]

ALTER DATABASE WideWorldImportersDW SET COMPATIBILITY_LEVEL = 130;
GO

SELECT
      Sale.[City Key],
      COUNT(*)
FROM fact.Sale
GROUP BY Sale.[City Key]
```

The execution plans that result from these sample queries provide an immediate clue that a significant performance difference occurred here, as seen in Figure 7-11.

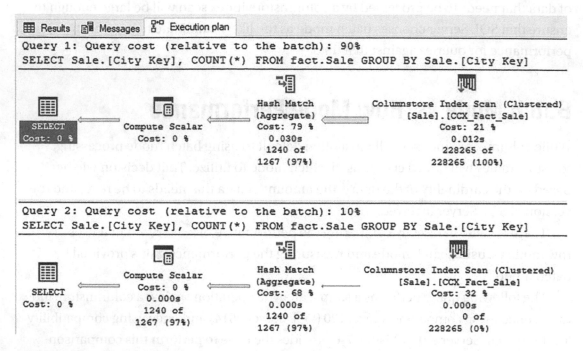

Figure 7-11. *Execution plans showing significant performance discrepancies*

The two execution plans appear nearly identical, except that the query cost for the first is 90%, whereas the second query is 10%. In addition, aggregate pushdown occurred, allowing the GROUP BY in our query to be processed in line with the columnstore index scan. This prevented the need to push all 228265 rows one at a time on to the hash match operation. Figure 7-12 compares the details for each columnstore index scan.

Columnstore Index Scan (Clustered)		Columnstore Index Scan (Clustered)	
Scan a columnstore index, entirely or only a range.		Scan a columnstore index, entirely or only a range.	
Physical Operation	Columnstore Index Scan	**Physical Operation**	Columnstore Index Scan
Logical Operation	Clustered Index Scan	**Logical Operation**	Clustered Index Scan
Actual Execution Mode	Row	**Actual Execution Mode**	Batch
Estimated Execution Mode	Row	**Estimated Execution Mode**	Batch
Storage	ColumnStore	**Storage**	ColumnStore
Actual Number of Rows for All Executions	228265	**Actual Number of Rows for All Executions**	0
Actual Number of Batches	0	**Actual Number of Batches**	0
Estimated Operator Cost	0.294806 (21%)	**Estimated Operator Cost**	0.0509048 (32%)
Estimated I/O Cost	0.0426157	**Estimated I/O Cost**	0.024838
Estimated CPU Cost	0.252191	**Estimated CPU Cost**	0.0260669
Estimated Subtree Cost	0.294806	**Estimated Subtree Cost**	0.0509048
Estimated Number of Executions	1	**Estimated Number of Executions**	1
Number of Executions	1	**Number of Executions**	1
Estimated Number of Rows for All Executions	228265	**Estimated Number of Rows for All Executions**	228265
Estimated Number of Rows Per Execution	228265	**Estimated Number of Rows Per Execution**	228265
Estimated Number of Rows to be Read	228265	**Estimated Number of Rows to be Read**	228265
Estimated Row Size	11 B	**Estimated Row Size**	11 B
Actual Rebinds	0	**Actual Rebinds**	0
Actual Rewinds	0	**Actual Rewinds**	0
Partitioned	True	**Partitioned**	True
Actual Partition Count	7	**Actual Partition Count**	0
Ordered	False	**Ordered**	False
Node ID	2	**Actual Number of Locally Aggregated Rows**	228265
		Node ID	2

Figure 7-12. *Execution plan details for row mode vs. batch mode operation*

There are a handful of notable differences between the expensive execution plan on the left and the efficient execution plan on the right:

- Batch mode was used successfully to process 228265 rows in the second plan.

- CPU consumption using batch mode is nearly ten times less than using row mode.

- Actual Number of Locally Aggregated Rows documents aggregate pushdown.

Making use of batch mode allows SQL Server to also take advantage of aggregate pushdown. The combination of these features was what allowed for CPU to be so greatly reduced.

This raises an important aspect of batch mode processing that further increases its effectiveness on analytic workloads: batch mode enables other powerful performance-improving features to be used when a query is optimized. Some of these features (along with earliest SQL Server versions they were enabled) include

- Adaptive joins (SQL Server 2017)

- Memory grant feedback (SQL Server 2017)

- Aggregate pushdown (SQL Server 2016)

109

Generally speaking, when SQL Server chooses to use batch mode, performance will be improved with its usage. Similarly, when additional intelligent query processing features are used (such as adaptive joins or aggregate pushdown), they will also have a positive impact on performance.

Testing batch mode vs. row mode processing can be challenging as forcing a query to use one over the other is not always straightforward. One way to make this testing easier is to use database scoped configuration changes to temporarily disable these features. The T-SQL in Listing 7-7 provides the syntax needed to disable batch mode on rowstore, as well as batch mode memory grant feedback and batch mode adaptive joins.

Listing 7-7. Query That Disables Optimization Features (for Testing Purposes Only)

```
ALTER DATABASE SCOPED CONFIGURATION SET BATCH_MODE_ON_ROWSTORE = OFF;

ALTER DATABASE SCOPED CONFIGURATION SET BATCH_MODE_MEMORY_GRANT_
FEEDBACK = OFF;

ALTER DATABASE SCOPED CONFIGURATION SET BATCH_MODE_ADAPTIVE_JOINS = OFF;
```

Note that these features should only be disabled for testing purposes only and should not be turned off in a production environment unless there are exceptional and well-documented reasons to do so.

Compatibility levels may also be adjusted for testing and demonstration purposes. This can help model the impact of an upgrade or to allow a SQL Server upgrade to functionally occur at a slower pace over time. By incrementally adjusting the compatibility level up by one level at a time from the original SQL Server version to the new version, risk can be isolated and mitigated in steps, rather than all at once. This process also provides a rollback mechanism, if needed, since compatibility modes can be lowered, in the event of an emergency.

CHAPTER 8

Bulk Loading Data

Any analytic data store requires the ability to perform data loads quickly and efficiently. Bulk loading is a reduced logging process that allows data to be inserted directly into a columnstore index. This not only bypasses the delta store, but results in a transaction size that reflects the compression of the target data, greatly reducing the amount of data written to the transaction log when this process is used.

Bulk Load Processes Explained

Traditional transactional workloads are fully logged. When fully logged, enough metadata is written to the transaction log so that SQL Server can recover from a failed transaction. In addition, data is written to the transaction log to ensure that point-in-time recovery is possible.

Fully logged transactions in OLTP scenarios are ideal as they allow a database to be rolled back to a specific point in time in the event of application problems. In addition, point-in-time recovery allows for research and forensics into the details of transactions, when needed.

Sometimes, transactional writes are intentionally subdivided into smaller batches to ensure that each transaction is short and fast and causes minimal contention with other queries against the same data.

The cost of fully logged transactions is that more data needs to be written to the transaction log, which results in

- More storage space consumed in the transaction log

- More storage space consumed in transaction log backup files

- More CPU/memory to process transaction log backups

- Longer query duration for write operations

111

© Edward Pollack 2022
E. Pollack, *Analytics Optimization with Columnstore Indexes in Microsoft SQL Server*,
https://doi.org/10.1007/978-1-4842-8048-5_8

Analytic workloads differ greatly in their recovery needs as data loads tend to be larger, less frequent, and asynchronous. When analytic data loads fail, the most common recourse is to investigate the problem, resolve it, and then rerun the data load. Point-in-time recovery within data load processes is less important than simply having recovery available to a point in time prior to the data load. Therefore, OLAP data loads can benefit greatly from minimally logged insert operations.

Outside of columnstore indexes, bulk loading data is limited to a handful of write operations, such as

- BCP

- Bulk insert operations

- Select into operations

- Partition switching

Because point-in-time recovery can be critical to transactional systems, any process that utilizes bulk loading needs to be documented well enough to not accidentally be used in a scenario where it is not desired.

Columnstore indexes use built-in bulk load processes that automatically insert larger batches directly into rowgroups without using the delta store. This greatly improves insert speeds for large analytic data loads and reduces transaction log bloat resulting from those processes.

Bulk Loading into Columnstore Indexes

The breakpoint for deciding whether to use a bulk load process or to use the delta store is 102,400 rows. Inserts of less than 102,400 rows will always be written to the delta store via a fully logged process, whereas inserts of 102,400 rows or more will be written directly to rowgroups in the columnstore index, bypassing the delta store. This decision can be shown in Figure 8-1.

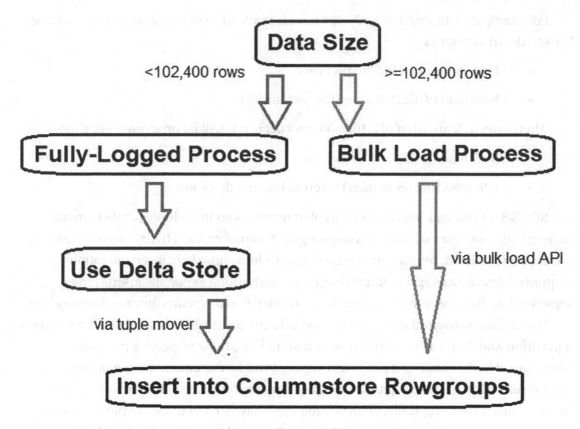

Figure 8-1. *Determination of process for bulk loading data into a columnstore index*

Unlike some of the other types of minimally logged insert operations in SQL Server, there are no prerequisites to take advantage of bulk loading data into a columnstore index. There is no need to adjust isolation levels, use explicit table locking, or adjust parallelism settings. Since bulk loading data will be the desired operation for large inserts into columnstore indexes, it is the default and will be used automatically when possible.

If an insert operation contains more than 2^{20} (1,048,576) rows, it will be subdivided into inserts in the following fashion:

1. Each batch of 2^{20} rows will be bulk inserted into the columnstore index until there are less than 2^{20} rows remaining to insert.

2. If the remainder of rows is greater than or equal to 102,400, it will also be bulk inserted into the columnstore index.

3. If the remainder of rows is less than 102,400, it will be inserted into the delta store.

113

For example, if an insert of 3,000,000 rows is made to a columnstore index, it will be broken down as follows:

- 2 bulk loads of 1,048,576 rows each

- 1 bulk load of 902,848 rows (the remainder)

Alternatively, if an insert of 2,100,000 rows occurs, it will be processed like this:

- 2 bulk loads of 1,048,576 rows each

- 2,848 rows (the remainder) inserted into the delta store

SQL Server can bulk load data into a columnstore index in multiple parallel threads so long as the data for each thread is targeting a different data file. This is automatic and requires no particular user action to accomplish. Columnstore bulk insert operations acquire exclusive locks against target rowgroups, and so long as parallel inserts target separate data files, they are guaranteed to not overlap the rowgroups they are inserting into.

When data is inserted into a partitioned columnstore index, that data is first assigned a partition and then each group of rows is inserted into their respective partitions. Therefore, whether bulk load processes are used will be dependent on the numbers of rows inserted into the target partition, rather than the total number of rows inserted by the source query. Typically, analytic tables will have a current/active partition that accepts new data, whereas the remaining partitions will contain older data that is no longer written to (outside of one-off data loads, software releases, or maintenance events).

Performance of Bulk Loading into Columnstore Indexes

To demonstrate the impact of bulk loading data into a columnstore index, a test will be conducted against a rowstore copy of *Fact.Sale*. The table's creation is not shown here, but is an identical copy, with only a clustered primary key and page compression, rather than a clustered columnstore index. This insert query is shown in Listing 8-1.

Listing 8-1. An Insert of 102,400 Rows into a Clustered Rowstore Index

```
INSERT INTO fact.Sale_Transactional
        ([Sale Key], [City Key],[Customer Key], [Bill To Customer Key],
        [Stock Item Key], [Invoice Date Key], [Delivery Date Key],
        [Salesperson Key], [WWI Invoice ID],
     Description, Package, Quantity, [Unit Price], [Tax Rate],
        [Total Excluding Tax], [Tax Amount], Profit, [Total Including Tax],
        [Total Dry Items],
        [Total Chiller Items], [Lineage Key])
SELECT TOP 102400
        *
FROM Fact.Sale;
```

The insert takes about 1 second. With the rows inserted, an undocumented but useful system function will be used to read the contents of the transaction log and determine the size of the transaction, as seen in Listing 8-2.

Listing 8-2. Query to Calculate the Transaction Size for a Clustered Rowstore Insert

```
SELECT
        fn_dblog.allocunitname,
        SUM(fn_dblog.[log record length]) AS log_size
FROM sys.fn_dblog (NULL, NULL)
WHERE fn_dblog.allocunitname = (
'Fact.Sale_Transactional.PK_Fact_Sale_Transactional')
GROUP BY fn_dblog.allocunitname;
```

The result is a single row that indicates the total log size for the insert transaction, as seen in Figure 8-2.

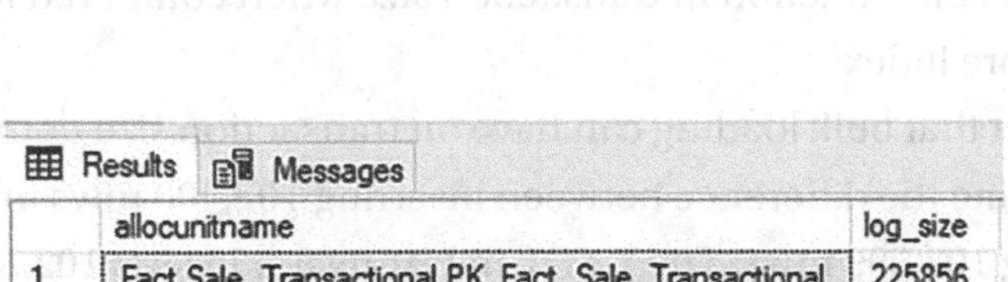

	allocunitname	log_size
1	Fact.Sale_Transactional.PK_Fact_Sale_Transactional	225856

Figure 8-2. Transaction size for an insert of 102,400 rows into a clustered rowstore index

The log size returned for the rowstore insert was 225,856 bytes, or about 220KB. The same insert will now be performed against a clean copy of the table with a columnstore index, as seen in Listing 8-3.

Listing 8-3. An Insert of 102,400 Rows into a Clustered Columnstore Index

```
INSERT INTO fact.Sale_CCI_Clean_Test
      ([Sale Key], [City Key],[Customer Key], [Bill To Customer Key],
      [Stock Item Key], [Invoice Date Key], [Delivery Date Key],
      [Salesperson Key], [WWI Invoice ID],
   Description, Package, Quantity, [Unit Price], [Tax Rate],
   [Total Excluding Tax], [Tax Amount], Profit, [Total Including Tax],
   [Total Dry Items],
   [Total Chiller Items], [Lineage Key])
SELECT TOP 102400
      *
FROM Fact.Sale;
```

This insert takes less than a second to complete. A new clean table is used to ensure that there are no residual transactions from previous demonstrations that would pollute the log. The results from *fn_dblog()* are seen in Figure 8-3.

	allocunitname	log_size
1	Fact.Sale_CCI_Clean_Test.CCI_Sale_CCI_Clean_Test	118192

Figure 8-3. *Transaction size for an insert of 102,400 rows into a clustered columnstore index*

Note that the transaction log size for the insert is 118,192 bytes, or about 115KB. This constitutes a significant reduction in transaction size when compared to a page compressed rowstore index.

With the impact that bulk loading can have on transaction size demonstrated, it is important to illustrate the difference between inserting 102,400 rows into a columnstore index and inserting 102,399 rows. The T-SQL in Listing 8-4 inserts 102,399 rows into a newly created clustered columnstore index.

Listing 8-4. An Insert of 102,399 Rows into a Clustered Columnstore Index

```
INSERT INTO fact.Sale_CCI_Clean_Test_2
        ([Sale Key], [City Key],[Customer Key], [Bill To Customer Key],
        [Stock Item Key], [Invoice Date Key], [Delivery Date Key],
        [Salesperson Key], [WWI Invoice ID],
     Description, Package, Quantity, [Unit Price], [Tax Rate],
        [Total Excluding Tax], [Tax Amount], Profit, [Total Including Tax],
        [Total Dry Items],
        [Total Chiller Items], [Lineage Key])
SELECT TOP 102399
        *
FROM Fact.Sale;
```

This takes about a second to execute. The query to pull data from *fn_dblog()* needs to be adjusted slightly to accommodate the log growth due to both the columnstore index itself and the delta store. This is shown in Listing 8-5.

Listing 8-5. Query to Calculate Log Growth for Columnstore Index and Delta Store

```
SELECT
        fn_dblog.allocunitname,
        SUM(fn_dblog.[log record length]) AS log_size
FROM sys.fn_dblog (NULL, NULL)
WHERE fn_dblog.allocunitname IN (
'Fact.Sale_CCI_Clean_Test_2.CCI_Sale_CCI_Clean_Test_2',
'Fact.Sale_CCI_Clean_Test_2.CCI_Sale_CCI_Clean_Test_2(Delta)')
GROUP BY fn_dblog.allocunitname;
```

Note that the delta store needs to be referenced separately to be included in the results. The transaction log space consumed by each object is seen in Figure 8-4.

	allocunitname	log_size
1	Fact.Sale_CCI_Clean_Test_2.CCI_Sale_CCI_Clean_Te...	456
2	Fact.Sale_CCI_Clean_Test_2.CCI_Sale_CCI_Clean_Te...	1300448

Figure 8-4. Transaction size for an insert of 102,399 rows into a clustered columnstore index

The insert into the delta store was significantly more expensive than any operation demonstrated thus far in this chapter, with a transaction size of 1,300,448, or about 1.2GB. As a result, there is a significant incentive to take advantage of bulk loading data into columnstore indexes when possible.

Trickle Insert vs. Staged Insert

While inserting into the delta store may seem expensive, it is nowhere near as costly as repeated inserts into a columnstore index would be. If an analytic table is often targeted with many smaller insert operations, there is significant value in collecting those rows into a temporary table first, prior to inserting into the columnstore index.

In workloads involving rowstore tables, large insert operations may be batched into small groups of rows in order to reduce contention and decrease the transaction size for each insert. Columnstore indexes do not benefit from micro-batching. When migrating code from rowstore tables to columnstore tables, resources can be saved by adjusting data load processes to operate on significantly larger batches. Batches of 2^{20} (1,048,576) rows are optimal, though a batch size greater than or equal to 102,400 will ensure that the delta store is not needed. If insert operations contain tens of millions of rows, then those inserts can be broken down into more manageable subunits to prevent a staging or temporary table from becoming too large.

The best practices for loading data into columnstore indexes are as follows:

1. Load at least 102,400 rows per insert operation.

2. When possible, load 1,048,576 rows per batch.

3. Only load less than 102,400 rows for the remaining rows at the end of the data load.

While this guidance may make it seem as though the delta store should be avoided at all costs, the goals of an analytic data store should not be compromised for this purpose. Delaying reporting data to prevent delta store usage is not worthwhile and will not save enough resources to be meaningful. Actively avoiding the insert of repeated small batches will ensure that insert performance is quite good. If the delta store is needed for the tail end of a data load process, then there is no reason to avoid it.

Other Data Load Considerations

Vertipaq optimization, which can greatly improve the effectiveness of columnstore index compression, is not used when a nonclustered rowstore index is present on a clustered columnstore index. Over time, this will result in rowgroups that will consume more resources than they would otherwise.

For scenarios where nonclustered rowstore indexes are required to support analytic processes, consider the following options for managing performance on the columnstore index.

Drop Nonclustered Indexes During Data Loads

A simple solution to ensure that Vertipaq optimization is always used is to drop nonclustered rowstore indexes during data loads and re-create them afterward. Building the nonclustered indexes is an online operation and will not interfere with other queries against the table. The downside to this approach is that any analytics that use the nonclustered indexes will be impacted during the data load process, until the nonclustered index rebuild is complete. Additional resources are also required to handle the nonclustered index build. This approach is most effective when the nonclustered indexes are small and relatively quick to build.

On partitioned tables, only the partitions with data that has changed require this consideration. Typically, partitions containing older data that is primarily static and unchanging in nature (not hot data) can be ignored.

For scenarios when nonclustered indexes are necessary and cannot be dropped, consider periodic maintenance to address inefficient compression over time. If a quarterly maintenance can be scheduled, then the following actions can be taken:

1. Drop nonclustered indexes on active partitions.

2. Rebuild the clustered columnstore index on active partitions.

3. Re-create nonclustered indexes.

As a planned maintenance event, these are relatively innocuous tasks that should not consume an unusual amount of time, even on a larger table.

Columnstore Reorganize Operations with Each Data Load

When a columnstore index is read, its contents plus the delta store are read together to produce the necessary output. While the delta store cannot get excessively large, columnstore indexes with periodic data loads can improve read speeds slightly by forcefully compressing the contents of the delta store into the columnstore index. The query in Listing 8-6 examines the contents of the small columnstore index created earlier.

Listing 8-6. Query to Return Details About the Structure of a Columnstore Index

```
SELECT
        tables.name AS table_name,
        indexes.name AS index_name,
        partitions.partition_number,
        column_store_row_groups.row_group_id,
        column_store_row_groups.state_description,
        column_store_row_groups.total_rows,
        column_store_row_groups.size_in_bytes,
        column_store_row_groups.deleted_rows,
        internal_partitions.internal_object_type_desc,
        internal_partitions.rows,
        internal_partitions.data_compression_desc
FROM sys.column_store_row_groups
INNER JOIN sys.indexes
ON indexes.index_id = column_store_row_groups.index_id
AND indexes.object_id = column_store_row_groups.object_id
INNER JOIN sys.tables
ON tables.object_id = indexes.object_id
INNER JOIN sys.partitions
ON partitions.partition_number = column_store_row_groups.partition_number
AND partitions.index_id = indexes.index_id
AND partitions.object_id = tables.object_id
```

```
LEFT JOIN sys.internal_partitions
ON internal_partitions.object_id = tables.object_id
WHERE tables.name = 'Sale_CCI_Clean_Test_2'
ORDER BY indexes.index_id, column_store_row_groups.row_group_id;
```

The results are found in Figure 8-5.

	table_name	index_name	partition_number	row_group_id	state_description	total_rows	size_in_bytes	deleted_rows	internal_object_type_desc	rows	data_compression_desc
1	Sale_CCI_Clean_Test_2	CCI_Sale_CCI_Clean_Test_2	1	0	OPEN	102399	23175168	NULL	COLUMN_STORE_DELETE_BITMAP	0	PAGE
2	Sale_CCI_Clean_Test_2	CCI_Sale_CCI_Clean_Test_2	1	0	OPEN	102399	23175168	NULL	COLUMN_STORE_DELTA_STORE	102399	NONE

Figure 8-5. *Rowgroup information for a small columnstore index*

Note that the entire contents of the columnstore index (102,399 rows) reside in the delta store. The delete bitmap exists as a default and is currently empty. If the operator wishes to move the contents of the delta store into columnstore rowgroups, this can be accomplished by the index maintenance command in Listing 8-7.

Listing 8-7. Index Reorganize Command to Compress Delta Store

```
ALTER INDEX CCI_Sale_CCI_Clean_Test_2 ON Fact.Sale_CCI_Clean_Test_2
REORGANIZE WITH (COMPRESS_ALL_ROW_GROUPS = ON);
```

Once complete, the delta store would be compressed and ready to move into the columnstore index, as seen in Figure 8-6.

	table_name	index_name	partition_number	row_group_id	state_description	total_rows	size_in_bytes	deleted_rows	internal_object_type_desc	rows	data_compression_desc
1	Sale_CCI_Clean_Test_2	CCI_Sale_CCI_Clean_Test_2	1	0	TOMBSTONE	102399	23175168	NULL	COLUMN_STORE_DELETE_BITMAP	0	PAGE
2	Sale_CCI_Clean_Test_2	CCI_Sale_CCI_Clean_Test_2	1	0	TOMBSTONE	102399	23175168	NULL	COLUMN_STORE_DELTA_STORE	102399	NONE
3	Sale_CCI_Clean_Test_2	CCI_Sale_CCI_Clean_Test_2	1	1	COMPRESSED	102399	1563728	0	COLUMN_STORE_DELETE_BITMAP	0	PAGE
4	Sale_CCI_Clean_Test_2	CCI_Sale_CCI_Clean_Test_2	1	1	COMPRESSED	102399	1563728	0	COLUMN_STORE_DELTA_STORE	102399	NONE

Figure 8-6. *Effects of index maintenance on a columnstore delta rowgroup*

The results show that the delta rowgroup affected by the index maintenance is now in an intermediary state. A new object has been created and compressed with the contents of the delta rowgroup inserted into it. The previous delta rowgroup (an uncompressed heap) is left in a tombstone state for the tuple mover to remove at a later point in time. Note the significant size difference between an uncompressed delta rowgroup and a compressed rowgroup.

At this time, running the same ALTER INDEX statement as before will force the tuple mover to complete this cleanup. Alternatively, waiting for a short amount of time to pass will achieve the same results. After 5 minutes have passed, the contents of this columnstore index are as seen in Figure 8-7.

	table_name	index_name	partition_number	row_group_id	state_description	total_rows	size_in_bytes	deleted_rows	internal_object_type_desc	rows	data_compression_desc
1	Sale_CCI_Clean_Test_2	CCI_Sale_CCI_Clean_Test_2	1	1	COMPRESSED	102399	1563728	0	COLUMN_STORE_DELETE_BITMAP	0	PAGE

Figure 8-7. *Columnstore index contents after the tuple mover executes*

Once the tuple mover completes its cleanup process, all that remains is a single compressed columnstore rowgroup.

Performing maintenance like this is not necessary but can improve query read speeds against a columnstore index after a data load is completed. Index maintenance will be discussed in far more detail in Chapter 14, including its use as part of data loads and other columnstore processes.

Summary

When loading data into a columnstore index, bulk loading ensures the fastest possible load speeds while minimizing server resource consumption. Bulk loading large numbers of rows in fewer batches is far more efficient than using trickle or small batch inserts.

By focusing data load processing around maximizing the use of compressed columnstore rowgroups and minimizing delta store usage, overall columnstore index performance can be improved, both for the data load processes and analytics that use the newly loaded data.

CHAPTER 9

Delete and Update Operations

Modifying data within a highly compressed structure is expensive and requires additional processes to manage it successfully. Whereas insert operations can benefit from bulk loading to streamline data load processes, delete and update operations require using the delete bitmap and delta store to manage changes to existing data.

The Cost of Modifying Data

In Chapter 5, columnstore compression was discussed in extensive detail. An important takeaway is that some forms of compression, such as run-length encoding, depend on the exact contents of the underlying data. Columnstore compression is exceptionally good at shrinking data by a considerable amount by applying a variety of encoding and compression algorithms and optimizations. Consider the sample data in Figure 9-1.

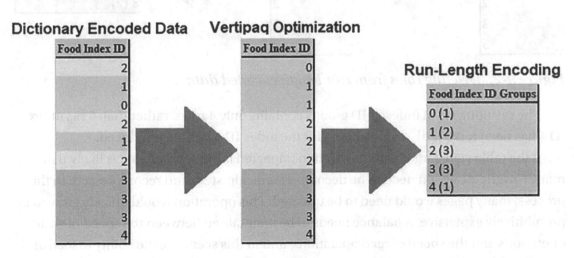

Figure 9-1. *Sample data encoded with run-length encoding*

123

E. Pollack, *Analytics Optimization with Columnstore Indexes in Microsoft SQL Server*,
https://doi.org/10.1007/978-1-4842-8048-5_9

The sample data is encoded with dictionary compression, reordered with Vertipaq optimization, and further compressed with run-length encoding. If a process deletes the last two rows in the table, then it is necessary to decompress the data fully, delete the rows, and then recompress it. Figure 9-2 shows how this process would impact the data.

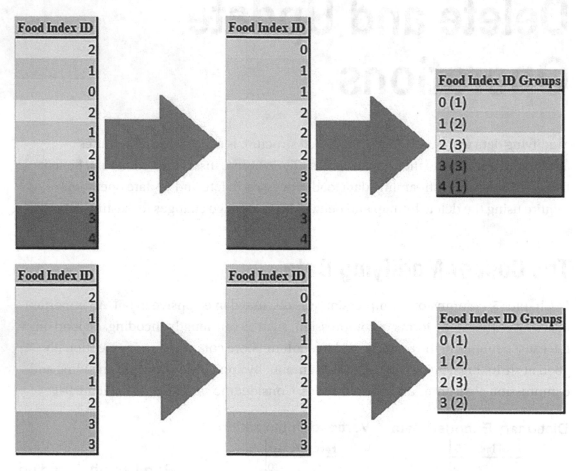

Figure 9-2. *Deleting rows from run-length encoded data*

The resulting set of indexed ID groups contains only 4 rows, rather than 5 (as index ID 4 has been removed), and the count for the index ID 3 has been reduced.

If the table were larger and the deletion impacted more rows, then it is likely that many rowgroups would need to be decompressed, adjusted, and recompressed. In the process, many pages would need to be updated. This operation would quickly grow to be prohibitively expensive. A balance needs to be maintained between the speed of write operations and the speed of read operations, and in this scenario, the ability to load and modify data quickly needs to be prioritized.

Delete Operations

In a columnstore index, the cost to decompress rowgroups, delete rows, and recompress them is prohibitively high. The more rowgroups a delete operation targets, the greater this cost would become. To mitigate this cost, a structure called the delete bitmap is used to track deletions from the columnstore index.

The delete bitmap is a heap that references the rows within underlying rowgroups. When a row is deleted, the data within the rowgroup remains unchanged and the delete bitmap is updated with a reference to the deleted row. As such, deleted rows in columnstore indexes can be seen as soft deleted, where removed rows are flagged, but not physically deleted.

Note that delete operations against rows in the delta store do not need to use the delete bitmap as the delta store is a rowstore heap and rows can simply be deleted from it as needed, without the need for soft deletes.

When a query is executed against a rowgroup containing deleted rows, the delete bitmap is consulted and deleted rows are excluded from the results. The delete bitmap may be visualized as seen in Figure 9-3.

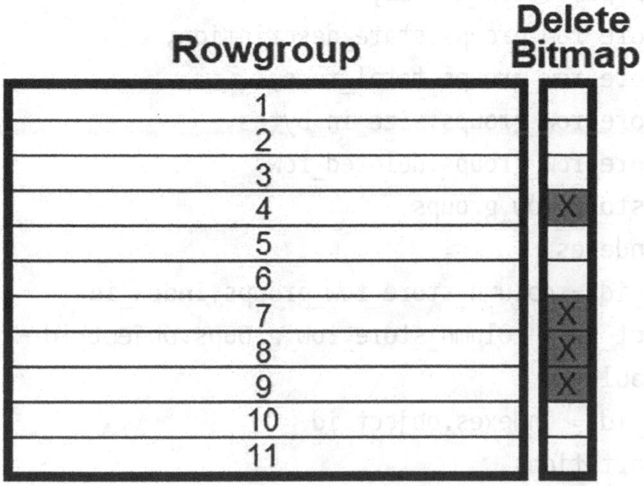

Figure 9-3. *The delete bitmap and its relationship to a columnstore index*

The underlying rows within the rowgroup are unchanged when a deletion occurs against them. Instead, the delete bitmap tracks which rows are deleted and is consulted when future queries are issued against this rowgroup. Because of this, deleting data in a columnstore index will not reclaim storage space.

Consider the query shown in Listing 9-1.

Listing 9-1. Query That Deletes Data from a Columnstore Index

```
DELETE
FROM Fact.Sale_CCI
WHERE [Invoice Date Key] = '1/1/2016';
```

When executed, this query will delete all sale data that was invoiced on 1/1/2016. Before doing so, the rowgroup metadata can be consulted to confirm that there are currently no deleted rows in the rowgroup. The query in Listing 9-2 will return metadata about rowgroups in this columnstore index, including the number of deleted rows, if any.

Listing 9-2. Query That Returns Metadata About Deleted Rows in Rowgroups

```
SELECT
        tables.name AS table_name,
        indexes.name AS index_name,
        partitions.partition_number,
        column_store_row_groups.state_description,
        column_store_row_groups.total_rows,
        column_store_row_groups.size_in_bytes,
        column_store_row_groups.deleted_rows
FROM sys.column_store_row_groups
INNER JOIN sys.indexes
ON indexes.index_id = column_store_row_groups.index_id
AND indexes.object_id = column_store_row_groups.object_id
INNER JOIN sys.tables
ON tables.object_id = indexes.object_id
INNER JOIN sys.partitions
ON partitions.partition_number = column_store_row_groups.partition_number
AND partitions.index_id = indexes.index_id
AND partitions.object_id = tables.object_id
WHERE tables.name = 'Sale_CCI'
ORDER BY indexes.index_id, column_store_row_groups.row_group_id;
```

The rowgroup metadata can be seen in Figure 9-4.

	table_name	index_name	partition_number	state_description	total_rows	size_in_bytes	deleted_rows
1	Sale_CCI	CCI_fact_sale_CCI	1	COMPRESSED	1048576	13027088	0
2	Sale_CCI	CCI_fact_sale_CCI	1	COMPRESSED	1048576	12997032	0
3	Sale_CCI	CCI_fact_sale_CCI	1	COMPRESSED	1048576	12997632	0
4	Sale_CCI	CCI_fact_sale_CCI	1	COMPRESSED	1048576	13084408	0
5	Sale_CCI	CCI_fact_sale_CCI	1	COMPRESSED	1048576	12984000	0
6	Sale_CCI	CCI_fact_sale_CCI	1	COMPRESSED	1048576	12991560	0
7	Sale_CCI	CCI_fact_sale_CCI	1	COMPRESSED	1048576	13024792	0
8	Sale_CCI	CCI_fact_sale_CCI	1	COMPRESSED	1048576	13025488	0
9	Sale_CCI	CCI_fact_sale_CCI	1	COMPRESSED	1048576	13001248	0

Figure 9-4. *Rowgroup metadata for a columnstore index, including deleted rows*

As is expected of a columnstore index that has had no delete operations executed against it, the *deleted_rows* column in *sys.column_store_row_groups* shows zero for each rowgroup. Executing the query in Listing 9-1 will delete a total of 15,400 rows from the columnstore index. Figure 9-5 shows the metadata details for the columnstore index after the deletion has completed.

	table_name	index_name	partition_number	state_description	total_rows	size_in_bytes	deleted_rows
1	Sale_CCI	CCI_fact_sale_CCI	1	COMPRESSED	1048576	13027088	618
2	Sale_CCI	CCI_fact_sale_CCI	1	COMPRESSED	1048576	12997032	666
3	Sale_CCI	CCI_fact_sale_CCI	1	COMPRESSED	1048576	12997632	765
4	Sale_CCI	CCI_fact_sale_CCI	1	COMPRESSED	1048576	13084408	564
5	Sale_CCI	CCI_fact_sale_CCI	1	COMPRESSED	1048576	12984000	629
6	Sale_CCI	CCI_fact_sale_CCI	1	COMPRESSED	1048576	12991560	698
7	Sale_CCI	CCI_fact_sale_CCI	1	COMPRESSED	1048576	13024792	593
8	Sale_CCI	CCI_fact_sale_CCI	1	COMPRESSED	1048576	13025488	679
9	Sale_CCI	CCI_fact_sale_CCI	1	COMPRESSED	1048576	13001248	596

Figure 9-5. *Rowgroup metadata after a deletion has occurred*

Each rowgroup now contains some number of deleted rows, depending on the number of rows within them that happen to have been invoiced on 1/1/2016. Note that the total rows in each rowgroup and the size in bytes have not changed. This is expected and reflects the fact that rows were soft deleted via the delete bitmap.

Because rows were removed from all rowgroups in the index, a deletion without the aid of the delete bitmap would have required a rebuild of the entire index, which would be a prohibitively expensive operation to perform while a process waits for a single day's worth of rows to be deleted. Instead, the delete of 15,400 rows completed exceptionally quickly, in under a second, thanks to the delete bitmap!

The only way to clean up deleted rows and free up the space consumed within rowgroups is to perform an index rebuild on the columnstore index or on any partitions impacted by the deletion. This is generally not needed unless the amount of deleted data becomes large with respect to the overall size of the index. Like with classic rowstore indexes, fragmentation is not problematic until there is too much of it, at which time a rebuild can resolve it. Note that index reorganize operations do not remove deleted rows from columnstore indexes! Chapter 14 dives into index maintenance in detail, discussing how and when it is needed, and best practices for its use.

Update Operations

In a columnstore index, an update is executed as two operations: a delete and an insert. While logically, the update will perform as a single atomic unit, under the covers it will consist of

1.   A set of deleted rows, flagged in the delete bitmap

2.   A set of newly inserted rows, written to the delta store

This means that an update operation will need to write to both the delete bitmap and the delta store in order to complete successfully. It is also important to note that the insert operations that result from an update operation against a columnstore index will exclusively use the delta store and cannot take advantage of bulk load processes.

Before continuing, a rebuild will be executed against the columnstore index to allow for easier visualization of the results. The query in Listing 9-3 will rebuild the index.

Listing 9-3. Query to Rebuild a Columnstore Index, Removing the Delete Bitmap

```
ALTER INDEX CCI_fact_sale_CCI ON Fact.Sale_CCI REBUILD;
```

With the data now clean, the query in Listing 9-4 can be used to return metadata about all rowgroups in the columnstore index, including both the delta store and delete bitmap.

Listing 9-4. Query to Return Delete Bitmap and Delta Store Metadata for Rowgroups in a Columnstore Index

```
SELECT
        tables.name AS table_name,
        indexes.name AS index_name,
        partitions.partition_number,
        column_store_row_groups.row_group_id,
        column_store_row_groups.state_description,
        column_store_row_groups.total_rows,
        column_store_row_groups.size_in_bytes,
        column_store_row_groups.deleted_rows,
        internal_partitions.internal_object_type_desc,
        internal_partitions.rows
FROM sys.column_store_row_groups
INNER JOIN sys.indexes
ON indexes.index_id = column_store_row_groups.index_id
AND indexes.object_id = column_store_row_groups.object_id
INNER JOIN sys.tables
ON tables.object_id = indexes.object_id
INNER JOIN sys.partitions
ON partitions.partition_number = column_store_row_groups.partition_number
AND partitions.index_id = indexes.index_id
AND partitions.object_id = tables.object_id
LEFT JOIN sys.internal_partitions
ON internal_partitions.object_id = tables.object_id
WHERE tables.name = 'Sale_CCI'
ORDER BY indexes.index_id, column_store_row_groups.row_group_id;
```

The results in Figure 9-6 show a clean columnstore index with no deleted rows or entries in the delta store.

	table_name	index_name	partition_number	row_group_id	state_description	total_rows	size_in_bytes	deleted_rows	internal_object_type_desc	rows
1	Sale_CCI	CCI_fact_sale_CCI	1	0	COMPRESSED	1048576	12975000	0	COLUMN_STORE_DELETE_BITMAP	0
2	Sale_CCI	CCI_fact_sale_CCI	1	1	COMPRESSED	1048576	13065744	0	COLUMN_STORE_DELETE_BITMAP	0
3	Sale_CCI	CCI_fact_sale_CCI	1	2	COMPRESSED	1048576	12913016	0	COLUMN_STORE_DELETE_BITMAP	0
4	Sale_CCI	CCI_fact_sale_CCI	1	3	COMPRESSED	1048576	13244208	0	COLUMN_STORE_DELETE_BITMAP	0
5	Sale_CCI	CCI_fact_sale_CCI	1	4	COMPRESSED	1048576	13121888	0	COLUMN_STORE_DELETE_BITMAP	0
6	Sale_CCI	CCI_fact_sale_CCI	1	5	COMPRESSED	1048576	13173112	0	COLUMN_STORE_DELETE_BITMAP	0
7	Sale_CCI	CCI_fact_sale_CCI	1	6	COMPRESSED	1048576	12946784	0	COLUMN_STORE_DELETE_BITMAP	0
8	Sale_CCI	CCI_fact_sale_CCI	1	7	COMPRESSED	1048576	13113216	0	COLUMN_STORE_DELETE_BITMAP	0
9	Sale_CCI	CCI_fact_sale_CCI	1	8	COMPRESSED	1048576	13108952	0	COLUMN_STORE_DELETE_BITMAP	0

Figure 9-6. *Metadata for rowgroups with no deletes/updates against them*

With a pristine columnstore index available, the effects of update operations can be easily visualized against it. Consider the query shown in Listing 9-5.

Listing 9-5. Query to Identify a Data Set to Update

```
SELECT
        *
FROM Fact.Sale_CCI
WHERE [Invoice Date Key] = '1/2/2016';
```

This SELECT query identifies a total of 18,150 rows in the table that match the filter criteria of an invoice date of 1/2/2016. Next, an update will be made against two columns in the table, as shown in Listing 9-6.

Listing 9-6. Query to Update Data from a Columnstore Index

```
UPDATE Sale_CCI
        SET [Total Dry Items] = [Total Dry Items] - 1,
            [Total Chiller Items] = [Total Chiller Items] + 1
FROM Fact.Sale_CCI
WHERE [Invoice Date Key] = '1/2/2016';
```

Returning to the rowgroup metadata query in Listing 9-4, the results of the UPDATE statement can be reviewed, with a sample seen in Figure 9-7.

	table_name	index_name	partition_number	row_group_id	state_description	total_rows	size_in_bytes	deleted_rows	internal_object_type_desc	rows
42	Sale_CCI	CCI_fact_sale_CCI	1	20	COMPRESSED	1048576	12977792	745	COLUMN_STORE_DELTA_STORE	18150
43	Sale_CCI	CCI_fact_sale_CCI	1	21	COMPRESSED	1048576	13034904	760	COLUMN_STORE_DELETE_BITMAP	18150
44	Sale_CCI	CCI_fact_sale_CCI	1	21	COMPRESSED	1048576	13034904	760	COLUMN_STORE_DELTA_STORE	18150
45	Sale_CCI	CCI_fact_sale_CCI	1	22	COMPRESSED	1048576	13001232	880	COLUMN_STORE_DELETE_BITMAP	18150
46	Sale_CCI	CCI_fact_sale_CCI	1	22	COMPRESSED	1048576	13001232	880	COLUMN_STORE_DELTA_STORE	18150
47	Sale_CCI	CCI_fact_sale_CCI	1	23	COMPRESSED	249279	3093384	155	COLUMN_STORE_DELETE_BITMAP	18150
48	Sale_CCI	CCI_fact_sale_CCI	1	23	COMPRESSED	249279	3093384	155	COLUMN_STORE_DELTA_STORE	18150
49	Sale_CCI	CCI_fact_sale_CCI	1	24	COMPRESSED	829623	10353896	633	COLUMN_STORE_DELETE_BITMAP	18150
50	Sale_CCI	CCI_fact_sale_CCI	1	24	COMPRESSED	829623	10353896	633	COLUMN_STORE_DELTA_STORE	18150
51	Sale_CCI	CCI_fact_sale_CCI	1	25	OPEN	18150	4169728	NULL	COLUMN_STORE_DELETE_BITMAP	18150
52	Sale_CCI	CCI_fact_sale_CCI	1	25	OPEN	18150	4169728	NULL	COLUMN_STORE_DELTA_STORE	18150

Figure 9-7. *Metadata for rowgroups after updating 18150 rows*

The metadata after the UPDATE was executed shows that every rowgroup in the columnstore index was impacted as 18,150 rows were deleted and 18,150 rows were then inserted. *Sys.internal_partitions* shows a delete bitmap and delta store object, each containing 18,150 total rows. The rowgroup detail illustrates how many rows were updated per rowgroup. In addition, the new rowgroup (number 25) shows the new open delta store that was created for the newly inserted rows.

The resulting structure underscores the fact that an UPDATE against a columnstore index executes as a combination of discrete delete and insert operations. Performing each of those operations sequentially would yield similar results.

Consider an update to all rows in this columnstore index for the range of invoice dates from 1/3/2016 up to 1/8/2016. A count of these rows shows a total of 148,170 that match that date filter. Before running an update, the columnstore index will be rebuilt, which will clean up the deleted rows and delta stores, allowing for a better demonstration. Listing 9-7 provides the query to rebuild the index and then update these rows.

Listing 9-7. Query to Update 148,170 Rows in a Columnstore Index After Rebuilding the Index

```
ALTER INDEX CCI_fact_sale_CCI ON Fact.Sale_CCI REBUILD;
GO

UPDATE Sale_CCI
        SET [Total Dry Items] = [Total Dry Items] - 1,
            [Total Chiller Items] = [Total Chiller Items] + 1
FROM Fact.Sale_CCI
WHERE [Invoice Date Key] >= '1/3/2016'
AND [Invoice Date Key] < '1/8/2016';
```

When updating 148,170 rows, the first thing to note is that it took 5 full seconds to execute! The previous update of 18,150 rows completed almost instantly after being executed. Viewing the metadata reveals the reason for this, as seen in Figure 9-8.

	table_name	index_name	partition_number	row_group_id	state_description	total_rows	size_in_bytes	deleted_rows	internal_object_type_desc	rows
43	Sale_CCI	CCI_fact_sale_CCI	1	21	COMPRESSED	1048576	13046592	7781	COLUMN_STORE_DELETE_BITMAP	148170
44	Sale_CCI	CCI_fact_sale_CCI	1	21	COMPRESSED	1048576	13046592	7781	COLUMN_STORE_DELTA_STORE	148170
45	Sale_CCI	CCI_fact_sale_CCI	1	22	COMPRESSED	1048576	12882040	4107	COLUMN_STORE_DELETE_BITMAP	148170
46	Sale_CCI	CCI_fact_sale_CCI	1	22	COMPRESSED	1048576	12882040	4107	COLUMN_STORE_DELTA_STORE	148170
47	Sale_CCI	CCI_fact_sale_CCI	1	23	COMPRESSED	991056	12197576	5714	COLUMN_STORE_DELETE_BITMAP	148170
48	Sale_CCI	CCI_fact_sale_CCI	1	23	COMPRESSED	991056	12197576	5714	COLUMN_STORE_DELTA_STORE	148170
49	Sale_CCI	CCI_fact_sale_CCI	1	24	COMPRESSED	87846	1098328	520	COLUMN_STORE_DELETE_BITMAP	148170
50	Sale_CCI	CCI_fact_sale_CCI	1	24	COMPRESSED	87846	1098328	520	COLUMN_STORE_DELTA_STORE	148170
51	Sale_CCI	CCI_fact_sale_CCI	1	25	OPEN	148170	33562624	NULL	COLUMN_STORE_DELETE_BITMAP	148170
52	Sale_CCI	CCI_fact_sale_CCI	1	25	OPEN	148170	33562624	NULL	COLUMN_STORE_DELTA_STORE	148170

Figure 9-8. *Metadata for rowgroups after updating 148,170 rows*

The key takeaway from the metadata following the larger update is that the delta store contains all 148,170 rows updated in the operation. Normally, any INSERT operations of 102,400 rows or more will benefit from a minimally logged bulk insert process, but UPDATE operations cannot benefit from it. Because the UPDATE is composed of both an INSERT and DELETE in the same transaction, it is not possible to fork the single transaction into a fully logged DELETE and a minimally logged INSERT.

Bulk insert processes on columnstore indexes can save immense resources when used, but are not allowed to violate the ACID (Atomic, Consistent, Isolated, and Durable) properties of a SQL Server database. Attempting to splice together a fully logged and minimally logged transaction into a single larger transaction would require the creation of a transaction that would provide point-in-time restore capabilities for the DELETE, but not the INSERT. While it is possible to conceive of ways for SQL Server to architect its way around that limitation, doing so would be confusing to anyone using a columnstore index and could result in unexpected results when restoring databases containing columnstore indexes that are subject to frequent UPDATE operations.

The key takeaway is that an UPDATE against a columnstore index will be comprised of a DELETE operation and a fully logged INSERT into the delta store. As the number of rows updated increases, the performance of those operations will decrease dramatically. The delta store was built to handle small numbers of rows – either trickle loads or the residual rows from a larger data load process. It was not built for large volumes of rows at one time and as a matter of course will perform poorly for those applications.

There is one final demonstration to underscore this challenge, and that is to update more rows than would fit into a single rowgroup. Consider the sample query in Listing 9-8.

Listing 9-8. Query to Count Rows with a Wide Date Range on a Columnstore Index

```
SELECT
        COUNT(*)
FROM Fact.Sale_CCI
WHERE [Invoice Date Key] >= '1/8/2016'
AND [Invoice Date Key] < '3/5/2016';
```

When executed, the result is 1,159,180 rows counted. This is greater than the 1,048,576 rows that can be stored in a single columnstore rowgroup. Listing 9-9 rebuilds the index once more and then performs an update against all 1,159,180 rows identified in Listing 9-9. This single UPDATE operation will result in the deletion of old rows, the insertion of new rows into the delta store, and the compression of most of the new rows into rowgroups.

Listing 9-9. Query to Update 1,159,180 Rows in a Columnstore Index After Rebuilding the Index

```
ALTER INDEX CCI_fact_sale_CCI ON Fact.Sale_CCI REBUILD;
GO

UPDATE Sale_CCI
        SET [Total Dry Items] = [Total Dry Items] - 1,
            [Total Chiller Items] = [Total Chiller Items] + 1
FROM Fact.Sale_CCI
WHERE [Invoice Date Key] >= '1/8/2016'
AND [Invoice Date Key] < '3/5/2016';
```

The update of 1,159,180 rows took almost a minute to complete. Figure 9-9 shows the resulting columnstore metadata immediately after this large UPDATE operation completes.

	table_name	index_name	partition_number	row_group_id	state_description	total_rows	size_in_bytes	deleted_rows	internal_object_type_desc	rows
73	Sale_CCI	CCI_fact_sale_CCI	1	24	COMPRESSED	827868	8575416	36672	COLUMN_STORE_DELETE_BITMAP	1159180
74	Sale_CCI	CCI_fact_sale_CCI	1	24	COMPRESSED	827868	8575416	36672	COLUMN_STORE_DELTA_STORE	1048576
75	Sale_CCI	CCI_fact_sale_CCI	1	24	COMPRESSED	827868	8575416	36672	COLUMN_STORE_DELTA_STORE	110604
76	Sale_CCI	CCI_fact_sale_CCI	1	25	CLOSED	1048576	237469696	NULL	COLUMN_STORE_DELETE_BITMAP	1159180
77	Sale_CCI	CCI_fact_sale_CCI	1	25	CLOSED	1048576	237469696	NULL	COLUMN_STORE_DELTA_STORE	1048576
78	Sale_CCI	CCI_fact_sale_CCI	1	25	CLOSED	1048576	237469696	NULL	COLUMN_STORE_DELTA_STORE	110604
79	Sale_CCI	CCI_fact_sale_CCI	1	26	OPEN	110604	25092096	NULL	COLUMN_STORE_DELETE_BITMAP	1159180
80	Sale_CCI	CCI_fact_sale_CCI	1	26	OPEN	110604	25092096	NULL	COLUMN_STORE_DELTA_STORE	1048576
81	Sale_CCI	CCI_fact_sale_CCI	1	26	OPEN	110604	25092096	NULL	COLUMN_STORE_DELTA_STORE	110604

Figure 9-9. *Metadata for rowgroups after updating 1,159,180 rows*

Note that there are multiple delta stores present. The open delta store (number 26) will remain open to accept future inserted data. The closed delta store will be processed by the tuple mover asynchronously and be compressed into a permanent columnstore rowgroup. Figure 9-10 shows the metadata for this columnstore index after a minute has passed and the tuple mover has executed.

	table_name	index_name	partition_number	row_group_id	state_description	total_rows	size_in_bytes	deleted_rows	internal_object_type_desc	rows
73	Sale_CCI	CCI_fact_sale_CCI	1	24	COMPRESSED	827868	8575416	36672	COLUMN_STORE_DELETE_BITMAP	1159180
74	Sale_CCI	CCI_fact_sale_CCI	1	24	COMPRESSED	827868	8575416	36672	COLUMN_STORE_DELTA_STORE	1048576
75	Sale_CCI	CCI_fact_sale_CCI	1	24	COMPRESSED	827868	8575416	36672	COLUMN_STORE_DELTA_STORE	110604
76	Sale_CCI	CCI_fact_sale_CCI	1	25	TOMBSTONE	1048576	237469696	NULL	COLUMN_STORE_DELETE_BITMAP	1159180
77	Sale_CCI	CCI_fact_sale_CCI	1	25	TOMBSTONE	1048576	237469696	NULL	COLUMN_STORE_DELTA_STORE	1048576
78	Sale_CCI	CCI_fact_sale_CCI	1	25	TOMBSTONE	1048576	237469696	NULL	COLUMN_STORE_DELTA_STORE	110604
79	Sale_CCI	CCI_fact_sale_CCI	1	26	OPEN	110604	25092096	NULL	COLUMN_STORE_DELETE_BITMAP	1159180
80	Sale_CCI	CCI_fact_sale_CCI	1	26	OPEN	110604	25092096	NULL	COLUMN_STORE_DELTA_STORE	1048576
81	Sale_CCI	CCI_fact_sale_CCI	1	26	OPEN	110604	25092096	NULL	COLUMN_STORE_DELTA_STORE	110604
82	Sale_CCI	CCI_fact_sale_CCI	1	27	COMPRESSED	1048576	840144	0	COLUMN_STORE_DELETE_BITMAP	1159180
83	Sale_CCI	CCI_fact_sale_CCI	1	27	COMPRESSED	1048576	840144	0	COLUMN_STORE_DELTA_STORE	1048576
84	Sale_CCI	CCI_fact_sale_CCI	1	27	COMPRESSED	1048576	840144	0	COLUMN_STORE_DELTA_STORE	110604

Figure 9-10. *Metadata for rowgroups after updating 1,159,180 rows and allowing the tuple mover to execute*

The rowgroup labeled in a state of "TOMBSTONE" (number 25) is no longer a logical part of the columnstore index and will be cleaned up in the future, either via the tuple mover or index maintenance. Rowgroup number 27 contains the contents of rowgroup number 25 when it was processed by the tuple mover. To summarize the changes made to the columnstore index by the update of 1,159,180 rows:

1.   1,159,180 rows were marked as deleted in the delete bitmap across all rowgroups.

2.   1,048,576 rows were inserted into one delta store, filling it to capacity.

3. 110,604 rows were inserted into another delta store and remain in an open state awaiting future inserted rows.

4. The 1,048,576 rows in the full delta store are processed by the tuple mover and compressed into a permanent rowgroup.

This is a significant amount of work for a single UPDATE statement, and it scales poorly with increasing row counts.

In general, updates should be limited to small row counts or avoided altogether. There is value in rethinking how code is written to refactor an UPDATE against a columnstore index into a set of deletes and inserts or to manage an update via intermediary processes that avoid it altogether. The performance of UPDATE operations on columnstore indexes will be unpredictable and a large enough row count will result in transactions large enough to create resource pressure on the SQL Server.

Chapter 15 (best practices) will discuss in greater detail how to avoid updates and a variety of tactics that can be used when migrating UPDATE code from rowstore indexes into columnstore indexes.

CHAPTER 10

Segment and Rowgroup Elimination

A key component to how columnstore indexes function is that every segment within the index is its own building block. Each may be read individually or in groups, but the number of segments read via any query can be reduced by efficient architecture and optimal query patterns. Reducing segments read directly reduces IO, improves query speed and memory-related performance metrics, such as page life expectancy.

Segment Elimination

Each segment represents data for a single column over a set of rows. When a query is executed against a columnstore index, SQL Server needs to determine which rowgroups are required to return the requested result set. Within those rowgroups, only the segments containing data for the selected columns will be read. Therefore, queries that select less columns will read fewer segments, thereby reducing IO, memory usage, and query runtimes.

© Edward Pollack 2022
E. Pollack, *Analytics Optimization with Columnstore Indexes in Microsoft SQL Server*,
https://doi.org/10.1007/978-1-4842-8048-5_10

Consider the columnstore index shown in Figure 10-1.

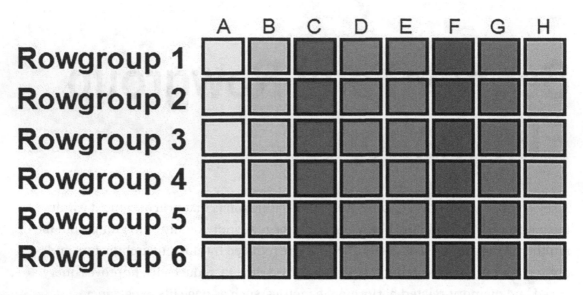

Figure 10-1. *Sample columnstore index with six rowgroups and eight columns*

With 6 rowgroups and 8 columns, this columnstore index contains a total of 48 segments. Because each column is broken into its own set of segments (one per rowgroup), it is not necessary to read segments for columns that are not needed for a query. If a sample query were to only read columns A and B, the result would be that the remaining segments can be automatically skipped, as shown in Figure 10-2.

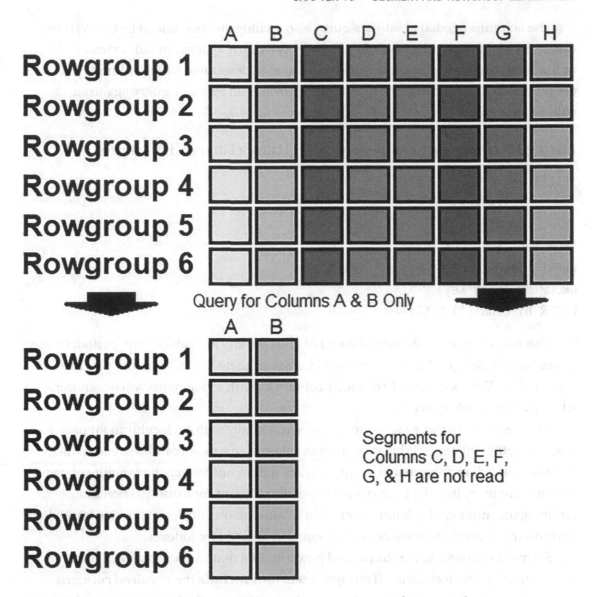

Figure 10-2. Impact of segment elimination on a query for two columns

By querying for only two of the possible eight columns, the number of segments read was reduced by 75%. This convention holds true for columnstore indexes with any number of columns. If this table had 24 columns, then reading only 2 of them would mean that 22 columns would not be read. The result of this feature is that the number of segments read in a columnstore index query will be proportional to the number of columns involved in the query.

The columns needed to satisfy a query also include any referenced by the WHERE clause, as well as in aggregates (GROUP BY/HAVING). If a query includes views or functions, then their contents will be evaluated to determine which columns are required to execute a query. Listing 10-1 provides an example query against a columnstore index.

Listing 10-1. Sample Columnstore Query Using a Filter and Aggregate

```
SELECT
        [City Key],
        COUNT(*)
FROM fact.Sale_CCI
WHERE [Invoice Date Key] >= '1/1/2016'
GROUP BY [City Key]
ORDER BY COUNT(*) DESC;
```

This analytic query calculates a count of sales per city for a given time period. Of the 21 columns in *Sale_CCI*, only 2 were required to complete this calculation: *City Key* and *Invoice Date Key*. As a result, 19 of the 21 column's worth of segments will be ignored when executing this query.

Alternatively, rowstore tables store rows sequentially with each column for each row stored together on pages. While reading less columns in rowstore indexes can reduce the amount of data presented to an application, it does not reduce the quantity of pages read into memory in order to retrieve the specific columns for a query. Therefore, reducing the number of columns queried in a columnstore index will provide immediate performance benefits that are not as pronounced in rowstore indexes.

Segment elimination is a simple and powerful tool that can be simplified into a single optimization technique: ***Write queries to only include the required columns***. Since rowgroups can contain up to 2^{20} rows, the cost of querying unnecessary columns can be quite high. Whereas transactional queries against rowstore tables often operate on small numbers of rows, analytic queries can access millions of rows at a time. Therefore, the perceived convenience of *SELECT* * queries will hinder performance on a columnstore index.

Consider the query in Listing 10-2.

Listing 10-2. A SELECT * Query Against a Columnstore Index

```
SELECT
    *
FROM fact.Sale_CCI
WHERE [Invoice Date Key] = '2/17/2016';
```

This SELECT * query returns all columns for sales on a specific date. While only 30,140 rows are returned, all 21 columns need to have their segments retrieved as part of the operation. Figure 10-3 provides the output of STATISTICS IO for this query.

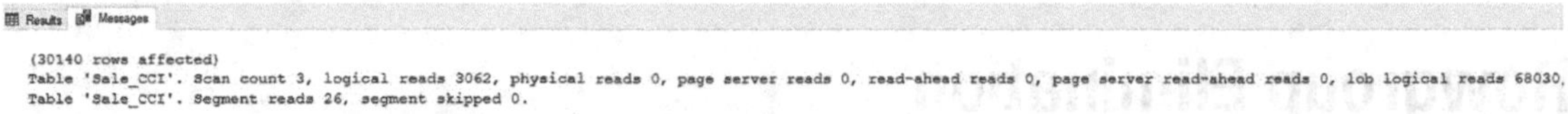

```
Results   Messages

(30140 rows affected)
Table 'Sale_CCI'. Scan count 3, logical reads 3062, physical reads 0, page server reads 0, read-ahead reads 0, page server read-ahead reads 0, lob logical reads 68030,
Table 'Sale_CCI'. Segment reads 26, segment skipped 0.
```

Figure 10-3. *IO for a sample SELECT * query*

Note that a total of 68,030 LOB logical reads are recorded. Listing 10-3 contains an alternative query in which only a small set of columns required by an application are returned.

Listing 10-3. A Query Against a Columnstore Index Requesting Only Three Columns

```
SELECT
    [Sale Key],
    [City Key],
    [Invoice Date Key]
FROM fact.Sale_CCI
WHERE [Invoice Date Key] = '2/17/2016';
```

Here, only three of the columns are requested, instead of all of them. The resulting IO can be viewed in Figure 10-4.

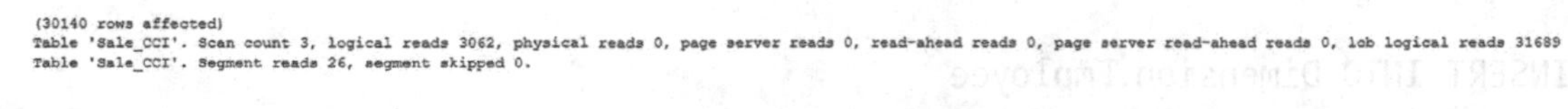

```
Results   Messages

(30140 rows affected)
Table 'Sale_CCI'. Scan count 3, logical reads 3062, physical reads 0, page server reads 0, read-ahead reads 0, page server read-ahead reads 0, lob logical reads 31689
Table 'Sale_CCI'. Segment reads 26, segment skipped 0.
```

Figure 10-4. *IO for a sample query requesting data from three columns*

When the column list was reduced to only those needed for the query, LOB logical reads were reduced from 68,030 to 31,689. The performance improvement for omitting columns will vary based on the data type, compression, and contents of each column. Omitting a text column with no repeated values will reduce IO far more than omitting a BIT column.

Segment elimination is an easy way to improve query speeds while also reducing resource consumption. Anyone writing queries against columnstore indexes should consider which columns are required for their workloads and ensure that no extra columns are returned.

Rowgroup Elimination

Unlike rowstore indexes, columnstore indexes have no built-in order. The data that is inserted into a columnstore index is added in the order it is received by SQL Server. As a result, the order of data within rowgroups is the direct result of the order it was inserted. Equally important is that UPDATE operations will reorder a columnstore index, removing rows from one set of rowgroups and inserting the new versions into the most current open rowgroups.

Because compressing rowgroups is a computationally expensive process, the cost to intrinsically maintain any form of data order would be prohibitively high. This is one of the most important concepts when architecting a columnstore index. Since data order is not enforced by SQL Server, it is the responsibility of the architect to determine data order up front and ensure that both data load processes and common query patterns maintain that agreed-upon data order.

Consider the table *Dimension.Employee* that contains a clustered rowstore index on the *Employee Key* column. If three new employees start work and are added to the table, the INSERT operations to add them could be represented by the T-SQL in Listing 10-4.

Listing 10-4. Query to Add Three New Employees to the Dimension.Employee Table

```
INSERT INTO Dimension.Employee
      ([Employee Key], [WWI Employee ID], Employee, [Preferred Name],
      [Is Salesperson], Photo, [Valid From], [Valid To], [Lineage Key])
VALUES
(   -1, -- Clustered Index
```

```
        289, N'Ebenezer Scrooge', N'Scrooge', 0, NULL, GETUTCDATE(),
        '9999-12-31 23:59:59.9999999', 3),
(       213, -- Clustered Index
        400, N'Captain Ahab', N'Captain', 0, NULL, GETUTCDATE(), '9999-12-31
        23:59:59.9999999', 3),
(       1017, -- Clustered Index
        501, N'Holden Caulfield', N'Phony', 0, NULL, GETUTCDATE(), '9999-12-31
        23:59:59.9999999', 3);
```

There are three rows inserted into the table, with clustered index ID values of -1, 213, and 1017. When inserted, SQL Server will place each row in the b-tree index in order with the rest of the rows, based on those *Employee Key* values. As a result, the table will remain ordered by the clustered index after the INSERT operation.

Imagine for a moment that this table did not have a rowstore index, but instead had a clustered columnstore index. In that scenario, the three rows would be inserted at the end of the open rowgroup(s) without any regard to the value of *Employee Key*. A query that searches for a specific range of IDs will need to examine any rowgroup that contains the IDs.

Columnstore metadata helps SQL Server locate rows based on the range of values for each column present in each rowgroup. Consider the metadata for the *Invoice Date Key* column in *Fact.Sale_CCI* using the query in Listing 10-5.

Listing 10-5. Query to Examine Metadata for a Single Column of a Columnstore Index

```
SELECT
        tables.name AS table_name,
        indexes.name AS index_name,
        columns.name AS column_name,
        partitions.partition_number,
        column_store_segments.segment_id,
        column_store_segments.min_data_id,
        column_store_segments.max_data_id,
        column_store_segments.row_count
FROM sys.column_store_segments
INNER JOIN sys.partitions
ON column_store_segments.hobt_id = partitions.hobt_id
```

143

```
INNER JOIN sys.indexes
ON indexes.index_id = partitions.index_id
AND indexes.object_id = partitions.object_id
INNER JOIN sys.tables
ON tables.object_id = indexes.object_id
INNER JOIN sys.columns
ON tables.object_id = columns.object_id
AND column_store_segments.column_id = columns.column_id
WHERE tables.name = 'Sale_CCI'
AND columns.name = 'Invoice Date Key'
ORDER BY tables.name, columns.name, column_store_segments.segment_id;
```

The results are shown in Figure 10-5.

	table_name	index_name	column_name	partition_number	segment_id	min_data_id	max_data_id	row_count
1	Sale_CCI	CCI_fact_sale_CCI	Invoice Date Key	1	0	734868	736114	1048576
2	Sale_CCI	CCI_fact_sale_CCI	Invoice Date Key	1	1	734868	736114	1048576
3	Sale_CCI	CCI_fact_sale_CCI	Invoice Date Key	1	2	734868	736114	1048576
4	Sale_CCI	CCI_fact_sale_CCI	Invoice Date Key	1	3	734868	736114	1048576
5	Sale_CCI	CCI_fact_sale_CCI	Invoice Date Key	1	4	734868	736114	1048576
6	Sale_CCI	CCI_fact_sale_CCI	Invoice Date Key	1	5	734868	736114	1048576
7	Sale_CCI	CCI_fact_sale_CCI	Invoice Date Key	1	6	734868	736114	1048576
8	Sale_CCI	CCI_fact_sale_CCI	Invoice Date Key	1	7	734868	736114	1048576

Figure 10-5. Metadata for the Invoice Date Key column of a columnstore index

Note that *min_data_id* and *max_data_id* are identical for each rowgroup. This means that the data contained for that column is unordered. If queries commonly filtered using *Invoice Date Key*, they would need to scan all rowgroups in the columnstore index in order to appropriately filter out the requested rows. As a columnstore index grows over time, the cost to scan all rowgroups will become burdensome. Even on a well-compressed columnstore index, queries will become slow, and the IO required to service an unfilterable query will be high.

STATISTICS IO provides a useful guide to the number of rowgroups read as part of a columnstore index scan. To demonstrate this, the query in Listing 10-6 will be used.

144

Listing 10-6. Query to Illustrate Rowgroup Reads in a Columnstore Index Scan

```
SELECT
    SUM([Quantity])
FROM Fact.Sale_CCI
WHERE [Invoice Date Key] >= '1/1/2016'
AND [Invoice Date Key] < '2/1/2016';
```

This is a classic analytic query that calculates the total sales quantity for a given month.

```
⊞ Results  📄 Messages

    (1 row affected)
    Table 'Sale_CCI'. Scan count 3, logical reads 3062, ph
    Table 'Sale_CCI'. Segment reads 26, segment skipped 0.
    Table 'Worktable'. Scan count 0, logical reads 0, phys
```

Figure 10-6. *STATISTICS IO for a sample unordered columnstore index scan*

When a columnstore index is scanned, STATISTICS IO will include a message in the output that indicates how many segments were read and skipped. This is a measure of the number of rowgroups that had to be scanned to determine which rows met the filter criteria and which could be automatically skipped. Figure 10-6 indicates that 26 segments were read and 0 were skipped. Because the underlying data is completely unordered, SQL Server cannot use columnstore metadata to skip any rowgroups. This represents a common real-world challenge, but one that is easy to solve.

Columnstore metadata allows rowgroups to be skipped when query filters do not include rows present in them. This process is called rowgroup elimination and is key to optimizing columnstore index performance. The easiest way to achieve this is by ordering data and maintaining that order over time. Data may be ordered by one or more columns that will represent the most common filters used in analytic queries. The most common dimension to order OLAP data by is time. Analytics often filter, aggregate, and visualize data using time-based units, such as hours, days, weeks, months, quarters, and years. Figure 10-7 shows the impact of rowgroup elimination on a query that requires only a narrow range of data based on filter criteria that honors ordered data.

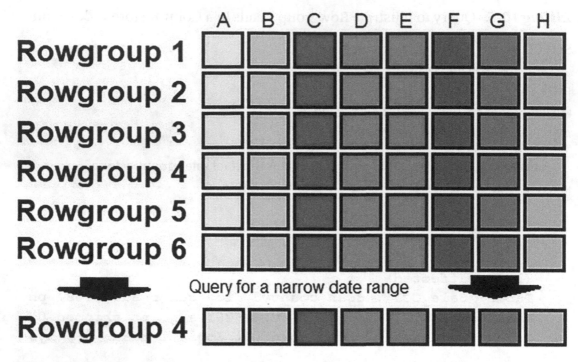

Figure 10-7. *Impact of rowgroup elimination on a narrow analytic query*

While this hypothetical index contains six rowgroups, only a single one is required to satisfy the filter criteria of the query. The power of rowgroup elimination is that it scales effectively as a columnstore index grows in size. A query that requests a narrow week of analytic data from a table with a month of data will perform similarly to that same query against a table with 10 years of data. This is the primary feature that allows columnstore indexes to scale effectively, even when billions of rows are present in a table.

In the example in Listing 10-6, a simple analytic query filtered on *Invoice Date Key*, but the unordered columnstore index data forced a full scan of the data to determine which rows met the filter criteria. If Invoice Date Key is the most common filter criteria for analysis of this data, then ordering by that column would allow for effective rowgroup elimination.

Listing 10-7. Query to Create a New Columnstore Index Ordered by Invoice Date Key

```
CREATE TABLE Fact.Sale_CCI_ORDERED
(       [Sale Key] [bigint] NOT NULL,
        [City Key] [int] NOT NULL,
```

```
     [Customer Key] [int] NOT NULL,
     [Bill To Customer Key] [int] NOT NULL,
     [Stock Item Key] [int] NOT NULL,
     [Invoice Date Key] [date] NOT NULL,
     [Delivery Date Key] [date] NULL,
     [Salesperson Key] [int] NOT NULL,
     [WWI Invoice ID] [int] NOT NULL,
     [Description] [nvarchar](100) NOT NULL,
     [Package] [nvarchar](50) NOT NULL,
     [Quantity] [int] NOT NULL,
     [Unit Price] [decimal](18, 2) NOT NULL,
     [Tax Rate] [decimal](18, 3) NOT NULL,
     [Total Excluding Tax] [decimal](18, 2) NOT NULL,
     [Tax Amount] [decimal](18, 2) NOT NULL,
     [Profit] [decimal](18, 2) NOT NULL,
     [Total Including Tax] [decimal](18, 2) NOT NULL,
     [Total Dry Items] [int] NOT NULL,
     [Total Chiller Items] [int] NOT NULL,
     [Lineage Key] [int] NOT NULL);
CREATE CLUSTERED INDEX CCI_fact_Sale_CCI_ORDERED ON Fact.Sale_CCI_ORDERED
([Invoice Date Key]);

INSERT INTO Fact.Sale_CCI_ORDERED
     ([Sale Key], [City Key], [Customer Key], [Bill To Customer Key],
      [Stock Item Key], [Invoice Date Key], [Delivery Date Key],
      [Salesperson Key], [WWI Invoice ID], Description, Package,
      Quantity, [Unit Price], [Tax Rate],
      [Total Excluding Tax], [Tax Amount], Profit, [Total Including Tax],
      [Total Dry Items],
      [Total Chiller Items], [Lineage Key])
SELECT
     Sale.[Sale Key], Sale.[City Key], Sale.[Customer Key], Sale.[Bill To
     Customer Key], Sale.[Stock Item Key], Sale.[Invoice Date Key],
     Sale.[Delivery Date Key],
```

```
        Sale.[Salesperson Key], Sale.[WWI Invoice ID], Sale.Description,
        Sale.Package, Sale.Quantity, Sale.[Unit Price], Sale.[Tax Rate],
        Sale.[Total Excluding Tax], Sale.[Tax Amount], Sale.Profit,
        Sale.[Total Including Tax], Sale.[Total Dry Items],
        Sale.[Total Chiller Items], Sale.[Lineage Key]
FROM fact.Sale
CROSS JOIN
Dimension.City
WHERE City.[City Key] >= 1 AND City.[City Key] <= 110;

-- Create a clustered columnstore index on the table, removing the existing
clustered rowstore index.
CREATE CLUSTERED COLUMNSTORE INDEX CCI_fact_Sale_CCI_ORDERED ON
Fact.Sale_CCI_ORDERED WITH (MAXDOP = 1, DROP_EXISTING = ON);
GO
```

Note that the data in the table created in Listing 10-7 is identical to the data
demonstrated earlier in this chapter, but has been subject to a clustered rowstore index
prior to being given a columnstore index. This additional step ensures that the initial
data set is ordered by *Invoice Date Key*. MAXDOP is intentionally set to 1 to avoid
parallelism as parallel threads may risk inserting data into the columnstore index in
multiple ordered streams rather than a single ordered stream.

Going forward, new data would be regularly inserted into this table via standard
data load processes. Assuming the new data contains the most recent values for
Invoice Date Key, then the columnstore index will remain ordered in the future as new
data is added to it.

To test the impact of data order on *Fact.Sale_CCI_ORDERED*, the query from
Listing 10-6 will be executed against it, with the output tab displayed in Figure 10-8.

```
 ⊞ Results   ▤ Messages

    (1 row affected)
    Table 'Sale_CCI_ORDERED'. Scan count 2, logical reads 0, physica:
    Table 'Sale_CCI_ORDERED'. Segment reads 2, segment skipped 22.
    Table 'Worktable'. Scan count 0, logical reads 0, physical reads
```

Figure 10-8. *STATISTICS IO for a sample filtered columnstore index scan*

Instead of reading every rowgroup in the columnstore index, SQL Server only needed to read two of them, with the remainder being skipped. Skipped segments in STATISTICS IO indicate that rowgroup elimination is being successfully implemented. The metadata query in Listing 10-5 can also be rerun against this ordered table to illustrate how data order impacts columnstore metadata, with the results being shown in Figure 10-9.

	table_name	index_name	column_name	partition_number	segment_id	min_data_id	max_data_id	row_count
1	Sale_CCI_ORDERED	CCI_fact_Sale_CCI_ORDERED	Invoice Date Key	1	0	734868	734930	1048576
2	Sale_CCI_ORDERED	CCI_fact_Sale_CCI_ORDERED	Invoice Date Key	1	1	734930	734984	1048576
3	Sale_CCI_ORDERED	CCI_fact_Sale_CCI_ORDERED	Invoice Date Key	1	2	734984	735038	1048576
4	Sale_CCI_ORDERED	CCI_fact_Sale_CCI_ORDERED	Invoice Date Key	1	3	735038	735091	1048576
5	Sale_CCI_ORDERED	CCI_fact_Sale_CCI_ORDERED	Invoice Date Key	1	4	735091	735150	1048576
6	Sale_CCI_ORDERED	CCI_fact_Sale_CCI_ORDERED	Invoice Date Key	1	5	735150	735207	1048576
7	Sale_CCI_ORDERED	CCI_fact_Sale_CCI_ORDERED	Invoice Date Key	1	6	735207	735266	1048576
8	Sale_CCI_ORDERED	CCI_fact_Sale_CCI_ORDERED	Invoice Date Key	1	7	735266	735322	1048576
9	Sale_CCI_ORDERED	CCI_fact_Sale_CCI_ORDERED	Invoice Date Key	1	8	735322	735373	1048576
10	Sale_CCI_ORDERED	CCI_fact_Sale_CCI_ORDERED	Invoice Date Key	1	9	735373	735422	1048576
11	Sale_CCI_ORDERED	CCI_fact_Sale_CCI_ORDERED	Invoice Date Key	1	10	735422	735474	1048576

Figure 10-9. *Metadata for the Invoice Date Key column of an ordered columnstore index*

The values of *min_data_id* and *max_data_id* for each rowgroup show a drastic change from that of an unordered columnstore index. Instead of the values being the same for each rowgroup, they progress from low values to high values as data progresses from the first rowgroup to the latter ones. To put this in perspective, if a hypothetical query required data for a data ID of 735270, it would only need to read the rowgroups associated with *segment_id* = 7 from this list of segments. Since the metadata indicates that the remaining segments do not contain this value, they (and their associated rowgroups) can automatically be skipped.

Ordering data by a key column is an easy way to enable rowgroup elimination, thereby reducing query resource consumption and improving the speed of any queries that can make use of that data order. Effective data order doesn't just reduce reads, but it can also save on storage space by improving the compression ratios of the underlying data. Listing 10-8 contains a script that will retrieve the data space used by the two columnstore indexes featured in this chapter.

Listing 10-8. Query to Retrieve Data Space Used for Two Columnstore Indexes

```
CREATE TABLE #storage_data
(       table_name VARCHAR(MAX),
        rows_used BIGINT,
        reserved VARCHAR(50),
        data VARCHAR(50),
        index_size VARCHAR(50),
        unused VARCHAR(50));

INSERT INTO #storage_data
        (table_name, rows_used, reserved, data, index_size, unused)
EXEC sp_MSforeachtable "EXEC sp_spaceused '?'";

UPDATE #storage_data
        SET reserved = LEFT(reserved, LEN(reserved) - 3),
                data = LEFT(data, LEN(data) - 3),
                index_size = LEFT(index_size, LEN(index_size) - 3),
                unused = LEFT(unused, LEN(unused) - 3);
SELECT
        table_name,
        rows_used,
        reserved / 1024 AS data_space_reserved_mb,
        data / 1024 AS data_space_used_mb,
        index_size / 1024 AS index_size_mb,
        unused AS free_space_kb,
        CAST(CAST(data AS DECIMAL(24,2)) / CAST(rows_used AS DECIMAL(24,2))
AS DECIMAL(24,4)) AS kb_per_row
FROM #storage_data
WHERE rows_used > 0
AND table_name IN ('Sale_CCI', 'Sale_CCI_ORDERED')
ORDER BY CAST(reserved AS INT) DESC;

DROP TABLE #storage_data;
```

The results are shown in Figure 10-10.

	table_name	rows_used	data_space_reserved_mb	data_space_used_mb	index_size_mb	free_space_kb	kb_per_row
1	Sale_CCI	25196150	342	342	0	176	0.0139
2	Sale_CCI_ORDERED	25109150	21	21	0	128	0.0009

Figure 10-10. *Space used by an ordered and unordered columnstore index*

The data space used for each table is dramatically different, with the ordered table consuming less than 10% of the space that the unordered table uses. This is an exceptionally dramatic example of how ordered data can be stored more efficiently than unordered data. Ordered data saves space because, typically, data is more similar to other data captured within a short timeframe of it than when compared to data that was collected years apart. Within any application, usage patterns change over time as new features are released, old features are retired, and user behavior changes. Because of this, data samples will look more and more different as time passes between them. These similarities translate into compression algorithms being able to take advantage of a data set with less distinct values for common dimensions. This also reduces dictionary size, which also helps to prevent dictionaries from filling up and forcing the creation of undersized rowgroups.

Real-world data may not compress as impressively as the sample here, but expect nontrivial savings that will have a positive impact on data load processes and on analytics speeds. It is important to remember that saving storage space also saves memory as data remains compressed until needed by an application. Therefore, if an ordered data set were to decrease in size by 25%, that would result in 25% less memory being consumed in the buffer pool by columnstore index pages. Furthermore, other common measures of server performance such as page life expectancy and latching would improve as smaller objects can be retrieved more quickly and will impact other data in memory less than larger objects.

An ordered columnstore index also improves UPDATE and DELETE speeds by allowing those operations to target less pages. For example, consider the queries on the ordered and unordered sales tables shown in Listing 10-9.

Listing 10-9. Query to Display Sample Row Counts for Two Columnstore Indexed Tables

```
SELECT COUNT(*) AS row_count FROM Fact.Sale_CCI WHERE [Invoice Date Key] =
'1/1/2015';
SELECT COUNT(*) AS row_count FROM Fact.Sale_CCI_ORDERED WHERE [Invoice Date
Key] = '1/1/2015';
```

The results show that in each table, the count of rows affected is identical, as seen in Figure 10-11.

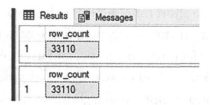

Figure 10-11. *Row counts for a sample query against ordered and unordered columnstore indexes*

For each table, 33,110 rows would be affected by an update using the same filter. Listing 10-10 provides a simple UPDATE statement against each table.

Listing 10-10. Query to Update 33,110 Rows in Two Columnstore Indexed Tables

```
UPDATE Sale_CCI
        SET [Total Dry Items] = [Total Dry Items] - 1,
                [Total Chiller Items] = [Total Chiller Items] + 1
FROM Fact.Sale_CCI_ORDERED -- Unordered
WHERE [Invoice Date Key] = '1/1/2015';
UPDATE Sale_CCI
        SET [Total Dry Items] = [Total Dry Items] - 1,
                [Total Chiller Items] = [Total Chiller Items] + 1
FROM Fact.Sale_CCI_ORDERED -- Ordered
WHERE [Invoice Date Key] = '1/1/2015';
```

The results in Figure 10-12 show the resulting IO and rowgroup usage for each UPDATE operation.

```
Messages
    Table 'Sale_CCI'. Scan count 4, logical reads 3570, physical re.
    Table 'Sale_CCI'. Segment reads 50, segment skipped 1.
    Table 'Worktable'. Scan count 0, logical reads 0, physical read

    (33110 rows affected)
    Table 'Sale_CCI_ORDERED'. Scan count 4, logical reads 509, phys.
    Table 'Sale_CCI_ORDERED'. Segment reads 2, segment skipped 23.
    Table 'Worktable'. Scan count 0, logical reads 0, physical read

    (33110 rows affected)
```

Figure 10-12. *STATISTICS IO output for updates against an ordered and unordered columnstore index*

Note the dramatic difference in IO, as well as segment reads for each operation. Because an UPDATE consists of both a DELETE and an INSERT, SQL Server had to perform the following tasks to complete each update:

1. Locate all rows matching the filter criteria.

2. Read all columns for all rows matching the filter criteria.

3. Mark these rows as deleted in the delete bitmap.

4. Insert new versions of these rows into the delta store.

In order to insert new versions of the updated rows, SQL Server needs to read the existing rows in their entirety, which is not a trivial operation. Once read, those rows are marked as deleted and the new versions are inserted into the delta store. This is an expensive process, but ordered data allows for far fewer rowgroups to be read, thereby reducing the work needed to set up the necessary data for the insert into the delta store.

DELETE operations are improved similarly, but require far less work as they simply need to

1. Locate all rows matching the filter criteria.

2. Mark these rows as deleted in the delete bitmap.

For both cases, an ordered columnstore index will immensely improve UPDATE and DELETE performance when the filter criteria honors the order used in the table. As an added bonus, an ordered columnstore index will allow for DELETE and UPDATE operations that cause less fragmentation. Instead of flagging rows as deleted in most (or all) rowgroups, the deletes can be isolated to a smaller number of rowgroups.

Combining Segment and Rowgroup Elimination

Segment elimination allows analytics that use less columns to automatically require less segments to be read, thereby reducing IO. Rowgroup elimination allows an ordered data set to facilitate analytic queries to use columnstore metadata to remove vast swaths of rowgroups from the result set, reducing IO significantly.

Optimal analytic workloads combine segment and rowgroup elimination to slice a table both vertically (rowgroup elimination) and horizontally (segment elimination). Consider the columnstore index introduced previously in Figure 10-1. If an analytic query were designed to only query for columns A and B and to also filter for a narrow date range, the resulting rowgroup reads would look similar to the results in Figure 10-13.

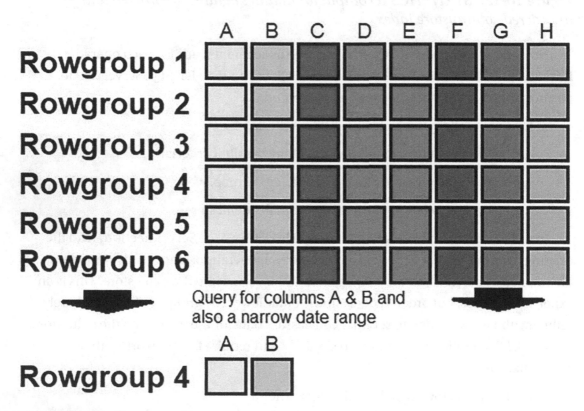

Figure 10-13. *Impact of segment and rowgroup elimination on a columnstore index*

Only querying for columns A and B allows columns C–H to be automatically skipped and all segments for those columns eliminated (36 segments in total). Querying for a narrow date range that only requires rows in rowgroup 4 allows rowgroups 1–3 and 5–6 to also be automatically skipped, eliminating another 10 segments. The result is a query that required only 2 out of the possible 48 segments in the table!

Combining segment and rowgroup elimination allows columnstore index queries to scale effectively, even as data grows larger or as more columns are added to the table.

CHAPTER 11

Partitioning

As an analytic table grows in size, it becomes apparent that newer data is read far more often than older data. While columnstore metadata and rowgroup elimination provide the ability to quickly filter out large amounts of columnstore index data, managing a table with millions or billions of rows can become cumbersome.

Equally important is the fact that older data tends to not change often. For a typical fact table, data is added onto the end of it in the order it is created, whereas older data remains untouched. If older data is modified, it is usually the result of software releases, upgrades, or other processes that fall squarely into the world of the data architect (that's us!) to manage.

Table partitioning is a natural fit for a clustered columnstore index, especially if it is large. Partitioning allows data to be split into multiple filegroups within a single database. These filegroups can be stored in different data files that reside in whatever locations are ideal for the data contained within them. The beauty of partitioning is that the table is logically unchanged, with its physical structure being influenced by the details of how it partitioned. This means that application code does not need to change in order to benefit from it. There are many benefits to partitioning, each of which is described in this chapter.

Maintain Hot/Warm/Cold Data

If older data is used far less often, then it can be stored in separate files that reside on slower storage. For example, reporting data from 10 years ago that is maintained for posterity but rarely used can be placed on inexpensive NAS storage, whereas new data can go on speedy SSD or flash storage.

The details will vary depending on the organization, but Figure 11-1 provides a simple representation of how an analytic table could be tiered to take advantage of different service levels.

© Edward Pollack 2022
E. Pollack, *Analytics Optimization with Columnstore Indexes in Microsoft SQL Server*,
https://doi.org/10.1007/978-1-4842-8048-5_11

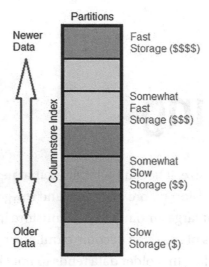

Figure 11-1. *How partitioning can influence storage speed and cost*

Partitioning allows storage to be tiered based on expected SLAs (service-level agreements). For partitions containing new data that is expected to be highly available and have low latency, fast and expensive storage can be used. For partitions containing older data that is rarely accessed, slower and cheaper storage can be used. The details are up to an organization, but the ability to efficiently divide up a large table automatically into different storage tiers is exceptionally useful and can save significant money in the long run.

Faster Data Movement/Migration

Having data divided up physically means that it can be copied and moved with ease. For example, consider a columnstore index with 50 billion rows that consumes 1TB of storage. If there was a need to migrate this table from its current server to a new server with minimal downtime, how would it be done? The simplest solutions involve database backups, copying data files, or using ETL to move the data slowly from one server to the other. All of these options work, but would be time-consuming and would involve the need to incur some downtime or make the table read-only once the data movement process starts.

Partitioning allows older/unchanging data to reside in separate data files, which in turn means that those files can be freely backed up/copied to the new server ahead of time. Assuming nothing changes within them, that process can occur days, weeks, or months prior to the migration. ETL or similar processes could be used on the day of the migration to catch up the target database with new data prior to permanently cutting over from the old data source to the new one.

Figure 11-2 illustrates the difference between migrating a large/monolithic table vs. a partitioned one.

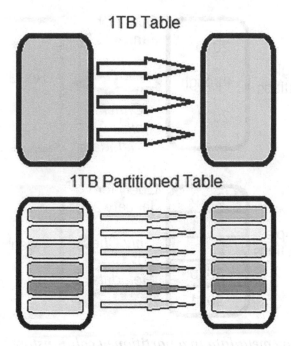

Figure 11-2. *Migration of a partitioned table vs. a nonpartitioned table*

Partitioning opens up the ability to subdivide the migration logically knowing that the physical storage of the table will facilitate the ability to copy/move each file one by one when needed. Instead of having to move a terabyte of data all at once or being forced to write ETL against the entire table, the table can be subdivided into smaller pieces, each of which is smaller and easier to move.

Partition Elimination

The logical definitions for each partition are not solely used for storage purposes. They also assist the query optimizer and allow it to automatically skip data when the filter in a query aligns with the partition function. For a query against a columnstore index, its filter can allow the metadata for rowgroups outside of the target partition to be ignored.

For example, if a columnstore index contains data ranging from 2010 through 2021 and is partitioned by year (with a single partition per year), then a query requesting rows from January 2021 would be able to automatically skip all rowgroups in partitions prior to 2021. Figure 11-3 shows how partition elimination can reduce reads and further speed up queries against columnstore indexes.

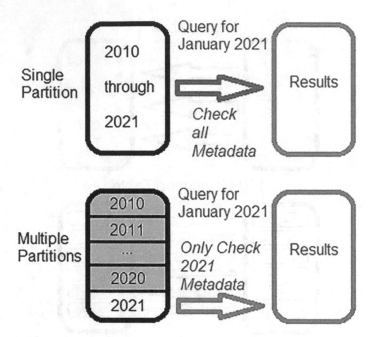

Figure 11-3. *Reading metadata in a partitioned columnstore index*

Partition functions are evaluated prior to columnstore metadata; therefore, data in irrelevant partitions is ignored when a query is executed. While columnstore metadata may be relatively lightweight, being able to skip the metadata for thousands of rowgroups can further improve analytic performance while reducing IO and memory consumption.

Database Maintenance

Some database maintenance tasks, such as backups and index maintenance, can be executed on a partition-by-partition basis. Since the data in older partitions rarely changes, it is less likely to require maintenance as often as newer data. Therefore, maintenance can be focused on the specific partitions that need it most. This also means that maintenance speeds can be greatly improved by no longer needing to operate on the entire table at one time.

In addition, how data is managed can vary partition to partition. Some ways in which data can be handled differently depending on the partition include

- **Compression** can be customized by partition. In a columnstore index, archive compression can be applied to older and less used partitions, whereas standard columnstore compression can be the default for newer data.

- Partitions can be **truncated** individually, allowing data to be removed from a portion of a table quickly, without having to use a DELETE statement.

- **Partition switching** allows data to be swapped in and out of a partitioned table quickly and efficiently. This can greatly speed up migrations, data archival, and other processes where a large volume of data needs to be moved at one time.

Partitioning in Action

To visualize how partitioning works, a new version of the test table *Fact.Sale_CCI* will be created. This version will be ordered by *Invoice Date Key* and also partitioned by year. Each partition needs to target a filegroup, which in turn will contain a data file. For this demonstration, a new filegroup and file will be created for each year represented in the table.

Listing 11-1 shows how new filegroups can be created that will be used to store data for the partitioned table.

Listing 11-1. Script That Creates a New Filegroup for Each Year of Data in the Table

```
ALTER DATABASE WideWorldImportersDW ADD FILEGROUP
WideWorldImportersDW_2013_fg;
ALTER DATABASE WideWorldImportersDW ADD FILEGROUP
WideWorldImportersDW_2014_fg;
```

```
ALTER DATABASE WideWorldImportersDW ADD FILEGROUP
WideWorldImportersDW_2015_fg;
ALTER DATABASE WideWorldImportersDW ADD FILEGROUP
WideWorldImportersDW_2016_fg;
ALTER DATABASE WideWorldImportersDW ADD FILEGROUP
WideWorldImportersDW_2017_fg;
```

Once executed, the presence of the new database filegroups can be confirmed by checking the Filegroups menu within the database's properties, as seen in Figure 11-4.

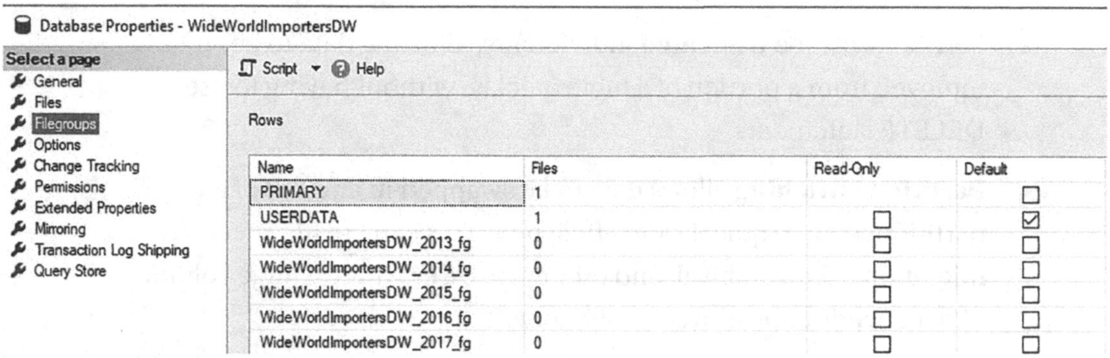

Figure 11-4. *New filegroups that will be used to store partitioned data*

While the five new filegroups are present in the database, they contain no files. The next step in this process is to add files to these filegroups (one file each). Listing 11-2 contains the code needed to add these files.

Listing 11-2. Script to Add Files to Each New Filegroup

```
ALTER DATABASE WideWorldImportersDW ADD FILE
        (NAME = WideWorldImportersDW_2013_data, FILENAME =
        'C:\SQLData\WideWorldImportersDW_2013_data.ndf',
         SIZE = 200MB, MAXSIZE = UNLIMITED, FILEGROWTH = 1GB)
TO FILEGROUP WideWorldImportersDW_2013_fg;
ALTER DATABASE WideWorldImportersDW ADD FILE
        (NAME = WideWorldImportersDW_2014_data, FILENAME =
        'C:\SQLData\WideWorldImportersDW_2014_data.ndf',
         SIZE = 200MB, MAXSIZE = UNLIMITED, FILEGROWTH = 1GB)
TO FILEGROUP WideWorldImportersDW_2014_fg;
```

```
ALTER DATABASE WideWorldImportersDW ADD FILE
       (NAME = WideWorldImportersDW_2015_data, FILENAME =
       'C:\SQLData\WideWorldImportersDW_2015_data.ndf',
       SIZE = 200MB, MAXSIZE = UNLIMITED, FILEGROWTH = 1GB)
TO FILEGROUP WideWorldImportersDW_2015_fg;
ALTER DATABASE WideWorldImportersDW ADD FILE
       (NAME = WideWorldImportersDW_2016_data, FILENAME =
       'C:\SQLData\WideWorldImportersDW_2016_data.ndf',
       SIZE = 200MB, MAXSIZE = UNLIMITED, FILEGROWTH = 1GB)
TO FILEGROUP WideWorldImportersDW_2016_fg;
ALTER DATABASE WideWorldImportersDW ADD FILE
       (NAME = WideWorldImportersDW_2017_data, FILENAME =
       'C:\SQLData\WideWorldImportersDW_2017_data.ndf',
       SIZE = 200MB, MAXSIZE = UNLIMITED, FILEGROWTH = 1GB)
TO FILEGROUP WideWorldImportersDW_2017_fg;
```

For this demonstration, each file has the same size and growth settings, but for a real-world table, these numbers will vary. By inspecting the size of the data that is to be partitioned, the amount of space needed for each year should be relatively easy to calculate. Note that once a table's data is migrated to a partitioned table, the data files that used to contain its data will now have additional free space that can be reclaimed, if needed. Figure 11-5 shows the new files listed under the Files menu within the database properties.

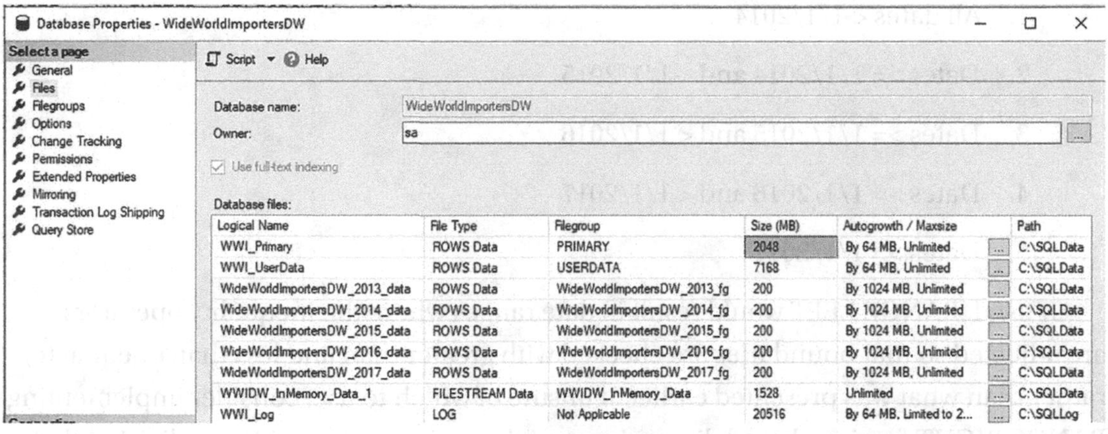

Figure 11-5. *New database files that will be used to store partitioned data*

New database files can be placed on any storage available to the server. This is where the table's data can be customized to meet whatever SLAs it is subject to. For this example, if data from prior to 2016 is rarely accessed, it could be placed into files on slower storage. Similarly, more recent data could be maintained on faster storage to support frequent analytics.

The next step in configuring partitioning is to determine how to slice up data from the table into the newly created files. This is achieved using a partition function. When working with a columnstore index, ensure that the column that the table is ordered by is also the same data type used for the partition function. This convention is the same with clustered rowstore indexes as well. If the data type for the partition function does not match the target column to order by in the table, an error will be thrown when the table is created. For this demonstration, the partition function will split up data using the DATE data type, which corresponds to the *Invoice Date Key* column that *Fact.Sale_CCI* is ordered by, as seen in Listing 11-3.

Listing 11-3. Creation of a Partition Function That Organizes Data by Date

```
CREATE PARTITION FUNCTION fact_Sale_CCI_years_function (DATE)
AS RANGE RIGHT FOR VALUES
        ('1/1/2014', '1/1/2015', '1/1/2016', '1/1/2017');
```

RANGE RIGHT specifies that the boundaries created will be defined using the dates provided as starting points. The result is that data will be divided into five buckets, like this:

1. All dates < 1/1/2014

2. Dates >= 1/1/2014 and < 1/1/2015

3. Dates >= 1/1/2015 and < 1/1/2016

4. Dates >= 1/1/2016 and < 1/1/2017

5. Dates >= 1/1/2017

If used, RANGE LEFT would result in date ranges where the inequality operators are adjusted so that boundaries are checked with greater than and less than or equal to, rather than what was presented earlier. If unsure of which to use, consider implementing RANGE RIGHT for time-based dimensions as it is typically a more natural division that cleanly divides up units of months, quarters, years, etc. The following list shows how the boundaries would be defined in the partition function in Listing 11-3 if RANGE LEFT were used:

1. All dates <= 1/1/2014

2. Dates > 1/1/2014 and <= 1/1/2015

3. Dates > 1/1/2015 and <= 1/1/2016

4. Dates > 1/1/2016 and <= 1/1/2017

5. Dates > 1/1/2017

This boundary configuration is somewhat counterintuitive for dates, but might be relevant for other data types.

The final step before partitioning can be implemented on a table is to create a partition scheme. A partition scheme is used to map the data boundaries defined in the partition function onto the filegroups defined earlier. This is where it can be decided which date ranges correspond to which physical database files. Listing 11-4 provides a partition scheme that assigns each date range defined by the partition function to one of the five newly created filegroups.

Listing 11-4. Creation of a Partition Scheme to Assign Dates to Database Filegroups

```
CREATE PARTITION SCHEME fact_Sale_CCI_years_scheme
AS PARTITION fact_Sale_CCI_years_function
TO (WideWorldImportersDW_2013_fg, WideWorldImportersDW_2014_fg,
WideWorldImportersDW_2015_fg, WideWorldImportersDW_2016_fg,
WideWorldImportersDW_2017_fg);
```

Note that the partition function will always specify one less boundary than there are filegroups. In this example, the partition function provides four dates that form date boundaries that define five distinct date ranges which are subsequently mapped onto the partition scheme and assigned filegroups. If the number of boundaries provided by the partition function is not one less than the partition scheme, an error will be returned, similar to what is seen in Figure 11-6.

```
Msg 7707, Level 16, State 1, Line 43
The associated partition function 'fact_Sale_CCI_years_function' generates more partitions than
there are file groups mentioned in the scheme 'fact_Sale_CCI_years_scheme_with_errors'.
```

Figure 11-6. *Error received if partition scheme contains too few filegroup entries*

The error is verbose enough to remind the user that the function generates too many or too few partitions than are afforded by the partition scheme. By writing out the time periods desired for the target table, the task of generating a partition function and partition scheme become far simpler.

With database files and filegroups defined, as well as a partition function and scheme, the final step to implementing partitioning is to create a table using the newly created partition scheme. Listing 11-5 creates a new version of *Fact.Sale* and partitions it using the *Invoice Date Key* column on *fact_Sale_CCI_years_scheme*.

Listing 11-5. Creation of a New Table That Is Partitioned by Year on a Date Column

```
CREATE TABLE Fact.Sale_CCI_PARTITIONED
(       [Sale Key] [bigint] NOT NULL,
        [City Key] [int] NOT NULL,
        [Customer Key] [int] NOT NULL,
        [Bill To Customer Key] [int] NOT NULL,
        [Stock Item Key] [int] NOT NULL,
        [Invoice Date Key] [date] NOT NULL,
        [Delivery Date Key] [date] NULL,
        [Salesperson Key] [int] NOT NULL,
        [WWI Invoice ID] [int] NOT NULL,
        [Description] [nvarchar](100) NOT NULL,
        [Package] [nvarchar](50) NOT NULL,
        [Quantity] [int] NOT NULL,
        [Unit Price] [decimal](18, 2) NOT NULL,
        [Tax Rate] [decimal](18, 3) NOT NULL,
        [Total Excluding Tax] [decimal](18, 2) NOT NULL,
        [Tax Amount] [decimal](18, 2) NOT NULL,
        [Profit] [decimal](18, 2) NOT NULL,
        [Total Including Tax] [decimal](18, 2) NOT NULL,
```

```
[Total Dry Items] [int] NOT NULL,
[Total Chiller Items] [int] NOT NULL,
[Lineage Key] [int] NOT NULL)
ON fact_Sale_CCI_years_scheme ([Invoice Date Key]);
```

The only difference in the definition of a partitioned table vs. a nonpartitioned table is the last line, where an ON clause defines the partition scheme to use and which column will be evaluated to determine which filegroups the data will be stored in. The data type of the partition column and partition function must match or an error will be returned, similar to what is shown in Figure 11-7.

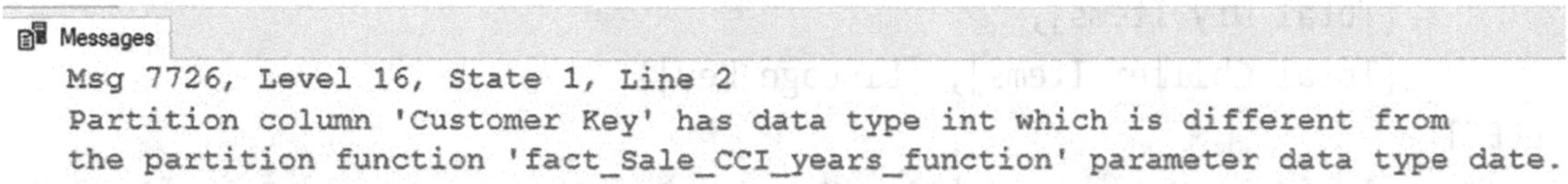

```
Messages
Msg 7726, Level 16, State 1, Line 2
Partition column 'Customer Key' has data type int which is different from
the partition function 'fact_Sale_CCI_years_function' parameter data type date.
```

Figure 11-7. *Error received if the data type of the partition column and partition function do not match*

Data types between the partition function and column must match exactly. DATE and DATETIME are not compatible, nor are other data types that may seem similar. SQL Server does not automatically convert between data types when evaluating partition functions and will instead throw an error when the table is created.

Once created, *Fact.Sale_CCI_PARTITIONED* is managed in the same fashion as *Fact.Sale_CCI_ORDERED* was:

1. A clustered rowstore index is created, ordered by *Invoice Date Key*.

2. Data is inserted into the table.

3. A clustered columnstore index is created, replacing the rowstore index.

The code in Listing 11-6 walks through each of these steps.

Listing 11-6. Populating a Partitioned Table with an Ordered Data Set

```
CREATE CLUSTERED INDEX CCI_fact_Sale_CCI_PARTITIONED ON
Fact.Sale_CCI_PARTITIONED ([Invoice Date Key]);

INSERT INTO Fact.Sale_CCI_PARTITIONED
        ([Sale Key], [City Key], [Customer Key], [Bill To Customer Key],
         [Stock Item Key], [Invoice Date Key], [Delivery Date Key],
         [Salesperson Key], [WWI Invoice ID], Description, Package,
         Quantity, [Unit Price], [Tax Rate],
         [Total Excluding Tax], [Tax Amount], Profit, [Total Including Tax],
         [Total Dry Items],
         [Total Chiller Items], [Lineage Key])
SELECT
        Sale.[Sale Key], Sale.[City Key], Sale.[Customer Key], Sale.[Bill To
        Customer Key], Sale.[Stock Item Key], Sale.[Invoice Date Key],
        Sale.[Delivery Date Key],
        Sale.[Salesperson Key], Sale.[WWI Invoice ID], Sale.Description,
        Sale.Package, Sale.Quantity, Sale.[Unit Price], Sale.[Tax Rate],
        Sale.[Total Excluding Tax], Sale.[Tax Amount], Sale.Profit,
        Sale.[Total Including Tax], Sale.[Total Dry Items],
        Sale.[Total Chiller Items], Sale.[Lineage Key]
FROM Fact.Sale
CROSS JOIN
Dimension.City
WHERE City.[City Key] >= 1 AND City.[City Key] <= 110;

CREATE CLUSTERED COLUMNSTORE INDEX CCI_Fact_Sale_CCI_PARTITIONED ON
Fact.Sale_CCI_PARTITIONED WITH (MAXDOP = 1, DROP_EXISTING = ON);
```

When complete, two tables will exist for demonstration purposes that are identical, except that one is partitioned and the other is not. Both are ordered by *Invoice Date Key* and will benefit from rowgroup elimination whenever filtered by that column. Listing 11-7 shows two queries that aggregate *Quantity* for a single month against each table.

Listing 11-7. Narrow Analytic Queries Executed Against Nonpartitioned and Partitioned Columnstore Indexes

```
SELECT
      SUM([Quantity])
FROM Fact.Sale_CCI_ORDERED
WHERE [Invoice Date Key] >= '1/1/2016'
AND [Invoice Date Key] < '2/1/2016';

SELECT
      SUM([Quantity])
FROM Fact.Sale_CCI_PARTITIONED
WHERE [Invoice Date Key] >= '1/1/2016'
AND [Invoice Date Key] < '2/1/2016';
```

While the queries are identical aside from the table name, the STATISTICS IO output illustrates the differences in execution between each, as seen in Figure 11-8.

```
▦ Results  ▣ Messages

  (1 row affected)
  Table 'Sale_CCI_ORDERED'. Scan count 3, logical reads 1425, physical reads
  Table 'Sale_CCI_ORDERED'. Segment reads 2, segment skipped 22.
  Table 'Worktable'. Scan count 0, logical reads 0, physical reads 0, page se

  (1 row affected)
  Table 'Sale_CCI_PARTITIONED'. Scan count 1, logical reads 0, physical read:
  Table 'Sale_CCI_PARTITIONED'. Segment reads 1, segment skipped 3.
```

Figure 11-8. *STATISTICS IO for a nonpartitioned columnstore index vs. a partitioned columnstore index*

The output of STATISTICS IO shows multiple ways in which query execution varied for each table. The most significant difference is in the reported segment reads. The nonpartitioned table read 2 segments while skipping 22, whereas the partitioned table read 1 segment while skipping 3. This IO reflects the original query that calculates a sum using only rows with an *Invoice Date Key* within January 2016.

For the table that is ordered and not partitioned, metadata needs to be reviewed from the entire table prior to using rowgroup elimination to skip segments. In the partitioned table, though, rowgroups that do not contain data from 2016 are automatically skipped. Since partition functions are evaluated prior to evaluating columnstore metadata, unrelated rowgroups are never read, including their metadata. This represents partition elimination in action. While partitioning is not intended to be a query optimization solution, it will have a positive impact on columnstore index IO and query speeds, especially on larger tables.

Partitioning also impacts the query optimizer, which will evaluate a query across less rowgroups and rows, which can simplify execution plans. Figure 11-9 shows the execution plans for the analytic queries demonstrated in Listing 11-7.

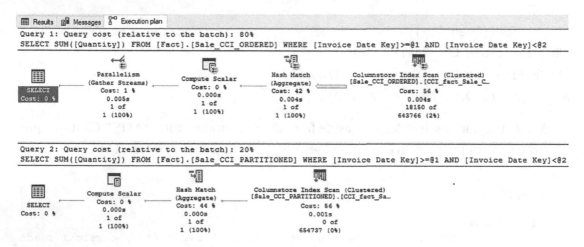

Figure 11-9. *Query execution plans for a nonpartitioned columnstore index vs. a partitioned columnstore index*

The execution plan for the nonpartitioned table is more complex as SQL Server determines that parallelism may help in processing the large number of rows. The execution plan for the partitioned table is simpler, as the optimizer chooses to not use parallelism. Note that the use of a hash match is to support the aggregate pushdown for the SUM operator into the columnstore index scan step. Also interesting to note is that the count of rows read in the execution plan is lower on a partitioned table (vs. a nonpartitioned table) when less partitions need to be read.

While the output of each query is identical and each execution plan produces the same result set, the ability to forgo parallelism saves computing resources, as is implied by the greatly reduced query cost for the partitioned table.

In addition to partition elimination, index maintenance can be adjusted to skip older, less updated partitions. For example, if a rebuild was deemed necessary for this columnstore index to clean it up after some recent software releases, the nonpartitioned table would need to be rebuilt en masse, as seen in Listing 11-8.

Listing 11-8. Query to Rebuild a Columnstore Index

```
ALTER INDEX CCI_fact_Sale_CCI_ORDERED ON Fact.Sale_CCI_ORDERED REBUILD;
```

The rebuild operation takes 61 seconds to complete. For a larger columnstore index, it could be significantly longer. If the portion of data impacted by the software release is limited to newer data only, it is very likely that only the most current partition needs to be rebuilt. Listing 11-9 shows how an index rebuild can be executed against a single partition.

Listing 11-9. Query to Rebuild the Current Partition in a Columnstore Index

```
ALTER INDEX CCI_fact_Sale_CCI_PARTITIONED ON Fact.Sale_CCI_PARTITIONED
REBUILD PARTITION = 5;
```

This rebuild only takes 1 second. This is because the most recent partition does not contain a full year of data. To provide a fairer assessment of rebuild times, Listing 11-10 shows a rebuild operation against a partition that contains a full year of data.

Listing 11-10. Query to Rebuild a Full Partition in a Columnstore Index

```
ALTER INDEX CCI_fact_Sale_CCI_PARTITIONED ON Fact.Sale_CCI_PARTITIONED
REBUILD PARTITION = 4;
```

This rebuild operation requires 11 seconds to complete. Each partition rebuild is significantly faster than being forced to rebuild the entire index. This can greatly reduce the performance impact of index maintenance, when it is needed.

Another unique feature that can be demonstrated is the use of the SWITCH option to move the contents of a partition from one table to another using a single DDL operation. Because the operation is a DDL metadata operation and not a fully logged data movement process, it will be significantly faster. This opens up a variety of options for speedy data load and maintenance processes that otherwise would be prohibitively expensive.

For example, if it were determined that all data in *Fact.Sale_CCI_PARTITIONED* had an error starting on 1/1/2016, correcting it would be a challenge if left in place. Updating a columnstore index is a slow and expensive process that results in heavy fragmentation and is therefore worth avoiding if possible.

An alternative to this would be to switch out the partition, modify the data, and then reinsert the data back into the table. This allows the data that is to be modified to be isolated prior to making any changes. The script in Listing 11-11 creates a new staging table with the same schema as *Fact.Sale_CCI_PARTITIONED* that will be used as the target for a partition switch.

Listing 11-11. Script to Create a Staging Table for Use in a Partition Switching Operation

```
CREATE TABLE Fact.Sale_CCI_STAGING
(       [Sale Key] [bigint] NOT NULL,
        [City Key] [int] NOT NULL,
        [Customer Key] [int] NOT NULL,
        [Bill To Customer Key] [int] NOT NULL,
        [Stock Item Key] [int] NOT NULL,
        [Invoice Date Key] [date] NOT NULL,
        [Delivery Date Key] [date] NULL,
        [Salesperson Key] [int] NOT NULL,
        [WWI Invoice ID] [int] NOT NULL,
        [Description] [nvarchar](100) NOT NULL,
        [Package] [nvarchar](50) NOT NULL,
        [Quantity] [int] NOT NULL,
        [Unit Price] [decimal](18, 2) NOT NULL,
        [Tax Rate] [decimal](18, 3) NOT NULL,
        [Total Excluding Tax] [decimal](18, 2) NOT NULL,
        [Tax Amount] [decimal](18, 2) NOT NULL,
        [Profit] [decimal](18, 2) NOT NULL,
        [Total Including Tax] [decimal](18, 2) NOT NULL,
        [Total Dry Items] [int] NOT NULL,
        [Total Chiller Items] [int] NOT NULL,
            [Lineage Key] [int] NOT NULL)
ON WideWorldImportersDW_2016_fg;
CREATE CLUSTERED COLUMNSTORE INDEX CCI_fact_Sale_CCI_STAGING ON
Fact.Sale_CCI_STAGING;
```

Note that the staging table is created on the same filegroup as the source data that is to be switched. If desired, the staging table could be created using the same partition scheme as *Fact.Sale_CCI_PARTITIONED*, which would allow the partition number to be specified in the partition switch, rather than having to explicitly provide a filegroup in the table create statement. The syntax is arbitrary and can be left to the convenience of the operator as to which is easier to implement.

Once the staging table is created, a partition on the 2016 filegroup can be switched from the source table into the staging table using the script in Listing 11-12.

Listing 11-12. Script to Switch a Partition from a Partitioned Columnstore Index into a Staging Table

```
ALTER TABLE Fact.Sale_CCI_PARTITIONED SWITCH PARTITION 4 TO
Fact.Sale_CCI_STAGING;
```

The partition switch executes in milliseconds as it is a minimally logged DDL operation. The results can be measured by validating the row count in the staging table, as shown in Listing 11-13.

Listing 11-13. Validating the Row Count in the Staging Table After the Partition Switch Operation Completes

```
SELECT COUNT(*) FROM Fact.Sale_CCI_STAGING;
```

The results of the count operation are shown in Figure 11-10.

Figure 11-10. *Count of rows in the newly populated staging table*

The result of the count query shows that over 3 million rows were switched from *Fact.Sale_CCI_PARTITIONED* to the staging table. From here, data can be modified in the staging table as needed to resolve whatever the identified issues are. Once the data is cleaned up, it can be inserted back into the original columnstore index, ensuring that the resulting data is clean with no fragmentation. Listing 11-14 shows a sample process for how this data modification could occur.

Listing 11-14. Example of Data Modification Using Staging Data. Data Is Moved Back into the Parent Table Using an INSERT Operation

```
UPDATE Sale_CCI_STAGING
        SET [Total Dry Items] = [Total Dry Items] + 1
FROM Fact.Sale_CCI_STAGING;

INSERT INTO Fact.Sale_CCI_PARTITIONED
        ([Sale Key], [City Key], [Customer Key], [Bill To Customer Key],
         [Stock Item Key], [Invoice Date Key], [Delivery Date Key],
         [Salesperson Key],
    [WWI Invoice ID], Description, Package, Quantity, [Unit Price],
    [Tax Rate], [Total Excluding Tax], [Tax Amount], Profit, [Total
    Including Tax],
    [Total Dry Items], [Total Chiller Items], [Lineage Key])
SELECT
        [Sale Key], [City Key], [Customer Key], [Bill To Customer Key],
        [Stock Item Key], [Invoice Date Key], [Delivery Date Key],
        [Salesperson Key],
    [WWI Invoice ID], Description, Package, Quantity, [Unit Price],
    [Tax Rate], [Total Excluding Tax], [Tax Amount], Profit, [Total
    Including Tax],
    [Total Dry Items], [Total Chiller Items], [Lineage Key]
FROM Fact.Sale_CCI_STAGING;

DROP TABLE Fact.Sale_CCI_STAGING;
```

The update is an expensive operation, but by isolating it to a staging table, the contention of the operation will not impact the larger columnstore index. Once the update is complete, the data can be inserted back into the partitioned table and the staging table dropped.

Alternatively, the INSERT operation can be replaced with another partition switch. The code in Listing 11-15 shows an alternative to the code in Listing 11-14.

Listing 11-15. Example of Data Modification Using Staging Data. Data Is Moved Back into the Parent Table Using Partition Switching

```
UPDATE Sale_CCI_STAGING
    SET [Total Dry Items] = [Total Dry Items] + 1
FROM Fact.Sale_CCI_STAGING;

ALTER TABLE Fact.Sale_CCI_STAGING SWITCH PARTITION 4 TO
Fact.Sale_CCI_PARTITIONED;

DROP TABLE Fact.Sale_CCI_STAGING;
```

This alternative code will be significantly faster as the partition switch is a speedy, minimally logged DDL operation, whereas the large INSERT in Listing 11-14 needs to incur the cost of writing all of this data back to *Fact.Sale_CCI_Partitioned*.

Partition switching is a versatile tool that can be used in a wide variety of data modification, archival, and deletion scenarios. Its use will vary between applications, but provides a fast way to shift data in and out of tables without the fragmentation and expense of a large write operation.

Partitioning Guidelines

While partitioning may sound like a win for any columnstore index, it should not be automatically implemented without research and foresight. Partitioning works well in larger tables, but does not provide value to small columnstore indexes. Therefore, capacity planning should be a step in the decision-making process to determine whether partitioning is a good fit or not for any given table.

Partition and Rowgroup Sizing

Because partitioning is applied to a table before rowgroups are created, partition boundaries will force rowgroups to be cut off. For example, if a nonpartitioned columnstore index contains 5,000,000 rows, those rows will likely reside in 5 rowgroups. If a new version of that table were created and partitioned on a date column that evenly spanned 10 years, then the result would be 500,000 rows per partition.

Rowgroups cannot span partitions, though. The new partitioned table would contain ten partitions, each of which consists of a single rowgroup. The result is a table with ten rowgroups instead of five.

Generally speaking, partitioning is not appropriate for a columnstore index unless the table contains at least tens or hundreds of millions of rows. Equally important, partitions need to be large enough to facilitate the use of filled-up rowgroups. Therefore, the partition function and partition scheme need to ensure that each partition contains at least 2^{20} (1,048,576) rows each. Undersized partitions will result in undersized rowgroups, which will lead to fragmentation over time.

The larger a columnstore index, the more it will benefit from partitioning. Aligning partition boundaries to organizational needs can also help in determining how to implement partitioning on a columnstore index. If an organization archives a billion rows of data each quarter, then partitioning by quarter makes perfect sense. If instead, the archival is organized by year, then partitioning by year would be more relevant.

Partition Column Choice

The column chosen for the partition function should be the same column that the columnstore index is ordered by. Partitioning and rowgroup elimination work best when they operate on the same data sets and that can only be accomplished when they use the same sort criteria. Therefore, if a columnstore index is ordered by a particular date column, then partitioning should also be configured on that column. Partitioning by another column may result in worse performance as SQL Server needs to scan more rowgroups across more partitions to retrieve the data it needs.

Storage Choice

If data within a columnstore index is accessed differently, the data files used for the partitioned table can mirror that usage. If older data is rarely accessed and can tolerate more latency, then it can be moved onto slower/less expensive hardware. If newer data needs to be highly available with minimal latency, then it can be placed on faster and more expensive storage.

As a result, a large table can be split up to save money. Every terabyte of data that lands on cheaper storage represents cost savings that can be easily quantified. While partitioning's primary purpose is not to save money, the ability to shift workloads via the strategic placement of data files can achieve this without significant effort.

When building a partitioned table, identify if the table has data that follows different usage patterns and assign data files based on that usage to slower or faster storage, when possible. If performance requirements change with time, data files can be moved between storage locations to ensure that SLAs are still met, even if data that was once rarely needed becomes critical to frequent analytic processes.

Additional Benefits

One of the greatest benefits of table partitioning is that it requires no application code changes. All partitioning structures are internal to SQL Server and have no bearing on an application beyond the performance experienced as the table is accessed. This also means that partitioning can be tested out for analytic data and kept or rolled back depending on the results of that testing. A "rollback" would consist of creating a second copy of data and swapping it into the production location, but is a reasonable process with analytic data where data load processes are well within the confines of data architecture. This allows partitioning to be tested with minimal impact on the code that developers write to consume this data.

Partitioning is an optional step when implementing a columnstore index, but can improve maintenance, speed up analytic workloads, and potentially save money. This feature should be targeted at larger tables with at least tens of millions of rows and that are expected to grow rapidly over time.

CHAPTER 12

Nonclustered Columnstore Indexes on Rowstore Tables

Clustered columnstore indexes provide a primary storage mechanism for analytic data. For tables that are intended for use as OLAP data sources, this is the optimal choice and will provide a data structure that facilitates fast and efficient reads and writes against analytic data.

For tables that are primarily transactional in nature, but also have analytic queries executed against them, a clustered columnstore index is not appropriate. There are a handful of options available to manage those additional analytic workloads, including

- Create covering rowstore indexes.

- Separate OLTP and OLAP.

- Create nonclustered columnstore indexes.

- Accept OLAP queries with no modifications to database schema.

Whereas a purely OLTP or OLAP workload can be managed with purely transactional or analytic data structures, a mixed workload is more complex and requires a more careful inspection of reads and writes to understand how to best manage it. This chapter will discuss each alternative and when they are most appropriate, providing guidance on how to choose the best storage methodology for a given workload.

Use Rowstore Indexes

This is the typical startup default for most transactional applications. Data begins small and grows over time. When row counts are low, running analytic queries against transactional data is performant enough that no significant modifications are needed to service them.

Relying on rowstore tables and single-column nonclustered rowstore indexes will suffice until data size and contention become significant enough to result in

- Locking

- Blocking

- Excessive resource consumption

- Long-running queries

Once that threshold has been reached, another solution is required. Generally speaking, running analytic processes against rowstore indexes will result in index scans, heavy reads, and high memory usage, and those costs do not scale well as data grows into millions or billions of rows. Figure 12-1 shows a simplification of the challenges of running mixed workloads against a rowstore table.

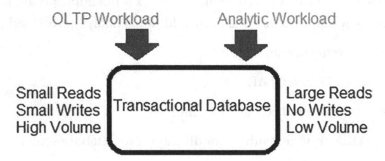

Figure 12-1. *The challenge of OLAP and OLTP queries against rowstore tables*

While mixing analytic and transactional needs works for small, less busy tables, challenges are guaranteed to arise when usage or size becomes significant. As a rule, it is generally advisable to avoid relying on rowstore tables for analytics if the table is expected to grow large.

Covering indexes allow for a rowstore index to completely cover an analytic query. This can offer improvement from clustered index scans and key lookups and is a good solution when analytics are limited in scope to a handful of well-understood queries.

For example, consider the query in Listing 12-1.

Listing 12-1. Example Analytic Query Against a Transactional Table

```
SELECT
      COUNT(*) AS sale_count,
      COUNT(DISTINCT SalespersonPersonID) AS sales_people_count,
      SUM(CAST(IsUndersupplyBackordered AS INT)) AS
      undersupply_backorder_count
FROM Sales.Orders
WHERE CustomerID = 90
AND OrderDate >= '1/1/2015'
AND OrderDate < '1/1/2016';
```

This query is a common example of analytics against transactional data. Figure 12-2 shows the execution plan for this query.

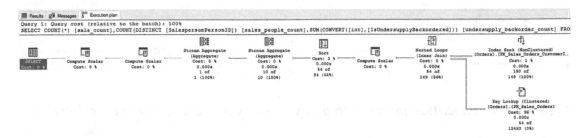

Figure 12-2. *Execution plan for an analytic query against a transactional table*

The execution plan shows an index seek that filters on the index for *CustomerID*. The key lookup retrieves the other columns from the clustered index that are needed to satisfy the query. The IO for the query as found in STATISTICS IO is shown in Figure 12-3.

```
(1 row affected)
Table 'Worktable'. Scan count 0, logical reads 0, physical reads 0,
Table 'Orders'. Scan count 1, logical reads 470, physical reads 0,
```

Figure 12-3. *STATISTICS IO for an analytic query against a transactional table*

Note that the key lookup incurred quite a bit of logical IO as SQL Server had to return to the clustered index to retrieve the *OrderDate*, *SalespersonPersonID*, and *IsUndersupplyBackordered* columns. If this query is executed often and does not vary significantly in form, a covering index can be an adequate way to manage it. Listing 12-2 creates an index that covers this sample query.

Listing 12-2. Nonclustered Rowstore Index That Fully Covers an Analytic Query

```
CREATE NONCLUSTERED INDEX NCI_Orders_covering
ON Sales.Orders (OrderDate, CustomerID)
INCLUDE (SalespersonPersonID, IsUndersupplyBackordered);
```

After creating this new covering index, the execution plan for the test query has been simplified to what is seen in Figure 12-4.

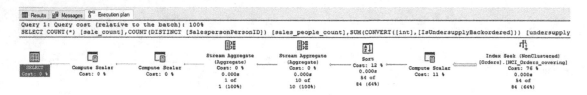

Figure 12-4. *Execution plan for an analytic query using a rowstore covering index*

The execution plan shows an index seek, rather than a seek plus a key lookup, as was the case before. The updated output of STATISTICS IO is shown in Figure 12-5.

```
(1 row affected)
Table 'Worktable'. Scan count 0, logical reads 0, physical reads 0,
Table 'Orders'. Scan count 1, logical reads 67, physical reads 0,
```

Figure 12-5. *STATISTICS IO for an analytic query using a rowstore covering index*

The new STATISTICS IO output shows a seven times decrease in IO, from 470 reads to 67. The covering index provides a significant performance boost to the analytic query, and as an added bonus can reduce contention as the new index is a separate object that can be read separately from the clustered index.

Covering indexes are great tools for analytic queries that are specific, consistent, and few in number. There is a danger in creating excessive numbers of covering indexes to try and keep up with new analytic queries. Over-indexing is a legitimate problem that can hamper write performance, waste storage, and consume significant memory. Similarly, covering indexes that contain too many columns are destined to waste space. For all intents and purposes, a covering index with too many columns can quickly devolve into a copy of the table, which is expensive to maintain.

The ideal scenarios where a covering index can be useful can be generalized as follows:

- Very limited number of specific, targeted analytic queries.

- Analytic queries that do not change often, if ever.

- Analytic queries that occur often enough to warrant some indexing action be taken.

- Column list is limited.

- Environment is conducive to removal of the index in the future, when no longer needed.

Separate OLAP and OLTP Processes

One solution to the challenge of running analytics against transactional tables is to separate OLAP data and processes from OLTP data and processes. There are many ways to tackle this challenge, including

- AlwaysOn Availability Groups

- Replication

- Separate analytic tables, fed by ETL

- Third-party analytics tools

- Third-party hardware solutions

Figure 12-6 shows a simple representation of workloads against an OLAP data copy.

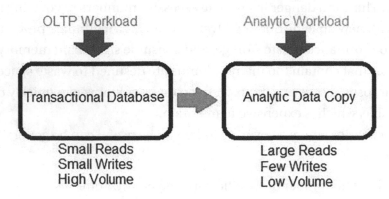

Figure 12-6. OLAP workloads targeted at a data copy

While separating transactional and analytic data is by far the most effective way of managing the challenge of mixed workloads, it is also the most disruptive.

AlwaysOn and Replication are mature tools that provide different ways to produce secondary copies of data for use by analytic processes. They require new components of SQL Server to be learned and implemented, as well as a commitment for additional hardware to support a new target for copies of OLTP data. They can also provide high availability, in the event that the primary transactional database fails.

If a database already uses AlwaysOn Availability Groups, then nonclustered columnstore indexes can be leveraged to off-load analytic queries to a readable secondary. Similarly, if Replication is used, the Replication target can be outfitted with a clustered or nonclustered columnstore index, if its primary purpose is to service analytic queries.

In addition to these built-in tools, an architect can create their own data copies and manage them via SQL Server Integration Services or some other data movement process. While manually building a data-copy process is a bit more labor intensive, it allows for the use of existing tools and for any amount of customization. This is often how organizations start their data warehousing environments.

Many third-party tools will perform similar tasks and allow for additional processing/management of data. The upside to investing in a tool by an outside organization is that the time, resources, and expertise needed to build and maintain it fall squarely on their shoulders, freeing up resources for other projects. The downsides are cost and investment in a new tool that may potentially be difficult to quit in the future if needed.

While solutions such as these incur latency, the latency can be controlled via configuration settings within each of them so that it remains within the bounds of organizational needs.

Nonclustered Columnstore Indexes

Introducing other solutions to analytic queries against transactional data sets the stage for how and when nonclustered columnstore indexes can effectively be used to manage analytic queries.

Nonclustered columnstore indexes are architected similarly to clustered columnstore indexes and exhibit similar behavior. Rowgroups, segments, and compression may be analyzed in the same fashion as with clustered columnstore indexes and best practices should be followed similarly. This means that they perform exceptionally well for analytic-style queries that aggregate millions of rows in a single operation. As with clustered columnstore indexes, though, DELETE and UPDATE operations can incur fragmentation and waste space over time, and UPDATE operations may perform poorly against large nonclustered columnstore indexes.

A huge difference between clustered and nonclustered columnstore indexes is that the nonclustered version allows for a column list to be specified. While data order is enforced by the rowstore clustered index, being able to pick and choose columns that are included can isolate those needed for analytics as opposed to those used primarily for transactional operations.

Note that the rowstore clustered index key columns are automatically included in nonclustered columnstore indexes by default and cannot be removed. They are required to support UPDATE and DELETE operations against existing rowgroups.

The primary benefits of nonclustered columnstore indexes are as follows:

- Allow real-time operational analytics.

- A column list can be specified.

- No app code changes are required.

- Columnstore index is stored on separate pages from rowstore indexes, thereby reducing contention.

- Index may be filtered, assigned compression delay, or off-loaded to an AlwaysOn replica.

Like clustered columnstore indexes, nonclustered columnstore indexes require some foresight to implement effectively. Because the clustered index is transactional in nature and the table is likely the target of frequent small write operations, considerations need to be made to the architecture of nonclustered columnstore indexes to ensure that the impact of write operations is managed effectively.

Figure 12-7 illustrates a simplified illustration of workloads against a table with both a clustered rowstore index and a nonclustered columnstore index.

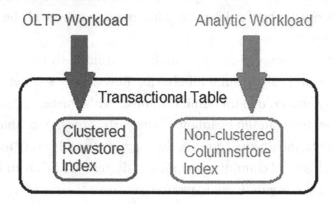

***Figure 12-7.** Mixed workloads against rowstore and columnstore indexes*

The takeaway from having both rowstore and columnstore indexes in a single table is that both can be used simultaneously, allowing transactional and analytic operations to execute side by side, rather than exclusively competing for resources.

To test the impact of nonclustered columnstore indexes on a transactional table, consider the script in Listing 12-3.

***Listing 12-3.** Creation of a Nonclustered Columnstore Index on a Rowstore Table*

```
CREATE NONCLUSTERED COLUMNSTORE INDEX NCCI_Orders ON Sales.Orders
(OrderDate, CustomerID, IsUndersupplyBackordered, SalespersonPersonID);
```

In the index creation statement, only columns involved in the analytic query were included. More can be added if needed for other common queries, but the goal is to ensure that analytics are used by the columnstore index without the need to refer to the clustered rowstore index.

Once added, the test query in Listing 12-1 can be executed again. The execution plan is shown in Figure 12-8.

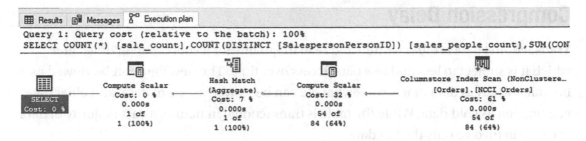

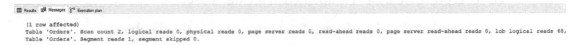

Figure 12-8. *Execution plan for an analytic query using a nonclustered columnstore index*

The execution plan shows that the columnstore index was exclusively used to return query results. Figure 12-9 shows the output of STATISTICS IO for the query.

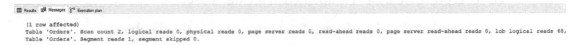

Figure 12-9. *STATISTICS IO for an analytic query using a nonclustered columnstore index*

Reads are about the same as with a covering index, with the added benefit that key lookups to the clustered index are avoided, ensuring no contention with other queries that are using it at the same time.

Managing Hot, Warm, and Cold Transactional Data

While nonclustered columnstore indexes can provide exceptional performance for real-time operational analytics, they have one glaring weakness: write operations. Transactional tables tend to incur small, incremental changes – inserts, updates, and deletes that affect a few rows at a time and that occur frequently. Columnstore indexes are designed for large bulk inserts, occasional deletes, and minimal updates.

Despite these immediate challenges, tools are available to manage these challenges when implementing nonclustered columnstore indexes to help maintain optimal performance.

Compression Delay

Transactional data is often written and read frequently for a short span of time, after which it is subject to less and less data access over time. The new data can be viewed as hot data, whereas data that is somewhat old can be viewed as warm data, and older data can be seen as cold data. While the table is transactional in nature, a vast majority of data access will involve only the hot data.

For example, consider an online order tracking system. The following is a summary of some of the steps involved in the order creation, processing, and completion, as well as notes on data access:

1. Order is placed for some cool swag. Data is written to a database.

2. Order is processed. Data is updated in the database.

3. Item is retrieved and packaged. Data is updated in the database.

4. Item is shipped. Data is updated in the database.

5. Item is tracked until delivery. Data is updated in the database with each shipping update.

6. Item is delivered. Data is updated in the database.

7. User leaves feedback on the order process and item.

8. User accesses this data read-only via the order history list in the future.

9. Eventually, the user rarely/never accesses this data again.

This flow of data indicates a clear progression from hot data (#1–6) to warm data (#7–8) to becoming cold data (#9). Analytic queries will most frequently address large swaths of historical data, which is more apparent starting at step #6 on the list. Tracking specific orders is undoubtedly a transactional need and applies most to steps #1–5 as they correlate most with someone that wants to know where their order is and when it will arrive.

A columnstore index will perform optimally the closer to the bottom of the list we go, whereas the frequent updates at the top of the list will be burdensome to compressed rowgroups. Each DELETE operation will flag a row as deleted in a rowgroup and waste space. Each UPDATE operation will delete a row and also insert a new row into the delta store.

To manage this challenge, compression delay can be used on a columnstore index. This feature delays the movement of data from the delta store into compressed segments by a preset amount of time. That timeframe is based on how long the data is expected to still be hot. During that period of time where compression is delayed, there will be no need to worry about the impact of DELETE or UPDATE operations against compressed rowgroups. Conversely, reads against the uncompressed delta store data will be slower than when the data ultimately is compressed. For a large table, though, the percentage of data that is hot will be small, whereas the amount of data that is warm or cold will comprise most of the table. Equally important is that the clustered rowstore index will service transactional queries, allowing data in the delta store to be avoided by those processes.

Consider the example of a columnstore index on *Sales.Orders* from Listing 12-3. If there typically was a period of 10 minutes in which the data was frequently updated, after which the data began to cool off and see less modifications, compression delay could be added to the index creation statement, as seen in Listing 12-4.

Listing 12-4. Nonclustered Columnstore Index Creation with Compression Delay

```
CREATE NONCLUSTERED COLUMNSTORE INDEX NCCI_Orders
ON Sales.Orders (OrderDate, CustomerID, IsUndersupplyBackordered,
SalespersonPersonID)
WITH (COMPRESSION_DELAY = 10 MINUTES);
```

The index will initially perform exactly as it did before. The difference will be when data is written to the delta store. Any rows inserted into the delta store will be retained for at least 10 minutes prior to writing to compressed rowgroups. Without compression delay, the tuple mover will periodically move rows from the delta store to compressed rowgroups With this feature, it will now wait at least 10 minutes before doing so.

The compression delay may be adjusted on an existing index, if needed, without the need for a rebuild. For example, if it is determined that data is hot for 30 minutes, rather than 10, an ALTER INDEX statement can adjust the compression delay accordingly, as seen in Listing 12-5.

Listing 12-5. Using an ALTER INDEX Statement to Adjust Compression Delay

```
ALTER INDEX NCCI_Orders ON Sales.Orders
SET (COMPRESSION_DELAY = 30 MINUTES);
```

Configuring compression delay is a balance between avoiding excessive writes against compressed rowgroups while ensuring that the delta store does not become so large that it adversely affects analytics. Ideally, rowstore indexes will service the transactional queries that operate on hot data, whereas the columnstore index handles analytic queries against larger volumes of data (that is mostly warm or cold).

Testing is necessary when determining the ideal value for compression delay, but the following is a set of guidelines to assist in finding a good starting point:

1. Measure new rows inserted over time. Ideally, the delta store would contain no more than a few rowgroups worth of data (a few million or less) that are not used heavily for analytics.

2. Measure update and delete operations and the period of time in which they most frequently occur. Try to set the compression delay to encompass that period of time.

3. If analytics do not target new data, then a higher compression delay is acceptable. Otherwise, it may need to be lowered to avoid frequent scans of the delta store.

4. If data load processes modify data heavily as part of insert operations, ensure that the compression delay period is long enough to encompass a typical data load. Alternatively, modify the data load process to use staging/temporary tables to modify data prior to its final insertion.

Compression delay can be a large or small number. If a transactional table has 1,000 new rows inserted per hour and those rows are heavily modified for 6 hours, then a compression delay of 360 minutes would be perfectly acceptable. In that scenario, the delta store would contain an average of 6,000 rows, which is small enough that scanning it would not be painful.

Alternatively, if a table has 2,000,000 rows inserted per hour, then compression delay would need to be more restrictive. If data in that table is hot for 2 hours, then an ideal compression delay value would be somewhere in the range of 30–120 minutes. Testing would be required to balance the needs of write processes vs. those of analytic read processes. The diagram in Figure 12-10 shows how compression delay impacts the flow of data for transactional and analytic queries with a nonclustered columnstore index.

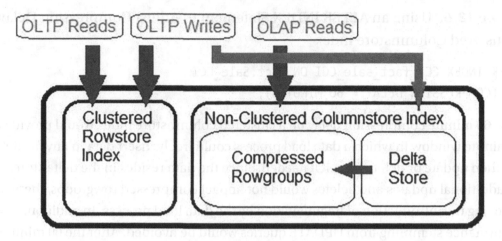

Figure 12-10. *Data flow for OLAP and OLTP queries against a nonclustered columnstore index with compression delay*

The goal represented in this data flow is for transactional queries to target the rowstore indexes and the delta store, whereas analytic queries target the columnstore index. Compression delay helps to ensure that OLTP writes are not impacting the performance of the compressed rowgroups within the nonclustered columnstore index. OLTP reads would be expected to target the rowstore indexes and would rarely make use of the columnstore index.

Compression delay can be applied to clustered columnstore indexes as well using the same syntax. This can be an excellent solution when data load processes fulfill one of these criteria:

- They have an overall long duration.

- Data is trickle loaded, rather than bulk loaded.

- Updates target data after it is initially inserted.

- A primarily analytic table is subject to OLTP queries as part of the data load process.

The query in Listing 12-6 alters the clustered columnstore index in *WideWorldImportersDW* to have a 60 minute compression delay.

Listing 12-6. Using an ALTER INDEX Statement to Adjust Compression Delay on a Clustered Columnstore Index

```
ALTER INDEX CCI_fact_sale_CCI ON Fact.Sale_CCI
SET (COMPRESSION_DELAY = 60 MINUTES);
```

A 60 minute compression delay on a clustered columnstore index would provide a 60 minute window in which a data load process could freely insert data in any fashion, and then update or delete from it if needed. Since the data resides in the delta store, the additional updates and deletes would not impact compressed rowgroups, therefore removing the introduction of fragmentation by the data load process. In addition, poor performance stemming from UPDATE queries would be avoided. After the 60 minute period has passed, the data would begin to be inserted into the columnstore index. Assuming the data load process has completed its data modifications against that data, then it would be inserted once and then left alone in its pristine compressed state.

The compression delay settings for columnstore indexes in a database can be retrieved using a query against *sys.indexes*, as shown in Listing 12-7.

Listing 12-7. Query to Return Index Compression Delay Information

```
SELECT
        tables.name AS table_name,
        indexes.name AS index_name,
        indexes.type_desc AS index_type,
        indexes.compression_delay
FROM sys.indexes
INNER JOIN sys.tables
ON tables.object_id = indexes.object_id
WHERE indexes.type_desc IN ('NONCLUSTERED COLUMNSTORE', 'CLUSTERED
COLUMNSTORE');
```

The column *compression_delay* provides a number (in minutes) indicating the current compression delay setting for that index. Zero indicates that no compression delay is used for an index. Note that the query filters exclusively on columnstore indexes. Other index types will have NULL entered for compression delay as it is not an option for any other index types aside from columnstore indexes.

Figure 12-11 shows the results of this query and the compression delay for each columnstore index in the database.

	table_name	index_name	index_type	compression_delay
1	Sale_CCI_ORDERED	CCI_fact_Sale_CCI_ORDERED	CLUSTERED COLUMNSTORE	0
2	Sale_CCI_PARTITIONED	CCI_fact_Sale_CCI_PARTITIONED	CLUSTERED COLUMNSTORE	0
3	Movement	CCX_Fact_Movement	CLUSTERED COLUMNSTORE	0
4	Sale_CCI	CCI_fact_sale_CCI	CLUSTERED COLUMNSTORE	60
5	Order	CCX_Fact_Order	CLUSTERED COLUMNSTORE	0
6	Purchase	CCX_Fact_Purchase	CLUSTERED COLUMNSTORE	0
7	Sale	CCX_Fact_Sale	CLUSTERED COLUMNSTORE	0
8	Sale_CCI_Normalized	CCI_Sale_CCI_Normalized	CLUSTERED COLUMNSTORE	0
9	Sale_CCI_Archive	CCI_Sale_CCI_Archive	CLUSTERED COLUMNSTORE	0
10	Stock Holding	CCX_Fact_Stock_Holding	CLUSTERED COLUMNSTORE	0
11	Transaction	CCX_Fact_Transaction	CLUSTERED COLUMNSTORE	0
12	Sale_CCI_Clean_Test	CCI_Sale_CCI_Clean_Test	CLUSTERED COLUMNSTORE	0
13	Sale_CCI_Clean_Test_2	CCI_Sale_CCI_Clean_Test_2	CLUSTERED COLUMNSTORE	0

Figure 12-11. *Compression delay for each columnstore index in a database*

Row 4 (circled) shows the index that was altered by the query in Listing 12-6 and confirms the compression delay setting of 60 minutes.

Fragmentation due to rows being deleted can be quantified using the percentage of rows being deleted, using the query shown in Listing 12-8.

Listing 12-8. Query to Return Index Fragmentation Due to Delete Operations

```
SELECT
        objects.name,
        partitions.partition_number,
        dm_db_column_store_row_group_physical_stats.row_group_id,
        dm_db_column_store_row_group_physical_stats.total_rows,
        dm_db_column_store_row_group_physical_stats.deleted_rows,
        CAST(100 * CAST(deleted_rows AS DECIMAL(18,2)) / CAST(total_rows AS
DECIMAL(18,2)) AS DECIMAL(18,2)) AS percent_deleted
FROM sys.dm_db_column_store_row_group_physical_stats
INNER JOIN sys.objects
ON objects.object_id = dm_db_column_store_row_group_physical_stats
.object_id
INNER JOIN sys.partitions
ON partitions.object_id = objects.object_id
```

```
AND partitions.partition_number = dm_db_column_store_row_group_physical_
stats.partition_number
AND partitions.index_id = dm_db_column_store_row_group_physical_stats
.index_id
WHERE objects.name = 'Sale_CCI'
ORDER BY dm_db_column_store_row_group_physical_stats.row_group_id;
```

This query specifically targets a single table (*Sale_CCI*) and returns the total rows, deleted rows, and percent deleted per rowgroup, as seen in Figure 12-12.

	name	partition_number	row_group_id	total_rows	deleted_rows	percent_deleted
1	Sale_CCI	1	0	1048576	47333	4.51
2	Sale_CCI	1	1	1048576	35479	3.38
3	Sale_CCI	1	2	1048576	80474	7.67
4	Sale_CCI	1	3	1048576	36388	3.47
5	Sale_CCI	1	4	1048576	69428	6.62
6	Sale_CCI	1	5	1048576	62487	5.96
7	Sale_CCI	1	6	1048576	32117	3.06
8	Sale_CCI	1	7	1048576	39962	3.81
9	Sale_CCI	1	8	1048576	48620	4.64
10	Sale_CCI	1	9	1048576	57274	5.46
11	Sale_CCI	1	10	1048576	49297	4.70

Figure 12-12. *Fragmentation due to deleted rows in a columnstore index*

In this example, fragmentation is approximately 5% across the index. Generally speaking, when deleted rows comprise more than 10% of a columnstore index, it may be considered fragmented enough to warrant further actions to be taken in order to remove and/or prevent further fragmentation.

Compression delay is an exceptionally useful setting when creating nonclustered columnstore indexes that can offset heavy transactional write operations against a table during the period of time when data is still hot. In addition to improving write performance, compression delay will reduce fragmentation, improve compression efficiency, and decrease memory consumption for the index.

Filtered Nonclustered Columnstore Indexes

Like nonclustered rowstore indexes, nonclustered columnstore indexes can have filters applied to them when created. This allows the columnstore index to be targeted, focused on cold and warm data while avoiding indexing hot data. These filters will often target columns that enumerate statuses, workflows, and location within the data life cycle.

Consider the example of an order processing system. In this system, orders are frequently manipulated up until a certain point in the process. Maybe it is when the order is picked, shipped, or received, but at some point in its life cycle, the data shifts from hot data to warm data and then later to cold data.

A filtered index can be used to target a nonclustered columnstore index to include only data that is no longer hot. For example, consider the index creation statement in Listing 12-9.

Listing 12-9. Creation of a Filtered Nonclustered Columnstore Index

```
CREATE NONCLUSTERED COLUMNSTORE INDEX NCCI_Orders
ON Sales.Orders (OrderDate, CustomerID, IsUndersupplyBackordered,
SalespersonPersonID)
WHERE PickedByPersonID IS NOT NULL;
```

This index will only include rows that happen to have a value for the *PickedByPersonID* column. As a result, rows will not be inserted into the columnstore index until they have been boxed and are ready to ship. Because of this, any data manipulation that occurs prior to this point in time will not impact the performance of the columnstore index.

Listing 12-10 calculates the number of rows that meet the filter criteria vs. the number that do not.

Listing 12-10. Calculating the Number of Rows That Meet the Filtered Index Criteria

```
SELECT
     SUM(CASE WHEN PickedByPersonID IS NULL THEN 1 ELSE 0 END) AS
     orders_not_picked,
     SUM(CASE WHEN PickedByPersonID IS NOT NULL THEN 1 ELSE 0 END) AS
     orders_picked
FROM Sales.Orders
```

The results in Figure 12-13 show that about 14% of the rows in the table are not picked and therefore are still classified as hot data.

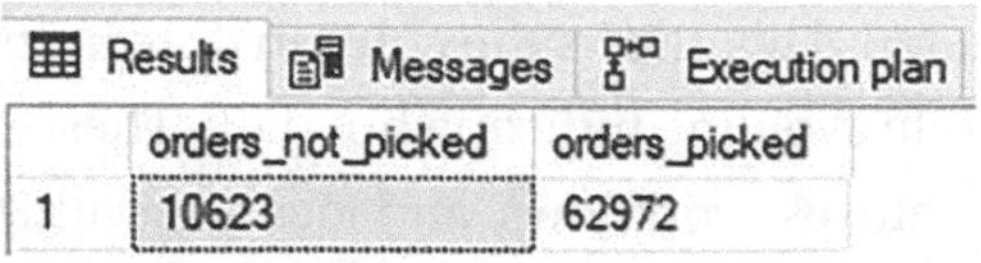

	orders_not_picked	orders_picked
1	10623	62972

Figure 12-13. *Count of rows that meet the filtered index criteria*

Typically, hot data will constitute a small fraction of data in the table. If a simple filter can be used to determine whether data is hot or not, then it can be applied to the nonclustered columnstore index to ensure that its performance is not negatively impacted by it.

Consider the analytic query presented in Listing 12-1. If this query was intended to only target data that is no longer hot, then adding the filter criteria used on the nonclustered columnstore index to this query would allow it to use the filtered version of the index, as seen in Listing 12-11.

Listing 12-11. Query That Uses a Filtered Nonclustered Columnstore Index

```
SELECT
        COUNT(*) AS sale_count,
        COUNT(DISTINCT SalespersonPersonID) AS sales_people_count,
        SUM(CAST(IsUndersupplyBackordered AS INT)) AS
        undersupply_backorder_count
FROM Sales.Orders
WHERE CustomerID = 90
AND OrderDate >= '1/1/2015'
AND OrderDate < '1/1/2016'
AND PickedByPersonID IS NOT NULL;
```

The execution plan for this query is shown in Figure 12-14.

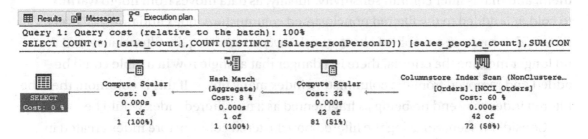

Figure 12-14. *Execution plan using a filtered nonclustered columnstore index*

As expected, the filtered nonclustered columnstore index was used to execute the query.

If needed, the query in Listing 12-12 shows all indexes in a database that have a filter defined on them, which can be used to review columnstore indexes and their details.

Listing 12-12. Query That Lists Indexes with Filters in a Given Database

```
SELECT
        indexes.name,
        indexes.type_desc,
        indexes.filter_definition
FROM sys.indexes
WHERE indexes.has_filter = 1;
```

The results of the query are useful in understanding what filters exist and their definitions, as shown in Figure 12-15.

	name	type_desc	filter_definition
1	NCCI_Orders	NONCLUSTERED COLUMNSTORE	([PickedByPersonID] IS NOT NULL)

Figure 12-15. *List of indexes with filters defined on them*

If the database contains many filtered indexes, the query could be further refined to omit rowstore indexes or other noise.

There is a single pitfall in filtered indexes that needs to be reviewed prior to using them, and that is filter column sensitivity. Ideally, as data moves from hot to warm to cold, it is added to the filtered nonclustered columnstore index and rarely (if ever) removed. If rows are capable of alternating between satisfying the filter clause and then no longer meeting the criteria, there is a danger that a single row in a table could be added and removed from the columnstore index many times. If this is common, then the filtered index may end up being as fragmented as a nonfiltered index would be.

Consider a scenario using the filtered nonclustered columnstore index created in Listing 12-9. If a row were assigned a value for *PickedByPersonID*, it would immediately be inserted into the delta store for the columnstore index where it would await compression via the tuple mover. If *PickedByPersonID* is then reset to NULL, it would be deleted from the columnstore index as it no longer meets the filter criteria. When designing any filtered index, there is value in ensuring that rows will not move in and out of the index often and that data follows a one-way journey from hot to warm to cold.

Compression delay can be combined with a filtered nonclustered columnstore index as a way to buffer out-of-band changes to data that cause it to move between hot and warm via routine processes. Listing 12-13 shows a filtered nonclustered columnstore index that includes compression delay.

Listing 12-13. Creation of a Filtered Nonclustered Columnstore Index with Compression Delay

```
CREATE NONCLUSTERED COLUMNSTORE INDEX NCCI_Orders
ON Sales.Orders (OrderDate, CustomerID, IsUndersupplyBackordered,
SalespersonPersonID)
WHERE PickedByPersonID IS NOT NULL
WITH (COMPRESSION_DELAY = 30 MINUTES);
```

This index provides additional buffering against the possibility that rows that have been assigned a *PickedByPersonID* might be

- Deleted

- Updated

- Have *PickedByPersonID* set back to NULL

A transactional table may make use of filtered nonclustered columnstore indexes, compression delay, or both and do so with success. The details as to which features to use and how to configure them should be driven by organizational need and its data life cycle. There is no one-size-fits-all solution in making these decisions. One table in one database for organization may benefit from a compression delay of 10 minutes, whereas 1,440 minutes might be optimal for another table. Filters might fully encapsulate a key use case in one workflow when others may be unable to easily be filtered for in an index.

Code Changes

If compression delay and filtered nonclustered columnstore indexes are unable to effectively manage analytic workloads against an OLTP table, it is possible that organizational logic, code, or both require review.

If application or database code can be improved in a way that supports both analytic and transactional workloads against the same table, then making those changes can allow an organization to prevent having to architect a more complex and expensive OLAP solution.

Ultimately, a solution exists for any analytic data challenge, but the ideal solution will be the one that costs the fewest resources while being capable of scaling most easily into the future. Real-time operational analytics are not appropriate for all workloads, and there will often be scenarios where a more expensive and resource-intensive solution (such as AlwaysOn or Replication) is the correct solution.

Vertipaq Optimization for Nonclustered Columnstore Indexes

In Chapter 5, columnstore compression was discussed in detail. An important issue that arose was that when a nonclustered rowstore index was added to a clustered columnstore index, rows that were inserted in the future could not benefit from Vertipaq optimization. Vertipaq optimization reorders rows, while SQL Server compresses a rowgroup, allowing like values to be grouped together and therefore compress more effectively. Without this feature available, newly inserted data would not compress as efficiently and both storage space and memory would be wasted over time.

A logical question to ask is, "Do nonclustered columnstore indexes benefit from Vertipaq optimization?" To test this and determine if Vertipaq optimization will be used or not, new rows will be inserted into *Sales.Orders*, as provided by the query in Listing 12-14.

Listing 12-14. Inserting Rows into Sales.Orders to Test Vertipaq Optimization

```
INSERT INTO Sales.Orders
(   OrderID, CustomerID, SalespersonPersonID, PickedByPersonID,
    ContactPersonID, BackorderOrderID, OrderDate, ExpectedDeliveryDate,
    CustomerPurchaseOrderNumber, IsUndersupplyBackordered, Comments,
    DeliveryInstructions, InternalComments, PickingCompletedWhen,
    LastEditedBy, LastEditedWhen)
SELECT
    73595 + ROW_NUMBER() OVER (ORDER BY OrderID) AS OrderID,
    CustomerID,
    SalespersonPersonID,
    PickedByPersonID,
    ContactPersonID,
    BackorderOrderID,
    OrderDate,
    ExpectedDeliveryDate,
    CustomerPurchaseOrderNumber,
    IsUndersupplyBackordered,
    Comments,
    DeliveryInstructions,
    InternalComments,
    PickingCompletedWhen,
    LastEditedBy,
    LastEditedWhen
FROM Sales.Orders;
```

This insert operation doubles the size of the table. Once complete, the query in Listing 12-15 can be executed to confirm the current state of rowgroups within the nonclustered columnstore index.

Listing 12-15. Query to Display Columnstore Rowgroup Metadata After a Large INSERT Operation

```
SELECT
        objects.name AS table_name,
        partitions.partition_number,
```

```
    dm_db_column_store_row_group_physical_stats.row_group_id,
    dm_db_column_store_row_group_physical_stats.has_vertipaq_
    optimization,
    dm_db_column_store_row_group_physical_stats.state_desc
FROM sys.dm_db_column_store_row_group_physical_stats
INNER JOIN sys.objects
ON objects.object_id = dm_db_column_store_row_group_physical_stats.
object_id
INNER JOIN sys.partitions
ON partitions.object_id = objects.object_id
AND partitions.partition_number = dm_db_column_store_row_group_physical_
stats.partition_number
AND partitions.index_id = dm_db_column_store_row_group_physical_stats.
index_id
WHERE objects.name = 'Orders'
ORDER BY dm_db_column_store_row_group_physical_stats.row_group_id;
```

The results in Figure 12-16 show both the existing compressed rowgroup and the newly created open rowgroup.

	table_name	partition_number	row_group_id	has_vertipaq_optimization	state_desc
1	Orders	1	0	1	COMPRESSED
2	Orders	1	1	NULL	OPEN

Figure 12-16. *Columnstore metadata after a large INSERT operation*

Data in the new rowgroup still resides in the delta store as a compression delay of 30 minutes was specified when the columnstore index was created. To avoid waiting 30 minutes for the rowgroup to be processed by the tuple mover, the T-SQL in Listing 12-16 will be used to enable that process immediately.

Listing 12-16. T-SQL to Enable the Tuple Mover to Process Open Delta Rowgroups

```
ALTER INDEX NCCI_Orders ON sales.Orders REORGANIZE WITH
(COMPRESS_ALL_ROW_GROUPS = ON);
```

The results in Figure 12-17 show the state of the columnstore index immediately after this script completed.

	table_name	partition_number	row_group_id	has_vertipaq_optimization	state_desc
1	Orders	1	0	1	COMPRESSED
2	Orders	1	1	NULL	TOMBSTONE
3	Orders	1	2	1	COMPRESSED

Figure 12-17. *Columnstore metadata after the open rowgroup is processed*

Note that the newly created rowgroup (row_group_id = 2) is compressed and is using Vertipaq optimization. If the metadata script in Listing 12-15 is executed again after a few minutes pass, then the rowgroup in the TOMBSTONE state will be removed, as shown in Figure 12-18.

	table_name	partition_number	row_group_id	has_vertipaq_optimization	state_desc
1	Orders	1	0	1	COMPRESSED
2	Orders	1	2	1	COMPRESSED

Figure 12-18. *Columnstore metadata after the tombstone rowgroup is automatically cleaned up*

The result of the INSERT operation is 2 rowgroups, one created alongside the initial creation of the columnstore index and the other created when a new set of rows were inserted and compressed. As shown in this example, Vertipaq optimization will be used for nonclustered columnstore indexes. This is a boon to columnstore compression and ensures that each segment is compressed as efficiently as possible, despite representing transactional data that may be subject to change more frequently than typical analytic tables.

It is the inclusion of the clustered rowstore index key columns in the nonclustered columnstore index that enables Vertipaq optimization to be used. Without the key columns included, linking rows within the columnstore index back to the rowstore index would be impossible and the columnstore index would need to be rebuilt whenever data is modified. Such a cost would be prohibitively high. Having clustered key columns available ensures that rows within the nonclustered columnstore index can be freely reordered without any danger that they could not easily be tied back to the clustered index.

Testing Nonclustered Columnstore Indexes

Because mixing analytic and transactional workloads incurs risk, testing is a key component of implementing nonclustered columnstore indexes. The following is a short list of guidelines to assist in testing nonclustered columnstore indexes.

- **Test trickle inserts**. Does inserting lots of single rows or small batches of rows perform similarly before and after the nonclustered columnstore index was added?

- **Test common updates**. Are UPDATE operations used against hot data? If so, test their performance before and after the columnstore index addition.

- **Test compression delay**. For OLTP rowstore tables, compression delay is likely a beneficial option to implement. Test different values of compression delay to find a sweet spot where write operations are as efficient as possible while generating little fragmentation in the columnstore index.

- **Test filters**. If a common delineation of hot data is defined by a column or set of columns, then adding a filter to the index can help isolate hot data from the data typically used for analytics. Test these carefully to ensure that analytic queries can use the index and that the filter columns do not get updated often.

- **Perform a before and after load test**. When in doubt, a general load test of common operations that compares performance before and after the nonclustered index is added can be helpful in understanding the impact of the new index. Ideally, a nonclustered columnstore index should greatly improve analytic performance while not negatively impacting write operations.

Nonclustered columnstore indexes provide an excellent tool for mixed workloads where transactional and analytic queries target a single table or set of tables. If the expense of separating OLAP from OLTP is too high, then this can be a cost-effective way to manage common analytic queries without the need to make significant architectural changes or change application code.

Don't Forget to Drop Unneeded Indexes!

Nonclustered columnstore indexes will often be implemented to replace one or many nonclustered rowstore indexes that previously serviced analytic queries. When this is the case, be certain to test and drop the old covering indexes when they are determined to no longer be needed.

If a nonclustered columnstore index can replace many covering rowstore indexes, then its addition may very well save computing resources after all of the old, unneeded indexes are dropped. The query in Listing 12-17 returns index usage statistics for a given table.

Listing 12-17. Script That Returns Index Usage Data for One Table

```
SELECT
        tables.name AS TableName,
        indexes.name AS IndexName,
        dm_db_index_usage_stats.user_seeks,
        dm_db_index_usage_stats.user_scans,
        dm_db_index_usage_stats.user_lookups,
        dm_db_index_usage_stats.user_updates,
        dm_db_index_usage_stats.last_user_seek,
        dm_db_index_usage_stats.last_user_scan,
        dm_db_index_usage_stats.last_user_lookup,
        dm_db_index_usage_stats.last_user_update
FROM sys.dm_db_index_usage_stats
INNER JOIN sys.tables
ON tables.object_id = dm_db_index_usage_stats.object_id
INNER JOIN sys.indexes
ON indexes.object_id = dm_db_index_usage_stats.object_id
AND indexes.index_id = dm_db_index_usage_stats.index_id
WHERE tables.name = 'Orders'
```

The results are provided in Figure 12-19.

	TableName	IndexName	user_seeks	user_scans	user_lookups	user_updates	last_user_seek	last_user_scan	last_user_lookup	last_user_update
1	Orders	NCCI_Orders	0	0	0	1	NULL	NULL	NULL	2021-12-02 15:11:48.383
2	Orders	PK_Sales_Orders	1	14	15	4	2021-11-10 10:44:33.257	2021-12-02 15:12:15.280	2021-12-02 15:11:47.457	2021-12-02 15:11:48.383
3	Orders	FK_Sales_Orders_CustomerID	5	0	0	4	2021-12-02 15:11:47.457	NULL	NULL	2021-12-02 15:11:48.383
4	Orders	FK_Sales_Orders_ContactPersonID	0	0	0	4	NULL	NULL	NULL	2021-12-02 15:11:48.383
5	Orders	FK_Sales_Orders_SalespersonPersonID	0	0	0	4	NULL	NULL	NULL	2021-12-02 15:11:48.383
6	Orders	FK_Sales_Orders_PickedByPersonID	8	3	0	4	2021-12-02 15:11:47.457	2021-12-02 15:11:48.070	NULL	2021-12-02 15:11:48.383

Figure 12-19. *Index usage statistics output*

The data returned by *sys.dm_db_index_usage_stats* is reset when SQL Server restarts, so it is important to either persist it somewhere permanent or take regular snapshots of it. Using the information returned, it can be quickly determined how often an index is used for reads (seeks, scans, lookups) vs. writes (updates). An index with zero or few reads over a long period of time can be safely dropped. Indexes with more frequent reads would need additional review to determine the impact of dropping them on the queries that regularly use them.

To summarize, the goal of secondary indexes on a clustered rowstore table is to produce the simplest, most compact and efficient solution possible. For analytic queries with a predictable and often repeated structure, nonclustered covering rowstore indexes an be sufficient to provide good performance with minimal change.

If analytic needs against rowstore tables are more diverse in structure, then a single nonclustered columnstore index can be a far more efficient way to cover them than creating many nonclustered rowstore indexes.

If filters can be applied to any secondary or covering indexes (rowstore or columnstore), then doing so can reduce their size and improve performance further by avoiding hot data that is written to often.

CHAPTER 13

Nonclustered Rowstore Indexes on Columnstore Tables

Clustered columnstore indexes provide effective enough compression and data access speeds that most typical analytic workloads will not require any other indexes to provide adequate performance.

The key to this performance lies in the underlying data order for a given analytic table. As long as queries using that data are able to filter based on the dimension that the data is ordered by (typically time), they can benefit from rowgroup elimination. For unusual queries that slice the data by other dimensions, the result will often be a full scan of the columnstore index. For large tables, this is prohibitively expensive and will necessitate another solution to help in optimizing these workloads.

Using Nonclustered Rowstore Indexes

Chapter 10 reviewed in detail the importance of data order in allowing for rowgroup elimination. When data is ordered by a dimension and analytic queries filter on that dimension, SQL Server can use columnstore metadata to automatically filter out unneeded rowgroups.

Nonclustered rowstore indexes can be created on clustered columnstore tables to provide additional support for common queries that do not follow along with the ordering of the data. Care must be taken when adding supporting indexes to a clustered columnstore index. The remainder of this chapter will discuss how nonclustered rowstore indexes can be best used when needed, as well as best practices for maintaining them.

207

© Edward Pollack 2022
E. Pollack, *Analytics Optimization with Columnstore Indexes in Microsoft SQL Server*,
https://doi.org/10.1007/978-1-4842-8048-5_13

Consider a clustered columnstore index on the table *Fact.Sale_CCI_Ordered* that is ordered by the column *Invoice Date Key*. This table is architected for filtering and aggregation across the time dimension provided by the column *Invoice Date Key*. The query in Listing 13-1 provides an analytic query that takes advantage of this natural data order.

Listing 13-1. Query That Filters and Aggregates Across the Time Dimension of an Ordered Clustered Columnstore Index

```
SELECT
      COUNT(*),
      SUM(Quantity) AS total_quantity
FROM Fact.Sale_CCI_ORDERED
WHERE [Invoice Date Key] >= '11/1/2015'
AND [Invoice Date Key] < '1/1/2016';
```

When executed, the result is returned quite quickly. Figure 13-1 shows the output of STATISTICS IO.

```
  Results    Messages    Execution plan


  (1 row affected)
  Table 'Sale_CCI_ORDERED'. Scan count 2, logical reads 0, physic
  page server read-ahead reads 0, lob logical reads 67, lob physi
  Table 'Sale_CCI_ORDERED'. Segment reads 4, segment skipped 21.
  Table 'Worktable'. Scan count 0, logical reads 0, physical read
  page server read-ahead reads 0, lob logical reads 0, lob physic
```

Figure 13-1. *STATISTICS IO output for a query against an ordered clustered columnstore index*

Note that the segment report shows 4 segments read and 21 skipped. In addition, the logical reads are quite low given that this table contains 25 million rows. Both of these are indicators that rowgroup elimination was used effectively and helped ensure that only a small slice of the table needed to be read in order to process the query and return results.

So long as the analytic queries line up filters, ordering, and aggregation with the column(s) that the table is ordered by, then performance like this is to be expected. Consider the very different query provided in Listing 13-2.

Listing 13-2. Analytic Query That Does Not Use a Table's Natural Ordering

```
SELECT
        COUNT(*),
        SUM(Quantity) AS total_quantity
FROM Fact.Sale_CCI_ORDERED
WHERE [Stock Item Key] = 186;
```

This query calculates quantity using *Stock Item Key* as the filter. Since the table is ordered by *Invoice Date Key*, SQL Server has no natural way to achieve rowgroup elimination. Figure 13-2 shows the STATISTICS IO output for this query.

```
田 Results  圓 Messages  ᵍ⁻ᵒ Execution plan

   (1 row affected)
   Table 'Sale_CCI_ORDERED'. Scan count 1, logical reads 0, physical reads 0,
   lob logical reads 378, lob physical reads 0, lob page server reads 0, lob
   Table 'Sale_CCI_ORDERED'. Segment reads 25, segment skipped 0.
```

Figure 13-2. *STATISTICS IO output for a query against an unordered column in an ordered clustered columnstore index*

This time, all rowgroups were read in the columnstore index and none were skipped. This performance can be attributed to there being a total of 227 values for *Stock Item Key* in the table, but those values being scattered across all rowgroups without any particular order. Listing 13-3 provides the query to return metadata about the *Stock Item Key* column contents in the columnstore index.

Listing 13-3. Query to Return Metadata About the Stock Item Key Column

```
SELECT
        tables.name AS table_name,
        indexes.name AS index_name,
        columns.name AS column_name,
        partitions.partition_number,
        column_store_segments.segment_id,
        column_store_segments.min_data_id,
        column_store_segments.max_data_id,
        column_store_segments.row_count
```

```
FROM sys.column_store_segments
INNER JOIN sys.partitions
ON column_store_segments.hobt_id = partitions.hobt_id
INNER JOIN sys.indexes
ON indexes.index_id = partitions.index_id
AND indexes.object_id = partitions.object_id
INNER JOIN sys.tables
ON tables.object_id = indexes.object_id
INNER JOIN sys.columns
ON tables.object_id = columns.object_id
AND column_store_segments.column_id = columns.column_id
WHERE tables.name = 'Sale_CCI_ORDERED'
AND columns.name = 'Stock Item Key'
ORDER BY tables.name, columns.name, column_store_segments.segment_id;
```

Figure 13-3 provides the output of this query, showing the minimum and maximum values for Stock Item Key for each rowgroup.

	table_name	index_name	column_name	partition_number	segment_id	min_data_id	max_data_id	row_count
1	Sale_CCI_ORDERED	CCI_fact_Sale_CCI_ORDERED	Stock Item Key	1	0	1	227	1048576
2	Sale_CCI_ORDERED	CCI_fact_Sale_CCI_ORDERED	Stock Item Key	1	1	1	227	1048576
3	Sale_CCI_ORDERED	CCI_fact_Sale_CCI_ORDERED	Stock Item Key	1	2	1	227	1048576
4	Sale_CCI_ORDERED	CCI_fact_Sale_CCI_ORDERED	Stock Item Key	1	3	1	219	1048576
5	Sale_CCI_ORDERED	CCI_fact_Sale_CCI_ORDERED	Stock Item Key	1	4	1	225	1048576
6	Sale_CCI_ORDERED	CCI_fact_Sale_CCI_ORDERED	Stock Item Key	1	5	1	219	1048576
7	Sale_CCI_ORDERED	CCI_fact_Sale_CCI_ORDERED	Stock Item Key	1	6	1	219	1048576
8	Sale_CCI_ORDERED	CCI_fact_Sale_CCI_ORDERED	Stock Item Key	1	7	1	219	1048576

Figure 13-3. *Columnstore segment metadata for the Stock Item Key columns*

It is readily apparent when viewing this segment metadata that each rowgroup has similarly wide ranges of values for *Stock Item Key*, and therefore SQL Server is unable to effectively use metadata to perform much filtering using this column. It is worth noting that a query for a value greater than 219 would allow for some rowgroup elimination as the *max_data_id* for some rowgroups is 219, rather than 227 or 225. Ignoring that small detail, it is safe to say that most queries that filter on *Stock Item Key* will be forced to scan all rowgroups in the columnstore index in order to return results.

If queries that filter on Stock Item Key are frequent and their current performance is unacceptably slow, then one solution to this challenge is to implement a nonclustered rowstore covering index on top of the columnstore index. To cover the query presented

here, it is necessary to order on *Stock Item Key* and include *Quantity*. The query in
Listing 13-4 creates this index.

Listing 13-4. Query to Create a Covering Rowstore Index

```
CREATE NONCLUSTERED INDEX IX_Sale_CCI_ORDERED
ON Fact.Sale_CCI_ORDERED ([Stock Item Key]) INCLUDE (Quantity);
```

The index creation query takes about 45 seconds to complete. Once complete,
executing the sample query in Listing 13-2 produces a new execution plan and new IO,
as seen in Figure 13-4.

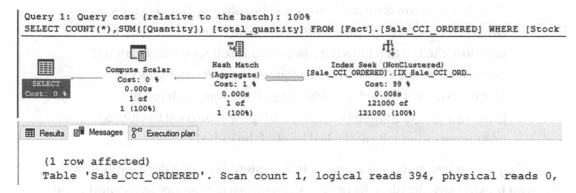

Figure 13-4. *Query execution plan and IO when using a covering index*

SQL Server exclusively uses the covering index to execute the query, resulting
in 394 reads and an index seek against the new index. This IO is slightly higher than
the previous example, but that should not be the sole decision-making metric when
determining indexing strategy. The query executes exceptionally fast as well. There are a
few key benefits to using a nonclustered rowstore index:

- Fast, predictable execution times, regardless of query parameters.

- Query reads against the covering index do not create contention with
  queries against the clustered columnstore index.

- Predictable execution plans and IO.

The benefits of covering nonclustered rowstore indexes are found exclusively on the reads. There are downsides to creating this index that must be understood before deciding to create a covering index like this:

- Write times are slowed down as the nonclustered index needs to be populated and mapped to the clustered columnstore index.

- Vertipaq optimization is not used when any nonclustered rowstore indexes are present. The mapping process to the clustered columnstore index makes reordering rows too inefficient of a process to execute on the fly.

- Nonclustered rowstore index sizes will be inflated. Data from the clustered index is duplicated within the nonclustered indexes. In addition, the key that links the rowstore index back to the clustered columnstore index is an 8-byte unique value that combines the 4-byte rowgroup ID and a 4-byte offset. If the nonclustered index is not unique, additional (variable) storage will be used to enforce uniqueness internally at the leaf level of the index.

Adding a nonclustered rowstore index to a clustered columnstore index is by no means an inexpensive decision. Its price is storage space, memory usage, and write speeds. Because of this, careful consideration must be taken prior to adding supporting indexes to a clustered columnstore index.

Enforcing Constraints

One common use of nonclustered rowstore indexes on clustered columnstore indexes is not performance related. Nonclustered rowstore indexes may be used to enforce uniqueness on a table, either via a primary key or by using a unique nonclustered index definition.

Creating unique constraints is no different than on a clustered rowstore table. Listing 13-5 shows the create statement for an existing nonclustered primary key over a clustered columnstore index.

Listing 13-5. Creating a Unique Nonclustered Rowstore Index on Top of a Clustered Columnstore Table

```
ALTER TABLE Fact.Sale ADD CONSTRAINT PK_Fact_Sale PRIMARY KEY NONCLUSTERED
(       [Sale Key] ASC,
        [Invoice Date Key] ASC);
```

This new index serves as a primary key for the underlying table, both enforcing uniqueness and allowing for foreign keys to be created on other tables that reference this table. For a scenario where either of these are important architectural requirements, then creating a primary key on the clustered columnstore index is a good solution to this problem.

The table *Fact.Sale* contains many nonclustered rowstore indexes defined on it. The query in Listing 13-6 returns the index size for each index on the table.

Listing 13-6. Query to Return Index Size for Each Index on Fact.Sale

```
SELECT
    indexes.name AS Index_Name,
    SUM(dm_db_partition_stats.used_page_count) * 8 Index_Size_KB,
    SUM(dm_db_partition_stats.row_count) AS Row_Count
FROM sys.dm_db_partition_stats
INNER JOIN sys.indexes
ON dm_db_partition_stats.object_id = indexes.object_id
AND dm_db_partition_stats.index_id = indexes.index_id
INNER JOIN sys.tables
ON tables.object_id = dm_db_partition_stats.object_id
INNER JOIN sys.schemas
ON schemas.schema_id = tables.schema_id
WHERE schemas.name = 'Fact'
AND tables.name = 'Sale'
GROUP BY indexes.name
ORDER BY indexes.name
```

The results of the index size query are shown in Figure 13-5.

	Index_Name	Index_Size_KB	Row_Count
1	CCX_Fact_Sale	5776	228265
2	FK_Fact_Sale_Bill_To_Customer_Key	5736	228265
3	FK_Fact_Sale_City_Key	5736	228265
4	FK_Fact_Sale_Customer_Key	5736	228265
5	FK_Fact_Sale_Delivery_Date_Key	5496	228265
6	FK_Fact_Sale_Invoice_Date_Key	4824	228265
7	FK_Fact_Sale_Salesperson_Key	5736	228265
8	FK_Fact_Sale_Stock_Item_Key	5736	228265
9	PK_Fact_Sale	6624	228265

Figure 13-5. *Index size details for one table*

In addition to the clustered columnstore index and the nonclustered rowstore primary key, there are another seven nonclustered rowstore indexes that each index a foreign key column. Note that the index size for each supporting index is close to the total size of the columnstore index itself. As a result, the table itself contains about 5.7MB of compressed columnstore data, but the total space used for data and index space is about 45MB.

This is an excellent example of an over-indexed table. If users truly search by that many dimensions without regard for a single data order, then a columnstore index might not be the ideal solution for this table. Alternatively, removing most of the extra indexes may still allow for performance that is fast enough, even in their absence.

Using a nonclustered rowstore index to enforce uniqueness on a clustered columnstore index can be a valuable tool when looking to enforce data integrity on OLAP data. It is generally inadvisable to implement multiple rowstore indexes on a clustered columnstore table unless the organizational need for those indexes greatly exceeds the cost.

Filtered Nonclustered Rowstore Indexes

One way to mitigate the cost of a nonclustered rowstore index on a columnstore index is to add a filter. Filtered indexes target a smaller portion of the table, consume less storage and memory, and can have a reduced impact on the compression and performance of the columnstore index.

Oftentimes, OLTP queries against an analytic table may target only a portion of the data – maybe newer, older, or based on some other useful filter. Consider the T-SQL that was tested in Listing 13-2. This query filters on Stock Item Key, which is not the column that then the columnstore index was ordered on. To mitigate the cost of this query, a nonclustered rowstore index was added, as was shown in Listing 13-4. What if this query never targeted new data, but exclusively was used to analyze older sales? Consider the updated index in Listing 13-7.

Listing 13-7. Example of a Filtered Nonclustered Rowstore Index on a Clustered Columnstore Index

```
CREATE NONCLUSTERED INDEX IX_Sale_CCI_ORDERED
ON Fact.Sale_CCI_ORDERED ([Stock Item Key], [Invoice Date Key]) INCLUDE
(Quantity)
WHERE [Invoice Date Key] <= '1/1/2016';
```

When a query is executed that uses this index and filters for data prior to 1/1/2016, it will use the filtered index rather than the columnstore index. Because the index is smaller, the number of rows that are read and the IO will be less than for the unfiltered version of this index.

One significant bonus of filtering a nonclustered rowstore index is that it allows the index to target more specifically hot vs. warm vs. cold data. This provides multiple benefits:

- Allows an index to target a specific use case, rather than all data

- Allows for better management of Vertipaq optimization

- Can facilitate the addition of multiple nonclustered indexes with less impact on write performance or resource consumption

If there is a need for secondary indexing on a clustered columnstore index, consider if filters can be added to reduce the size and impact of the nonclustered indexes. It's an easy way to improve performance and reduce storage and memory footprint, assuming queries that use the index can use the filters consistently.

Enabling Vertipaq Optimization

A downside of adding nonclustered rowstore indexes to a clustered columnstore index is that SQL Server will automatically forgo Vertipaq optimization. This will result in columnstore compression that is less effective than it could be if the feature were used. Note that Vertipaq optimization is only skipped for new data that is inserted into the table. Any data that existed in the columnstore index prior to the creation of the nonclustered indexes will benefit from the improved performance granted by it.

If a nonclustered rowstore index is needed on a clustered columnstore index, consider one of the following solutions that will allow for Vertipaq optimization to be maintained on compressed columnstore segments.

Add Filters to Nonclustered Rowstore Indexes

In addition to targeting relevant data when needed, filters can allow for hot data to be skipped when creating nonclustered indexes. This allows new data to be inserted into the clustered columnstore index using Vertipaq optimization, whereas older data can still be read using the nonclustered rowstore index.

Perform Periodic Index Maintenance

If nonclustered indexes are needed and filters cannot be applied, consider periodic maintenance in which the following steps are taken:

1. Drop nonclustered rowstore indexes.

2. Rebuild the clustered columnstore index.

3. Re-create the nonclustered rowstore indexes.

This can be time-consuming, especially for a larger table, but can allow columnstore indexes to be periodically rebuilt to be smaller and more efficient than before.

Note that partitioning can be a valuable tool here as index maintenance can target specific partitions. The query in Listing 13-8 shows how partitions can be filtered to show only those that contain rowgroups lacking Vertipaq optimization.

Listing 13-8. Query to Return Rowgroups That Are Not Benefitting from Vertipaq Optimization

```
SELECT DISTINCT
        objects.name,
        partitions.partition_number,
        dm_db_column_store_row_group_physical_stats.row_group_id,
        dm_db_column_store_row_group_physical_stats.has_vertipaq_
optimization
FROM sys.dm_db_column_store_row_group_physical_stats
INNER JOIN sys.objects
ON objects.object_id = dm_db_column_store_row_group_physical_stats.
object_id
INNER JOIN sys.partitions
ON partitions.object_id = objects.object_id
AND partitions.partition_number = dm_db_column_store_row_group_physical_
stats.partition_number
WHERE objects.name = 'Sale'
AND dm_db_column_store_row_group_physical_stats.has_vertipaq_optimization
IS NOT NULL
AND dm_db_column_store_row_group_physical_stats.has_vertipaq_
optimization = 0
ORDER BY dm_db_column_store_row_group_physical_stats.row_group_id;
```

The results are shown in Figure 13-6.

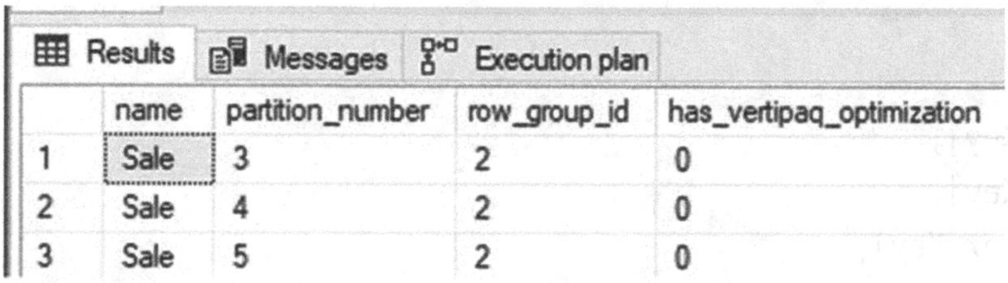

	name	partition_number	row_group_id	has_vertipaq_optimization
1	Sale	3	2	0
2	Sale	4	2	0
3	Sale	5	2	0

Figure 13-6. *Rowgroups lacking Vertipaq optimization*

The results show that only three partitions (3, 4, and 5) contain rowgroups that lack Vertipaq optimization. Therefore, periodic index maintenance could be targeted at only those partitions, skipping the rest. For less granular details, *row_group_id* can be omitted from the query to reduce the result set to a list of partitions that does not contain rowgroup IDs.

Indexed Views

It is possible to create indexed views on top of clustered columnstore indexes. While this represents an added layer of complexity, it allows for queries that do not follow the natural ordering of the columnstore index to be isolated into their own separate data structure. There, the view and its indexes can be modified freely without directly impacting the underlying table.

This can allow for more flexibility when performance testing supplementary indexes on data that is stored in a clustered columnstore index. The script in Listing 13-9 rebuilds the columnstore index on *Fact.Sale*, creates a schemabound view against it, and adds a pair of indexes to the new view.

Listing 13-9. Script to Rebuild a Table and Add an Indexed View to a Clustered Columnstore Index

```
ALTER INDEX [CCX_Fact_Sale] ON fact.sale REBUILD;
GO
CREATE VIEW Fact.v_Sale
WITH SCHEMABINDING
AS
SELECT
    [Sale Key],
    [City Key],
    [Customer Key],
    [Bill To Customer Key],
    [Stock Item Key],
    [Invoice Date Key],
    [Delivery Date Key],
    [Salesperson Key],
    [WWI Invoice ID],
```

```
    Description,
    Package,
    Quantity,
    [Unit Price],
    [Tax Rate],
    [Total Excluding Tax],
    [Tax Amount],
    Profit,
    [Total Including Tax],
    [Total Dry Items],
    [Total Chiller Items],
    [Lineage Key]
FROM Fact.Sale;
GO
CREATE UNIQUE CLUSTERED INDEX CI_v_sale
ON Fact.v_Sale ([Sale Key], [Invoice Date Key]);
GO
CREATE NONCLUSTERED INDEX IX_v_Sale
ON Fact.v_Sale ([Stock Item Key], Quantity)
GO
```

Rebuilding the columnstore index ensures that the index is in pristine condition prior to further testing. The view created in this demonstration includes all columns in the table, but could be revised to include less columns, join other tables, add computed columns, etc. The next step is to create a unique clustered index on the view. This step is necessary as nonclustered indexes on a view require a unique index as a prerequisite. Finally, a nonclustered covering index is added to handle queries against its columns.

Once complete, the analytic query in Listing 13-2 can be modified to target the view instead, as shown in Listing 13-10.

Listing 13-10. Analytic Query Targeting an Indexed View

```
SELECT
    COUNT(*),
    SUM(Quantity) AS total_quantity
FROM Fact.v_Sale
WHERE [Stock Item Key] = 186;
```

The results of the query are returned quickly. The execution plan and STATISTICS IO output are provided in Figure 13-7.

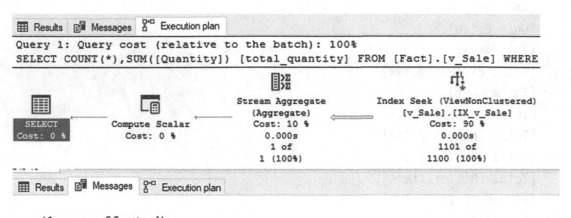

Figure 13-7 content:

Results | Messages | Execution plan

Query 1: Query cost (relative to the batch): 100%
SELECT COUNT(*),SUM([Quantity]) [total_quantity] FROM [Fact].[v_Sale] WHERE

| SELECT
Cost: 0 % | Compute Scalar
Cost: 0 % | Stream Aggregate
(Aggregate)
Cost: 10 %
0.000s
1 of
1 (100%) | Index Seek (ViewNonClustered)
[v_Sale].[IX_v_Sale]
Cost: 90 %
0.000s
1101 of
1100 (100%) |

Results | Messages | Execution plan

(1 row affected)
 Table 'v_Sale'. Scan count 1, logical reads 8, physical reads 0,

Figure 13-7. Execution plan and STATISTICS IO output for a query against an indexed view

The execution plan confirms that the nonclustered index on the view *v_Sale* was used. The IO output shows acceptably low reads against the view. There is an unexpected side effect of using an indexed view for managing select reads against a columnstore index: Vertipaq optimization is still used when new rows are inserted into the columnstore index!

While this is a useful benefit of indexed views against columnstore indexes, care should still be exercised when adding complexity to an existing table. Balance the needs of unusual workloads against a columnstore index vs. the cost of maintaining additional views and the indexes against those views.

Always test queries without supporting views or indexes first. Confirm their performance thoroughly and if needed test the impact of additional indexes or indexed views to confirm whether the additions are worth the cost.

Compression for Nonclustered Rowstore Indexes

Given the inflated size of nonclustered rowstore indexes when added to a clustered columnstore index, compression can be a valuable way to control the size of additional indexes and improve read performance against them.

Consider the nonclustered primary key defined on *Fact.Sale*. The index size data in Figure 13-5 shows that this index consumes 6,624KB. The script in Listing 13-11 drops this constraint and replaces it with a new version that uses page compression.

Listing 13-11. Script to Re-create a Nonclustered Primary Key with Page Compression

```
ALTER TABLE Fact.Sale DROP CONSTRAINT PK_Sale;
ALTER TABLE Fact.Sale ADD CONSTRAINT PK_Sale PRIMARY KEY NONCLUSTERED
([Sale Key], [Invoice Date Key])
WITH (DATA_COMPRESSION = PAGE);
```

When complete, the code in Listing 13-12 can be executed to confirm the new size of the index, after compression is applied.

Listing 13-12. Script to Check the Size of a Compressed Nonclustered Index

```
SELECT
    indexes.name AS Index_Name,
    SUM(dm_db_partition_stats.used_page_count) * 8 Index_Size_KB,
    SUM(dm_db_partition_stats.row_count) AS Row_Count
FROM sys.dm_db_partition_stats
INNER JOIN sys.indexes
ON dm_db_partition_stats.object_id = indexes.object_id
AND dm_db_partition_stats.index_id = indexes.index_id
INNER JOIN sys.tables
ON tables.object_id = dm_db_partition_stats.object_id
INNER JOIN sys.schemas
ON schemas.schema_id = tables.schema_id
WHERE indexes.name = 'PK_Sale'
GROUP BY indexes.name;
```

The results are shown in Figure 13-8.

	Index_Name	Index_Size_KB	Row_Count
1	PK_Sale	2736	228266

***Figure 13-8.** Index size for a page compressed nonclustered primary key*

The results show that the index now consumes only 2,736KB, a reduction of 3,888KB or about 59%. This is a significant space savings and illustrates the positive impact that compression can have when applied to secondary nonclustered indexes on a columnstore indexed table.

Nonclustered Rowstore Index Guidance

Adding nonclustered rowstore indexes to a clustered columnstore index is an effective way of managing frequent, unusual query patterns against analytic data. By splitting different reads onto both the clustered and nonclustered indexes, contention can be better managed by also splitting locks onto each index. Before making any indexing changes, ensure that new indexes are necessary and provide enough long-term benefits to necessitate their cost.

When possible, consider the use of filters to shrink the size of nonclustered indexes and decrease their impact on the underlying columnstore index. Similarly, consider partitioning if not already used as it can assist in streamlining and speeding up index maintenance processes.

Consider indexed views on top of columnstore indexes when there is added value in isolating unusual workloads away from the columnstore index and onto a separate object. The cost of maintaining them is in no way insignificant, but they can provide a convenient way to encapsulate specific workloads onto their own objects. Splitting workloads into separate objects helps to reduce contention as reads against each object target them separately, locking those objects separately from each other.

Regardless of how secondary indexes are created, consider compressing them. Compression can greatly reduce storage consumption, thereby decreasing memory footprint and speeding up read queries that use the compressed indexes.

As a rule of thumb, if the number of nonclustered rowstore indexes against a columnstore index increases past one (or two with an indexed view), consider alternative ways of storing this data, such as

- Clustered rowstore table with page compression and supporting indexes where needed.

- Clustered columnstore index with less nonclustered indexes.

- Separating workloads into separate tables that are managed independently of each other.

- Apply compression and/or filters to indexes to reduce size and upkeep of each, making them more manageable.

This chapter provided a variety of tactics toward finding a favorable configuration that allows wildly different workloads to coexist peacefully on a single table. There is no one-size-fits-all approach to secondary indexing on a clustered columnstore index, though. If unsure of the best way to proceed, test each alternative thoroughly to gain comfort with the pros and cons of each approach.

CHAPTER 14

Columnstore Index Maintenance

Depending on its usage, a columnstore index may require no maintenance at all, infrequent maintenance, or regular maintenance to ensure optimal storage, resource consumption, and performance.

Understanding how and when to use index maintenance will ensure that analytic queries continue to perform well both when a columnstore index is first created and years into the future.

What Causes Fragmentation?

There are three scenarios that can be used to describe fragmentation in columnstore indexes:

1. Wasted space due to deleted rows

2. Data that is inserted out of order

3. Multiple delta rowgroups present in the index

When data is deleted in a columnstore index, no rows are actually removed. The cost to decompress, delete rows, and recompress rowgroups is prohibitively expensive at runtime. Instead, SQL Server flags the rows as deleted using the delete bitmap, and when queries access that data, they use the bitmap to identify any rows that are deleted and need to be skipped.

Chapter 9 provides extensive detail as to how DELETE and UPDATE operations perform on columnstore indexes and outlines ways of managing them to avoid persistent performance challenges and minimize fragmentation. The net impact of deletion on columnstore indexes will be

- Space consumed by deleted data.

- More data needs to be read than is needed at runtime.

- Data is spread over more rowgroups than necessary.

The other cause of fragmentation is out-of-order data. A columnstore index should always be built and maintained with data that is ordered by a key column (or columns) that are used most frequently in filtering and aggregating queries.

Chapter 10 describes the importance of data order in columnstore indexes and how maintaining a data order that lines up with common query filters and aggregation can allow for exceptionally fast query performance.

Data that is inserted regularly in the desired columnstore index order will facilitate rowgroup elimination, thus allowing vast amounts of the index to be automatically skipped when filtered using the same column(s). When rows are inserted out of order, this forces more data to be read than should be necessary. Similarly, since an UPDATE operation is executed as the combination of a DELETE and INSERT, updating any older data in a columnstore index will result in it being reinserted at the tail end of the index alongside newer data.

Consider the example columnstore index in Figure 14-1, which is ordered by *Order_Date*.

Rowgroup #	Order Year	Row Count
1-10	2016	10mil
11-30	2017	20mil
31-50	2018	20mil
51-80	2019	30mil
81-100	2020	20mil
101-150	2021	50mil

Figure 14-1. *A columnstore index that is ordered by the date dimension*

This columnstore index is pristinely ordered by Order Year, with each set of rowgroups containing rows in ascending order by date. If a query is executed that calculates metrics for 2016, it can read the first ten rowgroups while ignoring the other 140.

Figure 14-2 shows the result of an UPDATE operation that alters data for 100,000 rows in 2016, 50,000 rows in 2017, and 25,000 rows in 2018.

Rowgroup #	Order Year	Row Count	Deleted Rows
1-10	2016	10mil	100k
11-30	2017	20mil	50k
31-50	2018	20mil	25k
51-80	2019	30mil	0
81-100	2020	20mil	0
101-150	2021	50mil	0
151	2016, 2017, 2018	175k	0

Figure 14-2. *Changes in rowgroup structure after an UPDATE operation*

When rows were updated, they remained in the columnstore index in their previous locations, but were flagged as deleted. A new rowgroup was created that contains the new versions of the deleted rows. The result is that there is now an open rowgroup that contains data for 2016, 2017, and 2018. In addition, when new data is inserted into the table, it will also be added to the open rowgroup, resulting in another year's worth of data being crammed into a single rowgroup.

Going forward, any query that requires data from 2016, 2017, 2018, or the current year will need to read this unordered rowgroup. If updates like this are common, then older rowgroups will quickly become logjammed with deleted rows, while newer rowgroups become unordered messes of data from many dates. The result will be wasted storage, wasted memory, and slower queries that need to read far more data than should be needed to return results.

Unordered inserts will have a similar impact as the INSERT portion of an UPDATE statement. Inserting data into the columnstore index in Figure 14-1 from 2015 would result in new rowgroups that contain both new and old data. Unordered inserts will, over a long period of time, result in the inability of SQL Server to take advantage of rowgroup elimination as more and more rowgroups contain data from all different time periods.

Delta rowgroups are a key part of columnstore index architecture and ensure that write operations can occur as quickly as possible. They slow down reads slightly, though, as rows reside in a b-tree structure and are not compressed with columnstore compression. The impact of the delta store on read performance is not significant, but administrators interested in maximizing columnstore read performance would be interested in compressing them as soon as possible after a data load process completes.

How Much Fragmentation Is Too Much?

Like with rowstore indexes, fragmentation does not require attention until it becomes significant enough to impact performance and waste a tangible amount of space. A columnstore index with 5 billion rows of which 1,000 are deleted should not be seen as problematic. Alternatively, if one billion of those rows were deleted, then the resulting fragmentation would be worth addressing.

Fragmentation should be broken out into two distinct calculations, of which each can be evaluated clinically and acted on appropriately. One is the percentage of a table that is comprised of deleted rows, and the other is a measure of unordered data within a columnstore index.

Quantifying Deleted Rows

Deleted rows are included in the view *sys.column_store_row_groups* and are relatively easy to report on. The query in Listing 14-1 returns a row per rowgroup within a single clustered columnstore index.

Listing 14-1. Query to Return Deleted Rows per Rowgroup

```
SELECT
      tables.name AS table_name,
      indexes.name AS index_name,
      partitions.partition_number,
      column_store_row_groups.row_group_id,
      column_store_row_groups.total_rows,
      column_store_row_groups.deleted_rows
FROM sys.column_store_row_groups
INNER JOIN sys.indexes
ON indexes.index_id = column_store_row_groups.index_id
AND indexes.object_id = column_store_row_groups.object_id
INNER JOIN sys.tables
ON tables.object_id = indexes.object_id
INNER JOIN sys.partitions
ON partitions.partition_number = column_store_row_groups.partition_number
AND partitions.index_id = indexes.index_id
```

```
AND partitions.object_id = tables.object_id
WHERE tables.name = 'Sale_CCI'
ORDER BY indexes.index_id, column_store_row_groups.row_group_id;
```

The results are shown in Figure 14-3.

	table_name	index_name	partition_number	row_group_id	total_rows	deleted_rows
1	Sale_CCI	CCI_fact_sale_CCI	1	0	1048576	47333
2	Sale_CCI	CCI_fact_sale_CCI	1	1	1048576	35479
3	Sale_CCI	CCI_fact_sale_CCI	1	2	1048576	80474
4	Sale_CCI	CCI_fact_sale_CCI	1	3	1048576	36388
5	Sale_CCI	CCI_fact_sale_CCI	1	4	1048576	69428
6	Sale_CCI	CCI_fact_sale_CCI	1	5	1048576	62487
7	Sale_CCI	CCI_fact_sale_CCI	1	6	1048576	32117
8	Sale_CCI	CCI_fact_sale_CCI	1	7	1048576	39962

Figure 14-3. *Deleted row counts per rowgroup for a columnstore index*

This detail shows how many rows are deleted per rowgroup. The results can be aggregated to show deleted rows per partition or for the entire table. If a table is partitioned, then knowing if the deleted rows exist only in one partition or all of them is useful for determining if all or only some partitions require attention.

In the example results outlined in Figure 14-3, about 5% of the columnstore index is comprised of deleted rows that are spread across the index relatively evenly. As a rough guideline, there is no urgent need for index maintenance to address this unless the percentage of deleted rows is at least 10% of the total rows in a partition or in the table.

Keep in mind that the performance impact of deleted rows is gradual over time. There will never be a scenario where a threshold is reached in which performance suddenly plummets. Therefore, automating index maintenance to occur when deleted rows exceed some set percentage is an effective way to avoid accidentally allowing an index to become absurdly fragmented.

Detailing Unordered Data

Understanding the effectiveness of ordered data is easy to see via querying segment metadata, but can be challenging to quantify. The query in Listing 14-2 shows how to retrieve the segment minimum and maximum data IDs for a given columnstore index and a single column.

Listing 14-2. Query to Retrieve Min/Max Data IDs for a Given Column in a Columnstore Index

```
SELECT
        tables.name AS table_name,
        indexes.name AS index_name,
        columns.name AS column_name,
        partitions.partition_number,
        column_store_segments.segment_id,
        column_store_segments.min_data_id,
        column_store_segments.max_data_id,
        column_store_segments.row_count
FROM sys.column_store_segments
INNER JOIN sys.partitions
ON column_store_segments.hobt_id = partitions.hobt_id
INNER JOIN sys.indexes
ON indexes.index_id = partitions.index_id
AND indexes.object_id = partitions.object_id
INNER JOIN sys.tables
ON tables.object_id = indexes.object_id
INNER JOIN sys.columns
ON tables.object_id = columns.object_id
AND column_store_segments.column_id = columns.column_id
WHERE tables.name = 'Sale_CCI'
AND columns.name = 'Invoice Date Key'
ORDER BY tables.name, columns.name, column_store_segments.segment_id;
```

The results of this query provide useful insight into the data order within this index, as shown in Figure 14-4.

	table_name	index_name	column_name	partition_number	segment_id	min_data_id	max_data_id	row_count
1	Sale_CCI	CCI_fact_sale_CCI	Invoice Date Key	1	0	734868	736114	1048576
2	Sale_CCI	CCI_fact_sale_CCI	Invoice Date Key	1	1	734868	736114	1048576
3	Sale_CCI	CCI_fact_sale_CCI	Invoice Date Key	1	2	734868	736114	1048576
4	Sale_CCI	CCI_fact_sale_CCI	Invoice Date Key	1	3	734868	736114	1048576
5	Sale_CCI	CCI_fact_sale_CCI	Invoice Date Key	1	4	734868	736114	1048576
6	Sale_CCI	CCI_fact_sale_CCI	Invoice Date Key	1	5	734868	736114	1048576
7	Sale_CCI	CCI_fact_sale_CCI	Invoice Date Key	1	6	734868	736114	1048576
8	Sale_CCI	CCI_fact_sale_CCI	Invoice Date Key	1	7	734868	736114	1048576

Figure 14-4. *Segment minimum/maximum value metadata for an unordered columnstore index*

In the metadata, note that the values for *min_data_id* and *max_data_id* are the same for each rowgroup. This means that queries that filter on the column *Invoice Date Key* will be forced to scan the entire table to return results as any value could be found in any rowgroup.

Consider an ordered version of this table, where the results are as seen in Figure 14-5.

	table_name	index_name	column_name	partition_number	segment_id	min_data_id	max_data_id	row_count
1	Sale_CCI_ORDERED	CCI_fact_Sale_CCI_ORDERED	Invoice Date Key	1	0	736022	736071	1048576
2	Sale_CCI_ORDERED	CCI_fact_Sale_CCI_ORDERED	Invoice Date Key	1	1	735969	736022	1048576
3	Sale_CCI_ORDERED	CCI_fact_Sale_CCI_ORDERED	Invoice Date Key	1	2	735920	736114	1048576
4	Sale_CCI_ORDERED	CCI_fact_Sale_CCI_ORDERED	Invoice Date Key	1	3	735871	735920	1048576
5	Sale_CCI_ORDERED	CCI_fact_Sale_CCI_ORDERED	Invoice Date Key	1	4	735822	735969	1048576
6	Sale_CCI_ORDERED	CCI_fact_Sale_CCI_ORDERED	Invoice Date Key	1	5	735729	735871	1048576
7	Sale_CCI_ORDERED	CCI_fact_Sale_CCI_ORDERED	Invoice Date Key	1	6	735777	735822	1048576
8	Sale_CCI_ORDERED	CCI_fact_Sale_CCI_ORDERED	Invoice Date Key	1	7	735634	735777	1048576

Figure 14-5. *Segment minimum/maximum value metadata for an ordered columnstore index*

This version of the table shows a progression of values for *min_data_id* and *max_data_id* that increases as the *segment_id* increases. Because each segment contains a distinct grouping of column values, this metadata can be effectively used to skip any rowgroups that contain values that are irrelevant to a query. The query in Listing 14-3 returns a complete list of all segments in a columnstore index that have any overlapping values. The inequalities are not inclusive as it is common that the start and end values in a rowgroup will overlap those in the next rowgroup.

Listing 14-3. Query to Return a List of Overlapping Segments

```
WITH CTE_SEGMENTS AS (
      SELECT
              tables.name AS table_name,
              indexes.name AS index_name,
              columns.name AS column_name,
              partitions.partition_number,
              column_store_segments.segment_id,
              column_store_segments.min_data_id,
              column_store_segments.max_data_id,
              column_store_segments.row_count
      FROM sys.column_store_segments
      INNER JOIN sys.partitions
      ON column_store_segments.hobt_id = partitions.hobt_id
      INNER JOIN sys.indexes
      ON indexes.index_id = partitions.index_id
      AND indexes.object_id = partitions.object_id
      INNER JOIN sys.tables
      ON tables.object_id = indexes.object_id
      INNER JOIN sys.columns
      ON tables.object_id = columns.object_id
      AND column_store_segments.column_id = columns.column_id
      WHERE tables.name = 'Sale_CCI_ORDERED'
      AND columns.name = 'Invoice Date Key')
SELECT
      CTE_SEGMENTS.table_name,
      CTE_SEGMENTS.index_name,
      CTE_SEGMENTS.column_name,
      CTE_SEGMENTS.partition_number,
      CTE_SEGMENTS.segment_id,
      CTE_SEGMENTS.min_data_id,
      CTE_SEGMENTS.max_data_id,
      CTE_SEGMENTS.row_count,
      OVERLAPPING_SEGMENT.partition_number AS
      overlapping_partition_number,
```

```
        OVERLAPPING_SEGMENT.segment_id AS overlapping_segment_id,
        OVERLAPPING_SEGMENT.min_data_id AS overlapping_min_data_id,
        OVERLAPPING_SEGMENT.max_data_id AS overlapping_max_data_id
FROM CTE_SEGMENTS
INNER JOIN CTE_SEGMENTS OVERLAPPING_SEGMENT
ON (OVERLAPPING_SEGMENT.min_data_id > CTE_SEGMENTS.min_data_id
AND OVERLAPPING_SEGMENT.min_data_id < CTE_SEGMENTS.max_data_id)
OR (OVERLAPPING_SEGMENT.max_data_id > CTE_SEGMENTS.min_data_id
AND OVERLAPPING_SEGMENT.max_data_id < CTE_SEGMENTS.max_data_id)
OR (OVERLAPPING_SEGMENT.min_data_id < CTE_SEGMENTS.min_data_id
AND OVERLAPPING_SEGMENT.max_data_id > CTE_SEGMENTS.max_data_id)
ORDER BY CTE_SEGMENTS.partition_number, CTE_SEGMENTS.segment_id
```

This query evaluates the boundaries for the minimum and maximum value of one column within each rowgroup and determines if any other rowgroups overlap those values.

The list returned by the query in Figure 14-6 may appear long at first glance, but it is important to note that any columnstore index that has been the target of UPDATE operations or unordered inserts will have entries here. Looking at the data returned, it can be seen that the out-of-order data is spread somewhat evenly across segments, with each segment containing 1–4 other segments that overlap at least one value with it.

	table_name	index_name	column_name	partition_number	segment_id	min_data_id	max_data_id	row_count	overlapping_partition_number	overlapping_segment_id	overlapping_min_data_id	overlapping_max_data_id
1	Sale_CCI_ORDERED	CCI_fact_Sale_CCI_ORDERED	Invoice Date Key	1	0	736022	736071	1048576	1	2	735920	736114
2	Sale_CCI_ORDERED	CCI_fact_Sale_CCI_ORDERED	Invoice Date Key	1	1	735969	736022	1048576	1	2	735920	736114
3	Sale_CCI_ORDERED	CCI_fact_Sale_CCI_ORDERED	Invoice Date Key	1	2	735920	736114	1048576	1	0	736022	736071
4	Sale_CCI_ORDERED	CCI_fact_Sale_CCI_ORDERED	Invoice Date Key	1	2	735920	736114	1048576	1	1	735969	736022
5	Sale_CCI_ORDERED	CCI_fact_Sale_CCI_ORDERED	Invoice Date Key	1	2	735920	736114	1048576	1	4	735822	735969
6	Sale_CCI_ORDERED	CCI_fact_Sale_CCI_ORDERED	Invoice Date Key	1	2	735920	736114	1048576	1	24	734868	735964
7	Sale_CCI_ORDERED	CCI_fact_Sale_CCI_ORDERED	Invoice Date Key	1	3	735871	735920	1048576	1	4	735822	735969
8	Sale_CCI_ORDERED	CCI_fact_Sale_CCI_ORDERED	Invoice Date Key	1	3	735871	735920	1048576	1	24	734868	735964
9	Sale_CCI_ORDERED	CCI_fact_Sale_CCI_ORDERED	Invoice Date Key	1	4	735822	735969	1048576	1	2	735920	736114
10	Sale_CCI_ORDERED	CCI_fact_Sale_CCI_ORDERED	Invoice Date Key	1	4	735822	735969	1048576	1	3	735871	735920

Figure 14-6. *List of overlapping values within rowgroups for the Invoice Date Key column*

While there is no precise way to measure the percentage of unordered data in the same way that it was possible to measure the percentage of rows in a columnstore index that are deleted, it is possible to gauge how effectively data order impacts query performance by performing metadata tests using COUNT(*) queries against the columnstore index. This could be done for every date in the table, which would result in a very thorough experiment. For the sake of a simple demonstration, eight sample dates will be chosen at random to test, as given by the query in Listing 14-4.

Listing 14-4. Sample Dates to Test How Ordered Data Is in a Columnstore Index

```
SELECT
        [Invoice Date Key],
        COUNT(*) AS Sale_Count
FROM Fact.Sale_CCI_ORDERED
WHERE [Invoice Date Key] IN ('5/1/2013', '9/5/2013', '1/17/2014',
'6/30/2014', '3/14/2015', '12/12/2015', '1/1/2016', '2/29/2016')
GROUP BY [Invoice Date Key]
ORDER BY [Invoice Date Key]
```

The results in Figure 14-7 provide row counts for each data.

	Invoice Date Key	Sale_Count
1	2013-05-01	20020
2	2013-09-05	30910
3	2014-01-17	15730
4	2014-06-30	15950
5	2015-03-14	17930
6	2015-12-12	15180
7	2016-01-01	15400
8	2016-02-29	37620

Figure 14-7. *List of sample dates for use in testing the effectiveness of columnstore data order*

Each data point chosen contains at most 0.1% of the data in the table as there are 25,109,150 total rows, of which these encompass eight of its dates. Based on the row counts and table size, an ideal ordered table would only require reading 1–2 rowgroups to retrieve data for any of those given dates. The query in Listing 14-5 executes separate COUNT(*) queries for each date identified earlier.

Listing 14-5. COUNT Queries to Test Rowgroup Reads

```
SET NOCOUNT ON;
SELECT COUNT(*) FROM Fact.Sale_CCI_ORDERED WHERE [Invoice Date Key] =
'5/1/2013';
SELECT COUNT(*) FROM Fact.Sale_CCI_ORDERED WHERE [Invoice Date Key] =
'9/5/2013';
```

```
SELECT COUNT(*) FROM Fact.Sale_CCI_ORDERED WHERE [Invoice Date Key] =
'1/17/2014';
SELECT COUNT(*) FROM Fact.Sale_CCI_ORDERED WHERE [Invoice Date Key] =
'6/30/2014';
SELECT COUNT(*) FROM Fact.Sale_CCI_ORDERED WHERE [Invoice Date Key] =
'3/14/2015';
SELECT COUNT(*) FROM Fact.Sale_CCI_ORDERED WHERE [Invoice Date Key] =
'12/12/2015';
SELECT COUNT(*) FROM Fact.Sale_CCI_ORDERED WHERE [Invoice Date Key] =
'1/1/2016';
SELECT COUNT(*) FROM Fact.Sale_CCI_ORDERED WHERE [Invoice Date Key] =
'2/29/2016';
```

Figure 14-8 shows the STATISTICS IO output for each preceding query.

```
Results   Messages
    Table 'Sale_CCI_ORDERED'. Scan count 1, logical reads 0, physic
    Table 'Sale_CCI_ORDERED'. Segment reads 4, segment skipped 21.
    Table 'Sale_CCI_ORDERED'. Scan count 1, logical reads 0, physic
    Table 'Sale_CCI_ORDERED'. Segment reads 4, segment skipped 21.
    Table 'Sale_CCI_ORDERED'. Scan count 1, logical reads 0, physic
    Table 'Sale_CCI_ORDERED'. Segment reads 4, segment skipped 21.
    Table 'Sale_CCI_ORDERED'. Scan count 1, logical reads 0, physic
    Table 'Sale_CCI_ORDERED'. Segment reads 4, segment skipped 21.
    Table 'Sale_CCI_ORDERED'. Scan count 1, logical reads 0, physic
    Table 'Sale_CCI_ORDERED'. Segment reads 3, segment skipped 22.
    Table 'Sale_CCI_ORDERED'. Scan count 1, logical reads 0, physic
    Table 'Sale_CCI_ORDERED'. Segment reads 3, segment skipped 22.
    Table 'Sale_CCI_ORDERED'. Scan count 1, logical reads 0, physic
    Table 'Sale_CCI_ORDERED'. Segment reads 3, segment skipped 22.
    Table 'Sale_CCI_ORDERED'. Scan count 1, logical reads 0, physic
    Table 'Sale_CCI_ORDERED'. Segment reads 3, segment skipped 22.
```

Figure 14-8. *STATISTICS IO output for COUNT queries in Listing 14-5*

For each of the eight COUNT(*) sample queries, 3–4 rowgroups are read in order
to retrieve the count. Based on the knowledge that these queries should read 1–2
rowgroups, it can be deduced that queries are generally reading two to three times more
rowgroups than is necessary. Depending on how often updates and unordered inserts

occur on the table, this may be acceptable or it may be unusual. Knowledge of the table's usage helps in understanding how extreme these numbers are and if reading three rowgroups instead of one is normal or worthy of attention.

Testing rowgroups read and skipped using STATISTICS IO is an effective way to gauge how ordered a columnstore index is. If there is a desire to be complete about this test and use count queries against many (or all) dates in the table, consider treating them as maintenance and performing that research at a predetermined time when running a lengthy maintenance script is acceptable.

The No-Maintenance Columnstore Index

An ideal columnstore index rarely requires maintenance. This is possible when the following are true:

- Rows are never deleted.

- Rows are never updated.

- Rows are always inserted in order.

If those three conditions can be met, then a columnstore index can be spared of nearly all maintenance. Whether any is performed is up to the whim of its administrator. Realistically, the only suboptimal scenario that can arise when the columnstore index is not the target of deletes, updates, or unordered inserts is that rowgroups may be undersized due to the use of the delta store to process small INSERT operations.

The impact of undersized rowgroups resulting from delta store usage is minor and should not be seen as an urgent problem in need of an immediate resolution. In these scenarios, waiting for infrequent maintenance periods to perform columnstore index maintenance would be more than effective enough to ensure that undersized rowgroups are merged effectively. Quarterly or yearly is likely often enough.

Now that the causes of fragmentation have been thoroughly detailed, using index maintenance operations to resolve fragmentation can be discussed.

Columnstore Reorganize

The fastest and simplest operation available for a columnstore index is the REORGANIZE. This is an online operation that accomplishes the following tasks:

- Combines undersized rowgroups via a columnstore index merge. This occurs when multiple rowgroups can combine to fit into a single new rowgroup (less than 1,024,576 or 2^{20} rows).

- May remove deleted rows via a self-merge. This only happens when more than 102,400 rows in a rowgroup are deleted.

If both of these tasks apply to a set of rowgroups, then a merge operation will be prioritized over a self-merge. Rowgroups that were trimmed due to dictionary pressure cannot be combined with other rowgroups, regardless of their row counts.

To demonstrate the merge and self-merge operations that can be used by a columnstore REORGANIZE operation, a large set of rows will be deleted from a columnstore index, as seen in Listing 14-6

Listing 14-6. Query to Delete a Large Portion of a Rowgroup

```
DELETE
FROM Fact.Sale_CCI_ORDERED
WHERE [Invoice Date Key] <= '1/17/2013';
```

Figure 14-9 shows the resulting set of deleted rows within the columnstore index's rowgroup metadata using the same query as provided in Listing 14-1.

	table_name	index_name	partition_number	row_group_id	total_rows	deleted_rows
20	Sale_CCI_ORDERED	CCI_fact_Sale_CCI_ORDERED	1	19	1048576	0
21	Sale_CCI_ORDERED	CCI_fact_Sale_CCI_ORDERED	1	20	1048576	0
22	Sale_CCI_ORDERED	CCI_fact_Sale_CCI_ORDERED	1	21	1048576	22880
23	Sale_CCI_ORDERED	CCI_fact_Sale_CCI_ORDERED	1	22	1048576	9020
24	Sale_CCI_ORDERED	CCI_fact_Sale_CCI_ORDERED	1	23	491180	159556
25	Sale_CCI_ORDERED	CCI_fact_Sale_CCI_ORDERED	1	24	500722	126444

Figure 14-9. *Deleted rows per rowgroup for a columnstore index*

The second column to the right shows total rows in the rowgroup, whereas the rightmost column provides the deleted row count. Of the rowgroups with deleted rows, only rowgroups 23 and 24 have more than 102,400 rows deleted and would qualify for a self-merge operation. These rowgroups are also valid targets for a columnstore merge operation as they can be combined, with the resulting rowgroup containing less than the row cap (2^{20} rows) for a columnstore rowgroup.

The syntax for a columnstore REORGANIZE operation is shown in Listing 14-7.

Listing 14-7. Syntax for a Columnstore Reorganize Operation

```
ALTER INDEX CCI_fact_Sale_CCI_ORDERED ON Fact.Sale_CCI_ORDERED REORGANIZE;
```

After the REORGANIZE operation is complete, the rowgroup metadata can be reviewed again, as shown in Figure 14-10.

	table_name	index_name	partition_number	row_group_id	total_rows	deleted_rows	state_description
21	Sale_CCI_ORDERED	CCI_fact_Sale_CCI_ORDERED	1	20	1048576	0	COMPRESSED
22	Sale_CCI_ORDERED	CCI_fact_Sale_CCI_ORDERED	1	21	1048576	22880	COMPRESSED
23	Sale_CCI_ORDERED	CCI_fact_Sale_CCI_ORDERED	1	22	1048576	9020	COMPRESSED
24	Sale_CCI_ORDERED	CCI_fact_Sale_CCI_ORDERED	1	23	491180	159556	TOMBSTONE
25	Sale_CCI_ORDERED	CCI_fact_Sale_CCI_ORDERED	1	24	500722	126444	TOMBSTONE
26	Sale_CCI_ORDERED	CCI_fact_Sale_CCI_ORDERED	1	25	419432	0	COMPRESSED
27	Sale_CCI_ORDERED	CCI_fact_Sale_CCI_ORDERED	1	26	286470	0	COMPRESSED

Figure 14-10. *Rowgroup metadata following an index REORGANIZE operation*

Note that rowgroups 23 and 24 are now flagged as TOMBSTONE and will be cleaned up by the tuple mover at some point in the near future. Two new rowgroups were created (25 and 26) that replace them, with the deleted rows removed. The self-merge operation essentially creates new rowgroups, copies all nondeleted rows into them, and swaps them in as the active rowgroups while the previous versions are flagged for cleanup. The resulting rowgroups are free of the burden of deleted rows. Remember that the self-merge only occurs when more than 102,400 rows in a rowgroup are deleted.

After a minute passes, the rowgroup metadata confirms that the rowgroups labeled as TOMBSTONE are now removed from the columnstore index, as seen in Figure 14-11. This is an automatic cleanup process that requires no operator intervention to trigger.

▦ Results ▣ Messages

	table_name	index_name	partition_number	row_group_id	total_rows	deleted_rows	state_description
19	Sale_CCI_ORDERED	CCI_fact_Sale_CCI_ORDERED	1	18	1048576	0	COMPRESSED
20	Sale_CCI_ORDERED	CCI_fact_Sale_CCI_ORDERED	1	19	1048576	0	COMPRESSED
21	Sale_CCI_ORDERED	CCI_fact_Sale_CCI_ORDERED	1	20	1048576	0	COMPRESSED
22	Sale_CCI_ORDERED	CCI_fact_Sale_CCI_ORDERED	1	21	1048576	22880	COMPRESSED
23	Sale_CCI_ORDERED	CCI_fact_Sale_CCI_ORDERED	1	22	1048576	9020	COMPRESSED
24	Sale_CCI_ORDERED	CCI_fact_Sale_CCI_ORDERED	1	25	419432	0	COMPRESSED
25	Sale_CCI_ORDERED	CCI_fact_Sale_CCI_ORDERED	1	26	286470	0	COMPRESSED

Figure 14-11. *Rowgroup metadata after the tuple mover removes TOMBSTONE rowgroups*

Rowgroups can only be combined if the reason they are undersized is not related to dictionary pressure. Figure 14-12 shows additional metadata from *sys.dm_db_column_store_row_group_physical_stats* for this columnstore index.

▦ Results ▣ Messages

	table_name	index_name	partition_number	row_group_id	state_desc	total_rows	deleted_rows	size_in_bytes	trim_reason_desc
1	Sale_CCI_ORDERED	CCI_fact_Sale_CCI_ORDERED	1	26	COMPRESSED	286470	0	1002256	REORG
2	Sale_CCI_ORDERED	CCI_fact_Sale_CCI_ORDERED	1	25	COMPRESSED	419432	0	1440408	DICTIONARY_SIZE
3	Sale_CCI_ORDERED	CCI_fact_Sale_CCI_ORDERED	1	22	COMPRESSED	1048576	9020	749248	NO_TRIM
4	Sale_CCI_ORDERED	CCI_fact_Sale_CCI_ORDERED	1	21	COMPRESSED	1048576	22880	762792	NO_TRIM
5	Sale_CCI_ORDERED	CCI_fact_Sale_CCI_ORDERED	1	20	COMPRESSED	1048576	0	756792	NO_TRIM
6	Sale_CCI_ORDERED	CCI_fact_Sale_CCI_ORDERED	1	19	COMPRESSED	1048576	0	754872	NO_TRIM
7	Sale_CCI_ORDERED	CCI_fact_Sale_CCI_ORDERED	1	0	COMPRESSED	1048576	0	750896	NO_TRIM

Figure 14-12. *Rowgroup metadata for a columnstore index, including rowgroup trim reason*

Because rowgroup 25 was trimmed due to dictionary pressure, it cannot be combined with rowgroup 26, even though their combined row counts could fit them into a single rowgroup.

Reorganize to Remove Delta Rowgroups

An additional option is available when issuing a columnstore index REORGANIZE command: the COMPRESS_ALL_ROW_GROUPS option. When used, SQL Server will initialize the tuple mover to process the contents of the delta store and move them into compressed rowgroups. This effectively empties the delta store, moving all data into compressed rowgroups.

The upside of this operation is that it ensures faster read operations, as there is no need to read the rowstore structure of the delta store when processing queries. The downside is that it is an additional maintenance option that requires time and resources to execute. Consider the INSERT operation shown in Listing 14-8.

Listing 14-8. Small INSERT Operation into a Columnstore Index

```
INSERT INTO Fact.Sale_CCI_ORDERED
    ([Sale Key], [City Key], [Customer Key], [Bill To Customer Key], [Stock
    Item Key], [Invoice Date Key], [Delivery Date Key],
    [Salesperson Key], [WWI Invoice ID], Description, Package, Quantity,
    [Unit Price], [Tax Rate], [Total Excluding Tax], [Tax Amount],
    Profit, [Total Including Tax], [Total Dry Items], [Total Chiller
    Items], [Lineage Key])
VALUES
(   6769, 69490, 0, 0, 26, '2013-02-10', '2013-02-11', 36, 2081, 'Coffee
    Mug', 'Each', 17, 12.42, 8.00, 211.14, 16.89, 75.00, 228.03,
        17, 0, 11);
```

One row is inserted into the columnstore index. Rowgroup metadata can confirm the new row that resides in an open delta rowgroup, as seen in Figure 14-13, using the same query as in Listing 14-1.

	table_name	index_name	partition_number	row_group_id	total_rows	deleted_rows	state_description
21	Sale_CCI_ORDERED	CCI_fact_Sale_CCI_ORDERED	1	20	1048576	0	COMPRESSED
22	Sale_CCI_ORDERED	CCI_fact_Sale_CCI_ORDERED	1	21	1048576	22880	COMPRESSED
23	Sale_CCI_ORDERED	CCI_fact_Sale_CCI_ORDERED	1	22	1048576	9020	COMPRESSED
24	Sale_CCI_ORDERED	CCI_fact_Sale_CCI_ORDERED	1	25	419432	0	COMPRESSED
25	Sale_CCI_ORDERED	CCI_fact_Sale_CCI_ORDERED	1	26	286470	0	COMPRESSED
26	Sale_CCI_ORDERED	CCI_fact_Sale_CCI_ORDERED	1	27	1	NULL	OPEN

Figure 14-13. *Rowgroup metadata for a newly inserted row into a delta rowgroup*

With a single row in the delta store, a REORGANIZE operation will be run using the COMPRESS_ALL_ROW_GROUPS option, as seen in Listing 14-9.

Listing 14-9. REORGANIZE Using the COMPRESS_ALL_ROW_GROUPS option

```
ALTER INDEX CCI_fact_Sale_CCI_ORDERED ON Fact.Sale_CCI_ORDERED REORGANIZE
WITH (COMPRESS_ALL_ROW_GROUPS = ON);
```

The resulting columnstore metadata after the index maintenance is shown in Figure 14-14.

	table_name	index_name	partition_number	row_group_id	state_desc	total_rows	deleted_rows	size_in_bytes	trim_reason_desc
1	Sale_CCI_ORDERED	CCI_fact_Sale_CCI_ORDERED	1	28	COMPRESSED	1	0	1760	REORG
2	Sale_CCI_ORDERED	CCI_fact_Sale_CCI_ORDERED	1	27	TOMBSTONE	1	0	16384	NULL
3	Sale_CCI_ORDERED	CCI_fact_Sale_CCI_ORDERED	1	26	COMPRESSED	286470	0	1002256	REORG
4	Sale_CCI_ORDERED	CCI_fact_Sale_CCI_ORDERED	1	25	COMPRESSED	419432	0	1440408	DICTIONARY_SIZE
5	Sale_CCI_ORDERED	CCI_fact_Sale_CCI_ORDERED	1	22	COMPRESSED	1048576	9020	749248	NO_TRIM
6	Sale_CCI_ORDERED	CCI_fact_Sale_CCI_ORDERED	1	21	COMPRESSED	1048576	22880	762792	NO_TRIM
7	Sale_CCI_ORDERED	CCI_fact_Sale_CCI_ORDERED	1	2	COMPRESSED	1048576	0	737808	NO_TRIM

Figure 14-14. *Rowgroup metadata immediately after index maintenance*

The metadata shows a single row in a compressed rowgroup, and the old delta store set to TOMBSTONE, awaiting cleanup. Figure 14-15 shows the rowgroup metadata after the TOMBSTONE rowgroup is cleaned up.

	table_name	index_name	partition_number	row_group_id	state_desc	total_rows	deleted_rows	size_in_bytes	trim_reason_desc
1	Sale_CCI_ORDERED	CCI_fact_Sale_CCI_ORDERED	1	28	COMPRESSED	1	0	1760	REORG
2	Sale_CCI_ORDERED	CCI_fact_Sale_CCI_ORDERED	1	26	COMPRESSED	286470	0	1002256	REORG
3	Sale_CCI_ORDERED	CCI_fact_Sale_CCI_ORDERED	1	25	COMPRESSED	419432	0	1440408	DICTIONARY_SIZE
4	Sale_CCI_ORDERED	CCI_fact_Sale_CCI_ORDERED	1	22	COMPRESSED	1048576	9020	749248	NO_TRIM
5	Sale_CCI_ORDERED	CCI_fact_Sale_CCI_ORDERED	1	21	COMPRESSED	1048576	22880	762792	NO_TRIM
6	Sale_CCI_ORDERED	CCI_fact_Sale_CCI_ORDERED	1	20	COMPRESSED	1048576	0	756792	NO_TRIM
7	Sale_CCI_ORDERED	CCI_fact_Sale_CCI_ORDERED	1	1	COMPRESSED	1048576	0	752856	NO_TRIM

Figure 14-15. *Rowgroup metadata after garbage collection*

A compressed rowgroup of a single row is silly, so another REORGANIZE will be executed against the columnstore index. The resulting metadata can be seen in Figure 14-16.

	table_name	index_name	partition_number	row_group_id	state_desc	total_rows	deleted_rows	size_in_bytes	trim_reason_desc
1	Sale_CCI_ORDERED	CCI_fact_Sale_CCI_ORDERED	1	29	COMPRESSED	286471	0	1002456	REORG
2	Sale_CCI_ORDERED	CCI_fact_Sale_CCI_ORDERED	1	25	COMPRESSED	419432	0	1440408	DICTIONARY_SIZE
3	Sale_CCI_ORDERED	CCI_fact_Sale_CCI_ORDERED	1	22	COMPRESSED	1048576	9020	749248	NO_TRIM
4	Sale_CCI_ORDERED	CCI_fact_Sale_CCI_ORDERED	1	21	COMPRESSED	1048576	22880	762792	NO_TRIM
5	Sale_CCI_ORDERED	CCI_fact_Sale_CCI_ORDERED	1	20	COMPRESSED	1048576	0	756792	NO_TRIM
6	Sale_CCI_ORDERED	CCI_fact_Sale_CCI_ORDERED	1	19	COMPRESSED	1048576	0	754872	NO_TRIM
7	Sale_CCI_ORDERED	CCI_fact_Sale_CCI_ORDERED	1	0	COMPRESSED	1048576	0	750896	NO_TRIM

Figure 14-16. *Rowgroup metadata after undersized rowgroups are combined*

241

Rowgroup 25 remains undersized due to dictionary pressure, but rowgroups 26 and 28 have been combined into the newly formed rowgroup 29. The trim reason description allows an operator to understand that this rowgroup was created and populated via an index REORGANIZE operation.

Index REORGANIZE operations are an excellent way to combine undersized rowgroups, assuming they do not suffer from dictionary size limitations. They can also remove deleted rows, assuming the number of deleted rows is greater than 102,400. Lastly, with the COMPRESS_ALL_ROW_GROUPS option, an index REORGANIZE can process the delta store contents into compressed rowgroups, which can later be combined via further REORGANIZE operations, if desired.

For a columnstore index that is not the target of UPDATE operations and does not experience out-of-order inserts, using index REORGANIZE operations will handle most fragmentation effectively and preclude the need for other regular index maintenance tasks. The simplest application of index maintenance is to run an index REORGANIZE operation after each data load and include the COMPRESS_ALL_ROW_GROUPS option. This will ensure that rowgroups remain relatively full and that delta stores are processed and not slowing down columnstore queries. For a stickler that wants perfection, a second REORGANIZE operation can be executed to further combine rowgroups resulting from processed delta stores. These are online, fast, and effective ways to manage fragmentation on an ongoing basis as a columnstore index grows via regular data load processes.

Columnstore Rebuild

Rebuilding a columnstore index functions similarly to rebuilding a rowstore index. When a REBUILD is issued, a completely new copy of the columnstore index is created, replacing the old index. While an expensive process, the results are

- Rowgroups that are filled to capacity, whenever possible.

- All deleted rows are eliminated.

- All delta stores are processed and compressed.

- Vertipaq optimization is applied, even if it previously was not.

In essence, a REBUILD is roughly equivalent to creating a columnstore index anew using a CREATE INDEX statement. The only difference is that the existing index structure will remain intact until the new index is built. For ONLINE rebuilds, this ensures that queries can continue to use the columnstore index, even as a rebuild operation is running.

Rebuilding a clustered columnstore index can only be accomplished as an online operation starting in SQL Server 2019. Nonclustered indexes can be rebuilt online regardless of SQL Server version.

Consider the columnstore index that has been tested recently in this chapter. The T-SQL in Listing 14-10 issues a REBUILD against that index.

Listing 14-10. REBUILD Statement Against a Clustered Columnstore Index

```
ALTER INDEX CCI_fact_Sale_CCI_ORDERED ON Fact.Sale_CCI_ORDERED REBUILD;
```

A REBUILD operation takes significantly longer than a REORGANIZE as the entire index must be re-created in its entirety. Alternatively, a REORGANIZE follows specific rules to determine what work to do and will usually only operate on a small portion of a columnstore index. Figure 14-17 shows a columnstore index after a REBUILD operation completes.

	table_name	index_name	partition_number	row_group_id	state_desc	total_rows	deleted_rows	size_in_bytes	trim_reason_desc
1	Sale_CCI_ORDERED	CCI_fact_Sale_CCI_ORDERED	1	24	COMPRESSED	410416	0	317264	RESIDUAL_ROW_GROUP
2	Sale_CCI_ORDERED	CCI_fact_Sale_CCI_ORDERED	1	23	COMPRESSED	263587	0	214808	RESIDUAL_ROW_GROUP
3	Sale_CCI_ORDERED	CCI_fact_Sale_CCI_ORDERED	1	22	COMPRESSED	1048576	0	726312	NO_TRIM
4	Sale_CCI_ORDERED	CCI_fact_Sale_CCI_ORDERED	1	21	COMPRESSED	1048576	0	694832	NO_TRIM
5	Sale_CCI_ORDERED	CCI_fact_Sale_CCI_ORDERED	1	20	COMPRESSED	1048576	0	725176	NO_TRIM
6	Sale_CCI_ORDERED	CCI_fact_Sale_CCI_ORDERED	1	19	COMPRESSED	1048576	0	733488	NO_TRIM
7	Sale_CCI_ORDERED	CCI_fact_Sale_CCI_ORDERED	1	0	COMPRESSED	1048576	0	765200	NO_TRIM

Figure 14-17. *Rowgroup metadata after a columnstore index REBUILD*

After a REBUILD, the columnstore index has no deleted rows, and rowgroups are mostly full. Oddly enough, the last two rowgroups (23 and 24) are undersized residuals and can be cleaned up via an index REORGANIZE operation. The metadata in Figure 14-18 shows the final results after the index is subject to an additional REORGANIZE after the REBUILD.

	table_name	index_name	partition_number	row_group_id	state_desc	total_rows	deleted_rows	size_in_bytes	trim_reason_desc
1	Sale_CCI_ORDERED	CCI_fact_Sale_CCI_ORDERED	1	25	COMPRESSED	674003	0	505624	REORG
2	Sale_CCI_ORDERED	CCI_fact_Sale_CCI_ORDERED	1	22	COMPRESSED	1048576	0	726312	NO_TRIM
3	Sale_CCI_ORDERED	CCI_fact_Sale_CCI_ORDERED	1	21	COMPRESSED	1048576	0	694832	NO_TRIM
4	Sale_CCI_ORDERED	CCI_fact_Sale_CCI_ORDERED	1	20	COMPRESSED	1048576	0	725176	NO_TRIM
5	Sale_CCI_ORDERED	CCI_fact_Sale_CCI_ORDERED	1	19	COMPRESSED	1048576	0	733488	NO_TRIM
6	Sale_CCI_ORDERED	CCI_fact_Sale_CCI_ORDERED	1	18	COMPRESSED	1048576	0	732536	NO_TRIM
7	Sale_CCI_ORDERED	CCI_fact_Sale_CCI_ORDERED	1	5	COMPRESSED	1048576	0	743128	NO_TRIM

Figure 14-18. *Rowgroup metadata after a columnstore index REBUILD and REORGANIZE*

Finally, the index is pristine, with 23 rowgroups that are completely full and 1 additional rowgroup that is leftover from the index maintenance operations.

Index REBUILD operations should be used infrequently to manage one of a few scenarios:

- Undersized rowgroups accumulated over a long period of time that cannot be combined via REORGANIZE operations.

- Extensive deleted rows that number less than 102,400 rows per rowgroup and cannot be addressed by REORGANIZE operations.

- Large amounts of out-of-order data exist in the columnstore index. This must be addressed in conjunction with work to reorder data, as shown in the next section.

Note that when an index REBUILD is issued, the compression type may be changed to or from columnstore archive compression, if needed. Because an index REBUILD is an expensive operation and is offline prior to SQL Server 2019, care should be taken to execute rebuilds during maintenance windows when such work is more tolerable to processes that use this data.

Sometimes, data can become heavily fragmented via software releases that make significant changes to the underlying schema and data. If this is anticipated, then scheduling an index REBUILD as a postprocessing step after the software release would be an excellent way to ensure that data continues to be efficiently delivered to analytic processes, even after a disruptive software release.

REBUILD operations may target a specific partition, thus allowing only data that is heavily fragmented to be rebuilt. For a large columnstore index in which only a small portion is actively written to, this is an excellent way to speed up rebuilds and minimize disruptions to the users of analytic data.

Columnstore Reorder and Rebuild

Clustered columnstore indexes do not enforce data order. It is up to the data architect that designs these tables to determine how to order data and to ensure that order is enforced via any processes that write to the table. The only way to effectively resolve the challenge of unordered columnstore data (without building new tables and structures) is to perform the following tasks:

1. Drop the columnstore index.

2. Create a clustered rowstore index with key columns that match the data order for the table.

3. Create a new clustered columnstore index with the DROP_EXISTING=ON option.

The clustered rowstore index is used to enforce a new data order on the contents of the table, whereas the new columnstore index replaces it, retaining the new data order.

This is an expensive and disruptive process that will result in analytic queries being unable to take advantage of the columnstore index from the point when the index is dropped until the new columnstore index is completely built. Therefore, it is a worthwhile process to implement during a maintenance window when causing trouble is more acceptable.

The script in Listing 14-11 performs these operations to reorder data from its current state to data that is ordered perfectly by Invoice Date Key.

Listing 14-11. Process to Fix Poorly Ordered Data in a Clustered Columnstore Index

```
/*      Step 1 */
DROP INDEX CCI_fact_Sale_CCI_ORDERED ON Fact.Sale_CCI_ORDERED;
/*      Step 2 */
CREATE CLUSTERED INDEX CCI_fact_Sale_CCI_ORDERED ON Fact.Sale_CCI_ORDERED
([Invoice Date Key]);
/*      Step 3 */
CREATE CLUSTERED COLUMNSTORE INDEX CCI_fact_Sale_CCI_ORDERED ON
Fact.Sale_CCI_ORDERED WITH (DROP_EXISTING=ON, MAXDOP=1);
```

Note that dropping a clustered columnstore index is not a speedy operation. It requires converting the columnstore structure into a b-tree/heap structure, which requires more computing resources than dropping a clustered rowstore index.

The process to fix data order on a columnstore index should be reserved for scenarios where fragmentation is high enough to negatively impact analytic processes and should be an infrequent operation.

If data becomes unordered quickly in a columnstore index, then consider ways to alter how data load processes operate to reduce fragmentation via those data loads. The following are a few helpful guidelines for doing so:

- Remove all UPDATE operations on columnstore indexes. Perform updates on staging tables instead (when possible).

- Avoid inserting data out of order. Use temporary or staging tables to ensure that data is ordered correctly prior to inserting new data.

Despite its complexity, the process to fix unordered data can be executed on a partition-by-partition basis, thus allowing only active partitions containing warm/hot data to be targeted with expensive index maintenance operations. For a columnstore index with many partitions, this can save considerable time and reduce disruption and downtime to analytic processes.

Columnstore Index Maintenance by Partition

The syntax to rebuild a specific partition of a columnstore index is shown in Listing 14-12.

Listing 14-12. Query to Rebuild a Single Partition of a Columnstore Index on a Partitioned Table

```
ALTER INDEX CCI_fact_Sale_CCI_PARTITIONED ON Fact.Sale_CCI_PARTITIONED
REBUILD PARTITION = 5;
```

In this example, if partition number 5 is identified as the only partition containing data that is being loaded/modified regularly, then rebuilding only it will save significant maintenance time as the other partitions can be skipped.

Index Maintenance in Nonclustered Columnstore Indexes

Nonclustered columnstore indexes are afforded less flexibility with regard to index maintenance. Data order is enforced by the clustered rowstore index, and therefore the quality of data order within a columnstore index is prescribed by its corresponding clustered rowstore index. If the table's clustered rowstore index happens to be the ordering column(s) for the columnstore index and that table is not subject to UPDATE operations, then the nonclustered columnstore index will maintain data order effectively.

Otherwise, index maintenance for nonclustered columnstore indexes will operate similarly to maintenance on clustered columnstore indexes:

- Use REORGANIZE operations to combine undersized rowgroups, process the delta store, and eliminate larger groups of deleted rows.

- Use REBUILD operations to eliminate undersized rowgroups and eliminate unordered data due to UPDATE operations.

The primary difference here is that a REBUILD can eliminate out-of-order data resulting from UPDATE operations. When rebuilt, a nonclustered columnstore index will be created using the order prescribed by the clustered rowstore index, which is not negatively impacted by UPDATE operations in the same way as a columnstore index.

Both REORGANIZE and REBUILD operations are available as online operations for nonclustered indexes, providing more flexibility when trying to schedule recurring (or one-time) maintenance. This means that real-time operational analytics that target a nonclustered columnstore index can continue efficiently, even as that index is being rebuilt.

Like with clustered columnstore indexes, maintenance on nonclustered columnstore indexes can be issued against any or all partitions, allowing active data to be targeted with maintenance while unchanging data can be skipped.

CHAPTER 15

Columnstore Index Performance

The ultimate measure of performance for any data structure is the speed in which data can be retrieved. In columnstore indexes, the time required to return data will be a function of two operations:

- Metadata reads

- Data reads

This chapter will walk through the steps needed to measure, assess, and tune columnstore index query performance, both for analytics and write operations. It will also introduce additional options for columnstore index usage and performance optimization.

Columnstore Metadata Reads

To determine what data to read and how to read it, the metadata for a columnstore index will be read prior to any columnstore index scans. This includes the metadata about the contents of rowgroups and segments. Consider the query in Listing 15-1.

Listing 15-1. Example Query Used in Performance Analysis

```
SELECT
        SUM(Quantity) AS Total_Quantity,
        SUM([Total Excluding Tax]) AS Total_Excluding_Tax
FROM Fact.Sale_CCI_PARTITIONED
WHERE [Invoice Date Key] = '7/17/2015';
```

© Edward Pollack 2022
E. Pollack, *Analytics Optimization with Columnstore Indexes in Microsoft SQL Server*,
https://doi.org/10.1007/978-1-4842-8048-5_15

Two columns are aggregated for a single value of *Invoice Date Key*. This table is both ordered and partitioned and therefore will benefit significantly from partition elimination and rowgroup elimination. When the query is executed, columnstore metadata is consulted to determine which segments need to be read.

The table *Fact.Sale_CCI_PARTITIONED* is partitioned on the *Invoice Date Key* column by year, with partitions assigned to the years 2013, 2014, 2015, 2016, and 2017. Listing 15-2 provides the definitions for both the partition scheme and function used in this demonstration.

Listing 15-2. Partition Function and Partition Scheme Definitions

```
CREATE PARTITION FUNCTION fact_Sale_CCI_years_function (DATE) AS RANGE
RIGHT FOR VALUES
('1/1/2014', '1/1/2015', '1/1/2016', '1/1/2017');

CREATE PARTITION SCHEME fact_Sale_CCI_years_scheme AS PARTITION
fact_Sale_CCI_years_function
TO (WideWorldImportersDW_2013_fg, WideWorldImportersDW_2014_fg,
WideWorldImportersDW_2015_fg,
WideWorldImportersDW_2016_fg, WideWorldImportersDW_2017_fg)
```

The table contains data ranging from 2013 through 2016 and therefore will not make use of the last partition. When executed, the query in Listing 15-1 will immediately check the filter against the partition function and then use the partition scheme to determine where data is located based on the function. Based on this information, it is determined that only data in the partition WideWorldImportersDW_2015_fg will be needed.

Columnstore metadata is stored separately for each partition, and therefore when executed, this query needs to only consult metadata relevant to the partition containing data for the year 2015. Figure 15-1 shows the segment metadata for *Invoice Date Key* in this columnstore index.

	index_name	partition_number	segment_id	encoding_type	row_count	min_data_id	max_data_id	primary_dictionary_id
1	CCI_fact_Sale_CCI_PARTITIONED	1	0	2	1048576	734868	734930	0
2	CCI_fact_Sale_CCI_PARTITIONED	1	1	2	1048576	734930	734984	0
3	CCI_fact_Sale_CCI_PARTITIONED	1	2	2	1048576	734984	735038	0
4	CCI_fact_Sale_CCI_PARTITIONED	1	3	2	1048576	735038	735091	0
5	CCI_fact_Sale_CCI_PARTITIONED	1	4	2	1048576	735091	735150	0
6	CCI_fact_Sale_CCI_PARTITIONED	1	5	2	1048576	735150	735207	0
7	CCI_fact_Sale_CCI_PARTITIONED	1	6	2	415024	735207	735232	0
8	CCI_fact_Sale_CCI_PARTITIONED	2	0	2	1048576	735233	735288	0

Figure 15-1. *Columnstore segment metadata for Invoice Date Key*

The metadata shows an exceptionally well-ordered columnstore index. Note that *min_data_id* and *max_data_id* progressively increase as values advance through each segment within each partition. An encoding type of 2 represents dictionary encoding for a nonstring data type, in this case a DATE. The primary dictionary used for this column has an ID of zero.

The query in Listing 15-3 provides a bit of additional detail on the dictionary used for this column.

Listing 15-3. Query to Return Information About a Columnstore Dictionary

```
SELECT
        partitions.partition_number,
        objects.name,
        columns.name,
        column_store_dictionaries.type,
        column_store_dictionaries.entry_count,
        column_store_dictionaries.on_disk_size
FROM sys.column_store_dictionaries
INNER JOIN sys.partitions
ON column_store_dictionaries.hobt_id = partitions.hobt_id
INNER JOIN sys.objects
ON objects.object_id = partitions.object_id
INNER JOIN sys.columns
ON columns.column_id = column_store_dictionaries.column_id
AND columns.object_id = objects.object_id
WHERE objects.name = 'Sale_CCI_PARTITIONED'
AND columns.name = 'Invoice Date Key'
AND column_store_dictionaries.dictionary_id = 0;
```

The results provide additional detail about the dictionary used for this column, as shown in Figure 15-2.

	partition_number	name	name	type	entry_count	on_disk_size
1	1	Sale_CCI_PARTITIONED	Invoice Date Key	1	313	1308
2	2	Sale_CCI_PARTITIONED	Invoice Date Key	1	313	1308
3	3	Sale_CCI_PARTITIONED	Invoice Date Key	1	313	1308

Figure 15-2.   Columnstore dictionary metadata

This shows that partitions 1–3 share a single dictionary that is a compact 1308 bytes. The scenario presented here is essentially the optimal columnstore index and query. The index is well ordered and partitioned and the query aligns perfectly with that order to minimize the amount of metadata read as part of its execution.

While columnstore metadata may not seem large when compared to the data itself, it is important to remember that a columnstore index with one billion rows will have approximately one thousand rowgroups. Each of those rowgroups will contain one segment per column. For this table which contains 21 columns, metadata will consist of about 21,000 segments per billion rows. Needing to read metadata on rowgroups, segments, dictionaries, and more can add up to a nontrivial amount of work for SQL Server. As with data itself, metadata needs to be loaded into memory before it can be read. Therefore, maintaining an ordered table and partitioning (if needed) can ensure that excessive metadata is not read when executing analytic queries.

Returning to the analytic query in Listing 15-1, it can be expected that it would execute quickly, resulting in minimal metadata reads, as well as minimal data reads. The STATISTICS IO output for the query is shown in Figure 15-3.

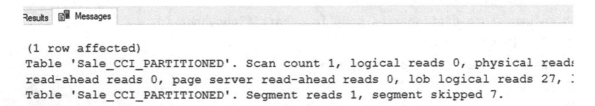

Figure 15-3.   Statistics IO output for a sample analytic query

This example was an ideal scenario where segment elimination, rowgroup elimination, and partitioning all combined to provide exceptionally low reads and a vast majority of segments skipped. While the real world will not always provide such optimal examples of columnstore performance, this illustrates the upper bound for what to compare performance against.

Columnstore Data Reads

Once columnstore metadata is read, the data itself is then read. It is critical to understand that the performance of queries against a columnstore index will ultimately be driven by the number of segments read when a query is executed. All other variables being equal, an analytic request that reads 1000 segments will be expected to perform approximately ten times slower than a query that reads 100 segments. While columnstore indexes may at times be seen as magical tools sprinkled with pixie dust, this is the one area in which there is no magic and performance will be guided by IO.

Segment reads equate to page reads which represent those IO operations. If the pages needed are already in memory, then the operations will be comprised of logical IO as segments are read directly from the buffer pool. If the required pages are not in memory yet (or are partially in memory), then physical reads will be required to copy pages from storage into the buffer pool.

Segment elimination and rowgroup elimination are the tools that limit segment reads and help ensure that only the amount of data needed to satisfy a query is read. The quality of columnstore compression applied to data helps squeeze data into as few pages as possible, thereby reducing IO.

At their most basic structure, columnstore indexes are bound by the same speed limitations that exist for rowstore tables. Reading pages from storage into the buffer pool takes time. Decompressing and reading data from the buffer pool takes additional time. Therefore, the less pages that need to be read, the faster columnstore index analytics can perform.

Other performance-boosting tools used by columnstore indexes (such as batch mode operation or filtered indexes) further improve query speeds by improving throughput or reducing IO. The focus throughout the step of reading columnstore data is to control IO via whatever means possible. Figure 15-4 illustrates how data and metadata are read from storage through to being used query results.

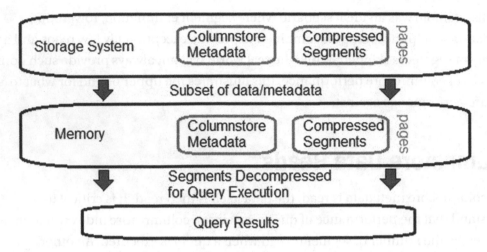

Figure 15-4. *Movement of columnstore data and metadata from storage to memory to usage by a query*

While the entire columnstore index resides on a storage system, typically only a fraction of it will be maintained in the buffer pool. Segments remain compressed throughout this entire IO process until they are needed by a query, at which time they are decompressed, and data is returned to SQL Server.

Memory Sizing

All of the performance discussions thus far have focused on reducing IO. Despite all efforts to minimize unnecessary IO, larger columnstore indexes will ultimately require reading significant numbers of segments from storage into memory.

The next step in ensuring highly performant columnstore indexes is to accurately estimate the amount of memory that should be allocated to SQL Server to support analytic queries.

Too little memory and data will be constantly removed from memory, only to be read back into the buffer pool when needed again soon. The process of reading data from storage (even fast storage) will be far greater than other steps in executing analytic queries.

Too much memory would represent unused computing resources, which translate into wasted money.

Allocating memory to SQL Server to support columnstore indexes requires a handful of steps:

1. Measure the size of the columnstore index.

2. Approximate how much of the index is comprised of hot data that should always reside in memory.

3. Approximate how much of the index represents warm data. This data will be in memory for some analytic needs, but not all.

4. Approximate data growth over time that will adjust the numbers calculated earlier.

Any data that is not hot or warm is expected to be cold and rarely used. It may still be valuable but is not accessed often enough to architect an entire system around it. Resources can be allocated at runtime by Azure, AWS, or other hosting services, if that level of flexibility is desired, but that is entirely optional and at the discretion of an organization and the importance of speedy access to cold data.

Consider a hypothetical columnstore index as shown in Listing 15-4.

Listing 15-4. Row Counts and Size for Data in a Columnstore Index

```
2017: 10,000,000 rows (1GB) - cold/rarely used
2018: 50,000,000 rows (3GB) - cold/rarely used
2019: 100,000,000 rows (5GB) - cold/rarely used
2020: 250,000,000 rows (10GB) - warm/sometimes used
2021: 500,000,000 rows (18GB) - hot/often used
```

This index shows a common trend in analytics by which the most recent year is heavily used for current reporting. The previous year is also accessed frequently for year-over-year analytics. All previous data is important and must be retained, but is not read very often when compared to newer data.

Based on the numbers provided, if the goal was to ensure that the most frequently used data was accounted for in memory allocation, then this columnstore index would warrant 18GB of memory to ensure that all 18GB of hot data can reside in memory, if needed.

If the 10GB of warm data were also important, then allocating some amount of memory up to 10GB would help ensure that data is not cycled in and out of memory too often and that it does not replace more important hot data in memory when requested.

If resources were plentiful, then allocating the full 10GB would accomplish the task in its entirety. Otherwise, the organization responsible for this data would need to determine how important the warm data is and allocate some amount of additional memory up to 10GB to cover it. For example, if it was estimated that the latter half of the 2020 data would be requested on a somewhat regular basis, but the earlier half would be far less used, then 5GB would be a good estimate of memory to allocate to this block of warm data.

The remaining 9GB of data from 2017 to 2019 would not receive any memory allocation as they are rarely read and would impact performance too infrequently to matter to most organizations. If infrequent analytics or reports are disruptive enough, an argument could be made to adding further memory to reduce that disruption, but this would be something that should be considered on a case-by-case basis.

This example also illustrates a fairly straightforward growth of about two times per year. If this rate of growth is expected to continue and the years with warm and hot data are expected to roll forward each year, then in a year, the current hot data (18GB) would become warm data, the current warm data (10GB) would become cold data, and next year's data (~35GB) would become the new hot data. Therefore, year-over-year growth would be represented by

$$(35GB + 18GB) - (18GB + 10GB) = \textbf{25GB}.$$

Note that the size of columnstore data used in memory will often not be the same as the total data size. A columnstore index with 20 columns may not see all columns used equally. It is quite possible that some columns may rarely get used. If this is the case, then memory estimations can adjust the amount needed downward to account for columns that are not needed in memory often. While these infrequently queried columns cannot be classified as cold data, they can be discounted from memory totals to ensure that memory estimates are not overinflated by segments that are rarely needed.

For example, if the 18GB of data for 2021 included 5GB of columns that are rarely queried, then the memory estimate for that data could be reduced from 18GB to as little as 13GB, if there is confidence in how infrequently those columns are used.

There is a great deal of estimation that goes into this work. At the absolute high end, a memory budget could encompass all space consumed by a columnstore index. At the lowest level, no memory could be allocated for these analytics. A realistic estimation will be somewhere in the middle and will be influenced by the performance required of this data and the availability/cost of computing resources.

Dictionary Size and Dictionary Pressure

Dictionary encoding is one of a multitude of ways in which SQL Server can improve columnstore compression effectiveness. Chapter 5 discussed encoding methods in detail and how dictionary encoding can be used by columnstore indexes to greatly reduce index size for columns that have repetitive values.

While dictionaries can be shared across many segments, a caveat to dictionary encoding is that they cap at 16 megabytes. As a result, if a column has wide values that do not repeat often, then the result may be that a dictionary fills up before a rowgroup could be completely written. The scenario when a dictionary fills up is known as dictionary pressure. While a dictionary is limited to 16MB, dictionary pressure will often occur at sizes well below that as the limitation is on how much space will be consumed there, rather than how much is currently used.

When a columnstore index experiences dictionary pressure, the rowgroup that is currently being written to will be closed and a new rowgroup will be created along with a new dictionary. This has two significant implications:

- **Dictionaries Consume Space:** The more dictionaries that are needed to support a columnstore index, and the larger they are, the more storage space and memory are required to read and write to them.

- **Undersized Rowgroups Create Fragmentation:** A rowgroup may contain up to 2^{20} (1,048,576) rows. When rowgroups are undersized by dictionary pressure (well below 2^{20} rows), then more rowgroups, segments, and dictionaries need to be maintained by SQL Server. This in turn wastes resources and slows down analytics that need these tables.

Fortunately, dictionary pressure is easy to diagnose. Once identified, a solution can be crafted to resolve it. Consider the rowgroup metadata shown in Figure 15-5.

	table_name	index_name	partition_number	row_group_id	state_desc	total_rows	deleted_rows	size_in_bytes	trim_reason_desc
1	Sale_CCI_ORDERED	CCI_fact_Sale_CCI_ORDERED	1	29	COMPRESSED	286471	0	1002456	REORG
2	Sale_CCI_ORDERED	CCI_fact_Sale_CCI_ORDERED	1	25	COMPRESSED	419432	0	1440408	DICTIONARY_SIZE
3	Sale_CCI_ORDERED	CCI_fact_Sale_CCI_ORDERED	1	22	COMPRESSED	1048576	0	749248	NO_TRIM
4	Sale_CCI_ORDERED	CCI_fact_Sale_CCI_ORDERED	1	21	COMPRESSED	1048576	22880	762792	NO_TRIM
5	Sale_CCI_ORDERED	CCI_fact_Sale_CCI_ORDERED	1	20	COMPRESSED	1048576	0	756792	NO_TRIM
6	Sale_CCI_ORDERED	CCI_fact_Sale_CCI_ORDERED	1	19	COMPRESSED	1048576	0	754872	NO_TRIM
7	Sale_CCI_ORDERED	CCI_fact_Sale_CCI_ORDERED	1	0	COMPRESSED	1048576	0	750896	NO_TRIM

Figure 15-5. *Example of dictionary pressure*

In this example, *row_group_id* 25 shows a trim reason of *DICTIONARY_SIZE* and a row count of 419,432 rows. In this rowgroup, SQL Server was loading rows into it when the dictionary reached a size where no more entries could be added without bringing it over the 16MB cap. If this were the only rowgroup like this, then dictionary pressure may not be seen as a serious issue. If many rowgroups were cut off at row counts this low, then dictionary pressure would without a doubt be inhibiting optimal performance and would be worth investigating and resolving.

There are two primary causes of dictionary pressure:

- Columns that are very wide

- Columns with many distinct values

The most common scenarios involving dictionary pressure are derived from columns that are both wide and have many distinct values. There is no one-size-fits-all solution to the challenge of dictionary pressure. The three most common solutions can be considered as the simplest ways of resolving this challenge:

- Normalize wide columns into a lookup (dimension) table.

- Sort on a different column.

- Partition the table.

Normalizing Wide Columns

The simplest solution requires schema changes and therefore may be disruptive, and that is to normalize a wide column that is identified as the source of dictionary pressure. Normalizing a column replaces a wide column (often string data) with a smaller numeric column. The lookup table would likely be stored using a clustered rowstore index and a supporting nonclustered rowstore index to handle queries against the text data.

When considering a columnstore index for a large analytic table, pay close attention to any wide columns, and as part of testing, run through the exercise of creating a columnstore index on the data. Once created, pay attention to rowgroup row counts and if dictionary pressure is occurring or not. If rowgroups are undersized by 10% or more, then consider normalizing the wide column if it is the culprit.

Lookup tables can contain other metadata that supports efficient searches against it, such as hashes, search criteria, or details that can be indexed and used to quickly reduce row counts before the text column needs to be interrogated.

Add or Change the Columnstore Sorting Column

Sometimes the way in which data is sorted within a columnstore index lends itself to poor dictionary encoding. If a columnstore index is unsorted or is sorted on a column that tends to group data together alongside nonsimilar values, then wider columns might become the source of dictionary pressure.

The column that a columnstore index is ordered on should always be the one that is most frequently used to filter queries. If there are a variety of common search criteria, then there may be other sorting options that provide better compression and performance.

This solution to dictionary pressure requires before-and-after testing of common analytic queries to ensure that one problem (dictionary pressure) is not being traded for another (poor analytic query performance).

Partitioning

One key element of partitioned columnstore indexes is that each partition contains its own distinct columnstore index. For example, a table that is broken into ten partitions will contain a separate columnstore structure in each partition. That includes separate dictionaries, as well!

When columnstore index row counts become large (hundreds of millions or billions of rows), partitioning can provide distinct performance and maintenance benefits in SQL Server. In addition to partition elimination, an added performance improvement can be seen in the separation of dictionaries across partitions. This solution is especially effective when the values for wide columns change slowly over time. In these scenarios, the data from one day to the next will have many repeated values, but across months or years will not.

When partitioning a table, be sensitive to the size of the partitions that are created. Because each represents a distinct, separate columnstore index, it is important that each be large enough to benefit from the key properties of columnstore indexes. Therefore, ensure that each partition has at least tens of millions of rows. Similarly, partitions that are exceptionally large (billions of rows) may suffer the same problems as an unpartitioned table with regard to dictionary pressure.

Testing is important in confirming the benefits of partitioning in a columnstore index. Generally speaking, if a table contains hundreds of millions of rows (or more), being able to subdivide it into smaller chunks using the columnstore ordering column as the partitioning column will allow performance benefits to be realized. If dictionary pressure exists, then this can become an effective way to manage it by splitting up dictionaries across partitions.

Chapter 11 dives into partitioning in detail, including demonstrations of how to implement it and how it can provide a host of benefits in addition to resolving dictionary pressure challenges.

In general, dictionaries are very efficient at storing their lookup data and columnstore indexes benefit greatly by using them. Dictionary pressure should be seen as an out-of-the-ordinary situation and only investigated if it is causing blatant performance problems.

Columnstore Indexes on Temporary Tables

For scenarios when analytic data needs to be crunched on the fly using temporary data, there can be value in adding columnstore indexes to temporary objects. This is a unique use case that will rarely be needed, but can provide exceptional value to ETL processes or any analytics in which an intermediary or temporary data set requires many expensive queries to be executed against it.

Adding a columnstore index to a temporary table works exactly as it does against a permanent table. Listing 15-5 shows an example of how to accomplish this task.

Listing 15-5. Query That Creates a Temporary Table, Populates It, and Adds a Columnstore Index

```
CREATE TABLE #Sales_Temp_Data
(      [Sale Key] BIGINT NOT NULL,
       [Customer Key] INT NOT NULL,
       [Invoice Date Key] DATE NOT NULL,
       Quantity INT NOT NULL,
       [Total Excluding Tax] DECIMAL(18,2) NOT NULL);

INSERT INTO #Sales_Temp_Data
       ([Sale Key], [Customer Key], [Invoice Date Key], Quantity, [Total
       Excluding Tax])
SELECT
```

```
    [Sale Key], [Customer Key], [Invoice Date Key], Quantity, [Total
    Excluding Tax]
FROM Fact.Sale_CCI_PARTITIONED;

CREATE CLUSTERED COLUMNSTORE INDEX CCI_Sales_Temp_Data ON #Sales_Temp_Data;
```

Once added, the newly indexed temporary table may be queried as effectively as a columnstore indexed permanent table, as seen in Listing 15-6.

Listing 15-6. Example Queries Against a Temporary Table with a Columnstore Index

```
SELECT
    COUNT(*)
FROM #Sales_Temp_Data;

SELECT
    SUM(Quantity) * SUM([Total Excluding Tax])
FROM #Sales_Temp_Data
WHERE [Invoice Date Key] >= '1/1/2015'
AND [Invoice Date Key] < '1/1/2016';
```

These queries execute relatively quickly, returning the requested results. Figure 15-6 shows the STATISTICS IO output from that pair of queries.

```
▦ Results  📄 Messages

  (1 row affected)
  Table '#Sales_Temp_Data_000000000090'. Scan count 1, logical reads 0, physic
  Table '#Sales_Temp_Data_000000000090'. Segment reads 25, segment skipped 0.

  (1 row affected)
  Table '#Sales_Temp_Data_000000000090'. Scan count 2, logical reads 0, physic
  Table '#Sales_Temp_Data_000000000090'. Segment reads 11, segment skipped 14.
  Table 'Worktable'. Scan count 0, logical reads 0, physical reads 0, page ser
```

Figure 15-6. *IO for queries against a temporary table with a columnstore index*

Note that the filtered query read almost half of the segments in the table, despite only reading about a quarter of its rows. When this temporary table was populated, no data order was enforced. As a result, data was inserted in whatever order SQL Server happened to read it from the source table, which was not optimal. Depending on how extensive the temporary table is to be used for analytics, taking the extra steps to order it prior to reading it may or may not be worth the time and resources needed to do so. That value will lie in whether or not the analytic processes are completing quickly enough and if they are using too much computing resources along the way.

Nonclustered columnstore index may also be created on temporary tables, if there is a need to slice data using both transactional and analytic methods. One benefit of doing so is that the clustered rowstore index can enforce data order on the table, even if further writes are made to it. Another benefit is that the column list for the columnstore index can be customized. This allows a small subset of columns to be subject to analytics when the remainder may be needed for other operations. Listing 15-7 shows the syntax for creating nonclustered columnstore indexes on a temporary table.

Listing 15-7. Illustrating the Use of Nonclustered Columnstore Indexes on Temporary Tables

```
CREATE TABLE #Sales_Temp_Data
(       [Sale Key] BIGINT NOT NULL,
        [Customer Key] INT NOT NULL,
        [Invoice Date Key] DATE NOT NULL,
        Quantity INT NOT NULL,
        [Total Excluding Tax] DECIMAL(18,2) NOT NULL);

INSERT INTO #Sales_Temp_Data
        ([Sale Key], [Customer Key], [Invoice Date Key], Quantity, [Total
        Excluding Tax])
SELECT
        [Sale Key], [Customer Key], [Invoice Date Key], Quantity, [Total
        Excluding Tax]
FROM Fact.Sale_CCI_PARTITIONED;

CREATE CLUSTERED INDEX CI_Sales_Temp_Data ON #Sales_Temp_Data ([Sale Key]);

CREATE NONCLUSTERED COLUMNSTORE INDEX NCCI_Sales_Temp_Data ON
#Sales_Temp_Data ([Invoice Date Key], Quantity, [Total Excluding Tax]);
```

The syntax for nonclustered columnstore indexes is identical for temporary tables and permanent tables, and once created, they can be used in the same fashion.

Note that columnstore indexes are not allowed on table variables. The T-SQL in Listing 15-8 shows an attempt to do so.

Listing 15-8. A Script That Attempts to Add a Columnstore Index to a Table Variable

```
DECLARE @Sales_Temp_Data TABLE
(       [Sale Key] BIGINT NOT NULL,
        [Customer Key] INT NOT NULL,
        [Invoice Date Key] DATE NOT NULL,
        Quantity INT NOT NULL,
        [Total Excluding Tax] DECIMAL(18,2) NOT NULL);

INSERT INTO @Sales_Temp_Data
        ([Sale Key], [Customer Key], [Invoice Date Key], Quantity, [Total
        Excluding Tax])
SELECT
        [Sale Key], [Customer Key], [Invoice Date Key], Quantity, [Total
        Excluding Tax]
FROM Fact.Sale_CCI_PARTITIONED;

CREATE CLUSTERED COLUMNSTORE INDEX CCI_Sales_Temp_Data ON @Sales_Temp_Data;
```

This query won't even compile and will immediately generate the error shown in Figure 15-7 when parsed.

```
Messages
    Msg 102, Level 15, State 1, Line 200
    Incorrect syntax near '@Sales_Temp_Data'.
```

Figure 15-7. *Parsing error when trying to create a columnstore index on a table variable*

SQL Server provides the courtesy of raising an error during parsing, before the table variable is created and populated.

Using columnstore indexes on temporary tables will not be a frequently applied use case, but specific processes that rely heavily on the crunching of temporary data may be able to use them effectively. Performance testing can be the ultimate test of whether this is a helpful solution or one that does not provide enough value to be of worth.

Memory-Optimized Columnstore Indexes

A common use case for columnstore indexes is real-time operational analytics. Nonclustered columnstore indexes provide the ability to execute analytic queries against OLTP/rowstore tables efficiently. By being able to choose the columns to index, the columnstore index can be used to target problematic OLAP queries in scenarios where analytics cannot easily be off-loaded to other systems.

Memory-optimized tables are the ultimate in OLTP solutions. They provide exceptional speed for heavily transactional workloads while eliminating the latching and locking that typically accompanies contentious workloads. They can be targeted with columnstore indexes, too, allowing analytics to be run against highly transactional tables in memory. This is a niche use-case that can provide exceptional speeds for a select few scenarios that will be discussed in this section.

Demonstrating Memory-Optimized Columnstore Indexes

Before diving into columnstore index queries, it is important to configure a database with the necessary filegroup, file, and snapshot isolation setting needed to allow memory-optimized tables to be created. Listing 15-9 provides the necessary configuration changes to allow memory-optimized tables in SQL Server.

Listing 15-9. Enabling Memory-Optimized Tables in SQL Server

```
ALTER DATABASE WideWorldImporters ADD FILEGROUP WideWorldImporters_moltp
CONTAINS MEMORY_OPTIMIZED_DATA;
ALTER DATABASE WideWorldImporters ADD FILE (name='WideWorldImporters_moltp',
filename='C:\SQLData\WideWorldImporters_moltp') TO FILEGROUP
WideWorldImporters_moltp;
ALTER DATABASE WideWorldImporters SET
MEMORY_OPTIMIZED_ELEVATE_TO_SNAPSHOT = ON;
```

Only one memory-optimized filegroup is allowed per database. If a database already has one, then trying to add another will result in an error like the one shown in Figure 15-8.

🔳 Messages

```
Msg 10797, Level 15, State 2, Line 205
Only one MEMORY_OPTIMIZED_DATA filegroup is allowed per database.
```

Figure 15-8. *Error encountered when adding a memory-optimized filegroup to a database that already has one*

With these basic configuration steps complete, we can experiment with a memory-optimized table that contains a columnstore index. The script in Listing 15-10 shows the creation of an example table.

Listing 15-10. Initial (Imperfect) Creation of a Memory-Optimized Table with a Columnstore Index

```
CREATE TABLE Sales.Orders_MOLTP
(       OrderID INT NOT NULL CONSTRAINT PK_Orders_MOLTP PRIMARY KEY
        NONCLUSTERED HASH WITH (BUCKET_COUNT = 150000),
        CustomerID INT NOT NULL,
        SalespersonPersonID INT NOT NULL,
        PickedByPersonID INT NULL,
        ContactPersonID INT NOT NULL,
        BackorderOrderID INT NULL,
        OrderDate DATE NOT NULL,
        ExpectedDeliveryDate DATE NOT NULL,
        CustomerPurchaseOrderNumber NVARCHAR(20) NULL,
        IsUndersupplyBackordered BIT NOT NULL,
        Comments NVARCHAR(MAX) NULL,
        DeliveryInstructions NVARCHAR(MAX) NULL,
        InternalComments NVARCHAR(MAX) NULL,
        PickingCompletedWhen DATETIME2(7) NULL,
        LastEditedBy INT NOT NULL,
        LastEditedWhen DATETIME2(7) NOT NULL,
        INDEX CCI_Orders_MOLTP CLUSTERED COLUMNSTORE)
WITH (MEMORY_OPTIMIZED = ON, DURABILITY = SCHEMA_AND_DATA);
```

This definition appears valid, but when executed, an error is returned, as shown in Figure 15-9.

```
Messages
  Msg 35343, Level 16, State 1, Line 213
  The statement failed. Column 'Comments' has a data type that cannot participate in a columnstore index.
  Msg 1750, Level 16, State 1, Line 213
  Could not create constraint or index. See previous errors.
```

Figure 15-9. *Error due to LOB columns included in memory-optimized columnstore index definition*

Columns of MAX length are not allowed in a memory-optimized columnstore index. To allow its creation, these columns need to be normalized into another table or shrunk to a smaller size. Listing 15-11 shows a revised script where the MAX length columns have been reduced in size to accommodate this limitation.

Listing 15-11. Second (Imperfect) Creation of a Memory-Optimized Table with a Columnstore Index

```
CREATE TABLE Sales.Orders_MOLTP
(     OrderID INT NOT NULL CONSTRAINT PK_Orders_MOLTP PRIMARY KEY
      NONCLUSTERED HASH WITH (BUCKET_COUNT = 150000),
      CustomerID INT NOT NULL,
      SalespersonPersonID INT NOT NULL,
      PickedByPersonID INT NULL,
      ContactPersonID INT NOT NULL,
      BackorderOrderID INT NULL,
      OrderDate DATE NOT NULL,
      ExpectedDeliveryDate DATE NOT NULL,
      CustomerPurchaseOrderNumber NVARCHAR(20) NULL,
      IsUndersupplyBackordered BIT NOT NULL,
      Comments NVARCHAR(2000) NULL,
      DeliveryInstructions NVARCHAR(2000) NULL,
      InternalComments NVARCHAR(2000) NULL,
      PickingCompletedWhen DATETIME2(7) NULL,
      LastEditedBy INT NOT NULL,
      LastEditedWhen DATETIME2(7) NOT NULL,
      INDEX CCI_Orders_MOLTP CLUSTERED COLUMNSTORE)
WITH (MEMORY_OPTIMIZED = ON, DURABILITY = SCHEMA_AND_DATA);
```

With the NVARCHAR(MAX) columns replaced with NVARCHAR(2000), the script is executed, resulting in a new error, as seen in Figure 15-10.

```
Messages
Msg 41307, Level 16, State 1, Line 234
Warning: The row size limit of 8060 bytes for memory optimized tables has been exceeded and will not work
on subscribers running SQL Server 2014 or earlier. Please simplify the table definition.
```

Figure 15-10. *Error due to a memory-optimized columnstore index containing more than 8060 bytes per row*

While this error message appears to provide a glimmer of hope that this table definition would work if it is executed on a version of SQL Server later than SQL Server 2014, the result is still failure. After some review, a table definition is crafted that accommodates these limitations and allows a table to (finally) be created, as seen in Listing 15-12.

Listing 15-12. Working Table Creation for a Memory-Optimized Columnstore Index

```
CREATE TABLE Sales.Orders_MOLTP
(      OrderID INT NOT NULL CONSTRAINT PK_Orders_MOLTP PRIMARY KEY
       NONCLUSTERED HASH WITH (BUCKET_COUNT = 150000),
       CustomerID INT NOT NULL,
       SalespersonPersonID INT NOT NULL,
       PickedByPersonID INT NULL,
       ContactPersonID INT NOT NULL,
       BackorderOrderID INT NULL,
       OrderDate DATE NOT NULL,
       ExpectedDeliveryDate DATE NOT NULL,
       CustomerPurchaseOrderNumber NVARCHAR(20) NULL,
       IsUndersupplyBackordered BIT NOT NULL,
       Comments NVARCHAR(500) NULL,
       DeliveryInstructions NVARCHAR(250) NULL,
       InternalComments NVARCHAR(500) NULL,
       PickingCompletedWhen DATETIME2(7) NULL,
       LastEditedBy INT NOT NULL,
       LastEditedWhen DATETIME2(7) NOT NULL,
       INDEX CCI_Orders_MOLTP CLUSTERED COLUMNSTORE)
WITH (MEMORY_OPTIMIZED = ON, DURABILITY = SCHEMA_AND_DATA);
```

Success! This table contains a handful of features that are not present on disk-based tables:

- Nonclustered hash index is used as the primary key.

- MEMORY_OPTIMIZED = ON.

- DURABILITY = SCHEMA_AND_DATA.

The durability setting determines if this table's data can be recovered when the server is restarted or if only the schema is persisted. SCHEMA_ONLY is significantly faster as there is no need to persist data to disk storage. In addition, startup is faster as no data needs to be loaded into the table for it to be available. SCHEMA_ONLY is typically used for tables that contain temporary data such as session, ETL, or transient information that is not needed again once processed. SCHEMA_ONLY does not support columnstore indexes, though, and therefore is out of scope for any further discussion here.

Note that the columnstore index is labeled as a clustered columnstore index, but it is not truly a clustered index. The primary storage mechanism for a memory-optimized table is always the set of rows in memory. The columnstore index is an additional structure on top of the memory-optimized object that is also persisted to disk storage. These caveats incur quite a bit of overhead by SQL Server to maintain a columnstore index alongside a memory-optimized table.

Also worthy of highlighting is the fact that this memory-optimized clustered columnstore index contains numerous wide columns that are not ideal for dictionary encoding. *CustomerPurchaseOrderNumber*, *Comments*, *DeliveryInstructions*, and *InternalComments* are string columns that are unlikely to be repetitive. Therefore, they are not likely to compress well and may cause dictionary pressure, resulting in undersized rowgroups and further reduction in columnstore efficiency. This is not a deal-breaker, but is essential to understand when considering implementing a memory-optimized columnstore index. Tables that are built primarily for OLTP workloads will often contain text data that is essential for transactional processing, but that may be suboptimal for analytics. One possibility that could resolve a situation like this would be to split the table into two, with the string columns and supporting data in one table and the numbers and metrics in the other. This would allow one to be given a memory-optimized columnstore index and the other to remain with its memory-optimized rowstore structure.

Nonclustered columnstore indexes are not supported on memory-optimized tables, and therefore the option to choose which columns to include in the index is not available.

With a memory-optimized columnstore index created, the script in Listing 15-13 can be executed to populate it with the same data as in the disk-based table *Sales.Orders*.

Listing 15-13. Script to Populate a Memory-Optimized Columnstore Index with Data

```
INSERT INTO Sales.Orders_MOLTP
(      OrderID, CustomerID, SalespersonPersonID, PickedByPersonID,
       ContactPersonID, BackorderOrderID, OrderDate, ExpectedDeliveryDate,
   CustomerPurchaseOrderNumber, IsUndersupplyBackordered, Comments,
   DeliveryInstructions, InternalComments, PickingCompletedWhen,
   LastEditedBy, LastEditedWhen)
SELECT
       OrderID, CustomerID, SalespersonPersonID, PickedByPersonID,
       ContactPersonID, BackorderOrderID, OrderDate, ExpectedDeliveryDate,
   CustomerPurchaseOrderNumber, IsUndersupplyBackordered, Comments,
   DeliveryInstructions, InternalComments, PickingCompletedWhen,
   LastEditedBy, LastEditedWhen
FROM Sales.Orders;
```

With table creation and population complete, the sizes of the original *Sales.Orders* table can be compared to its memory-optimized counterpart. Note the index contents of each table:

Sales.Orders:

- A one-column primary key index

- Four single-column indexes

- One four-column index

Sales.Orders_MOLTP:

- A one-column primary key index

- A columnstore index (on all columns)

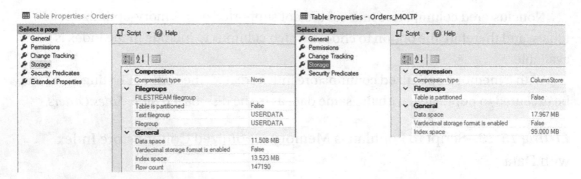

Figure 15-11. *Size comparison of a disk-based table vs. a memory-optimized table with a clustered columnstore index*

Note in Figure 15-11 the significant size difference between the disk-based table (25MB) and the memory-optimized table (117MB). That is a hefty space penalty and underscores the fact that mapping a memory-optimized structure to a columnstore structure is even more complex an operation than mapping a nonclustered rowstore index to a clustered columnstore index. Before continuing, one additional memory-optimized table will be created, as shown in Listing 15-14.

Listing 15-14. Table Creation for a Memory-Optimized Table Without a Columnstore Index

```
CREATE TABLE Sales.Orders_MOLTP_NO_CCI
(     OrderID INT NOT NULL CONSTRAINT PK_Orders_MOLTP_NO_CCI PRIMARY KEY
      NONCLUSTERED HASH WITH (BUCKET_COUNT = 150000),
      CustomerID INT NOT NULL,
      SalespersonPersonID INT NOT NULL,
      PickedByPersonID INT NULL,
      ContactPersonID INT NOT NULL,
      BackorderOrderID INT NULL,
      OrderDate DATE NOT NULL INDEX IX_Orders_MOLTP_NO_CCI_OrderDate
      NONCLUSTERED,
      ExpectedDeliveryDate DATE NOT NULL,
      CustomerPurchaseOrderNumber NVARCHAR(20) NULL,
      IsUndersupplyBackordered BIT NOT NULL,
      Comments NVARCHAR(500) NULL,
      DeliveryInstructions NVARCHAR(250) NULL,
```

```
        InternalComments NVARCHAR(500) NULL,
        PickingCompletedWhen DATETIME2(7) NULL,
        LastEditedBy INT NOT NULL,
        LastEditedWhen DATETIME2(7) NOT NULL)
WITH (MEMORY_OPTIMIZED = ON, DURABILITY = SCHEMA_AND_DATA);
GO
```

This table is identical to the previously created memory-optimized table, except that the columnstore index has been swapped out for a nonclustered index on *OrderDate*. The new table's total size is 20MB, which is about one-sixth of the size of the columnstore table, representing a significant space savings.

Consider a test analytic query that is executed against all three test tables, as shown in Listing 15-15.

Listing 15-15. Test Analytic Query Against Each Orders Table

```
SELECT
        COUNT(*) AS OrderCount,
        COUNT(DISTINCT(CustomerID)) AS DistinctCustomerCount
FROM Sales.Orders
WHERE OrderDate >= '1/1/2015'
AND OrderDate < '4/1/2015';

SELECT
        COUNT(*) AS OrderCount,
        COUNT(DISTINCT(CustomerID)) AS DistinctCustomerCount
FROM Sales.Orders_MOLTP_NO_CCI
WHERE OrderDate >= '1/1/2015'
AND OrderDate < '4/1/2015';

SELECT
        COUNT(*) AS OrderCount,
        COUNT(DISTINCT(CustomerID)) AS DistinctCustomerCount
FROM Sales.Orders_MOLTP
WHERE OrderDate >= '1/1/2015'
AND OrderDate < '4/1/2015';
```

Results are returned from each query. The execution plans can be seen in Figure 15-12.

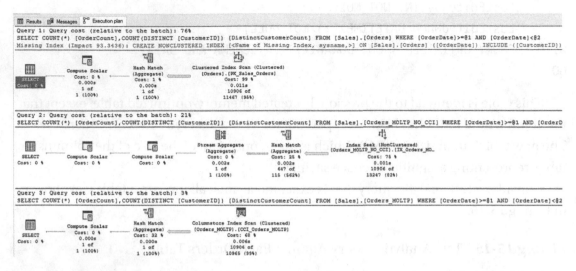

Figure 15-12. *Execution plans for a test analytic query against multiple tables*

The disk-based execution plan suggests a covering index to avoid a clustered index scan that incurs a total of 1383 reads. The memory-optimized table without a columnstore index uses an index seek to return results, whereas the memory-optimized table with a columnstore index uses a columnstore index scan to return the same results.

The columnstore index scan is by far the least expensive and fastest option out of the three of these example tables. That being said, the cost of maintaining a memory-optimized columnstore index is not trivial. There are a variety of limitations imposed on this structure, beyond what has already been introduced:

- ALTER TABLE cannot be used on a memory-optimized columnstore index to add columns, create indexes, change data types, or many of the other common DDL changes made after a table is initially created.

- The columnstore index is replicated to disk as a matter of necessity, to help speed up database recovery after a server restart.

- Just as with disk-based tables, mixing clustered columnstore and nonclustered rowstore indexes removes SQL Server's ability to automatically apply Vertipaq optimization.

- Computed columns are not allowed on memory-optimized columnstore indexes.

- Because memory-optimized columnstore indexes are only allowed as clustered indexes, filters may not be applied to them.

- Index maintenance is extremely limited. Rebuilds may only be used to adjust hash index bucket counts (if needed) and reorganize operations are not allowed. *Sys.sp_memory_optimized_cs_migration* can be used to process the contents of the delta store, if needed.

- Columnstore archive compression is not allowed on memory-optimized columnstore indexes.

The list of caveats related to memory-optimized columnstore indexes is significant and makes it clear that this is not a feature that should be used without careful consideration. The ideal scenario for putting a columnstore index is as follows:

- OLTP table with high concurrency.

- OLTP table that is identified as an exceptional candidate for migration to a memory-optimized table.

- Table is targeted with frequent analytic queries that cause heavy scans and unacceptable resource consumption.

- OLTP and OLAP operations cannot be split into separate data sources.

Even if a table meets these criteria, be sure to test thoroughly and be able to quantify that the performance benefits of the memory-optimized columnstore index outweigh the limitations and drawbacks. This is a unique architectural feature that will only be applicable to a small fraction of high-volume, highly concurrent OLTP tables. More often than not, other alternatives will be more feasible, such as

- Disk-based table with a clustered rowstore index and a nonclustered columnstore index.

- Memory-optimized table with additional covering nonclustered indexes.

- Separate OLTP/OLAP data processing/storage systems.

Optimization Strategies

Generally speaking, optimization is a process that should begin with solutions that address the most common use cases. Tweaking and implementing additional layers of complexity should only occur when one or more of the following are true:

- Other solutions have failed to provide sufficient performance gains.

- The situation can be classified as an exception to the rules or an edge case.

- Testing and QA of new strategies proves worthwhile gains (in performance, resource savings, or both).

There is no one-size-fits-all solution to any set of architectural challenges, and therefore it is important to use caution when applying techniques introduced in this chapter (or anywhere for that matter). Keep it simple and only when simple fails should less simple solutions be considered.

Index

A

AlwaysOn Availability Groups, 183, 184
Analytic data
    characteristics, 18
    OLAP vs. OLTP data access patterns, 16
    size, 2–4
    structure, 4, 5
Analytic query pattern, 101
Analytic sales order table, 3
Analytic workloads, 112, 179

B

Backups, 30, 111, 158, 160
Batch mode execution
    columnstore aggregation query, 101
    execution plan
        clustered index scan, 105
        columnstore index, 100
        fact and dimension tables, 102
        performance discrepancies, 108
        row counts, 105
        row mode vs. batch mode
          operation, 109
    performance, 107–110
    query, 100
Batch mode processing, 98, 105–107
Batch mode *vs.* row mode processing, 110
Binary tree structure, 37, 45
Bit array compression, 66, 67

Brute-force approach, 17
Bulk insert processes, 45, 132
Bulk loading
    columnstore indexes, 112, 114
    performance, columnstore
        indexes, 114–118
    processes, 111, 112

C

Clustered columnstore index, 179, 207
    compressed segments, 46
    data storage, 24
Clustered rowstore index, 23
    data storage, 21
    structure, 46
Columnstore archive compression,
    68–70, 244, 273
Columnstore compression
    algorithms
        dictionary encoding, 54–60
        row order (vertipaq)
          optimization, 62–65
        run-length encoding, 65, 66
        string data normalization, 60, 62
        value encoding, 51–54
    data stored by columns, 49
    data structure, 50
    life cycle, 71
    repeated values, 50
    repetitive columns, 49

Columnstore indexes
    aggregating single column, 25
    analytic table, 25
    architectural components
        delete bitmap, 41
        delta store, 40, 41
        rowgroups and segments, 36–39
        sample data set, 33, 35, 36
    benefits, 24
    compression, 69
    data stored, 24
    internal partitions, 93
    loading data, practices, 118
    maintenance by partition, 246
    memory usage
        access_count, 91
        object_load_time, 91, 92
        object_type_desc, 90
        Sale_CCI Table, 89
    partitioning, 259
    physical storage on pages, 43–47
    reorder and rebuild, 245, 246
    vs. rowstore clustered index, 24
    SQL Server
        compression, 29, 30
        data loads, 30
        faster analytic reads, 30
        native analytic data, 26, 27
        scalability, 27–29
    temporary tables, 260–263
Columnstore metadata, 143, 145
    rowgroup, 73–75
    rowgroup operational statistics, 84–88
    rowgroup physical, 79–84
    segment, 75–79
Columnstore segments, 67, 76–79, 90, 210
COMPRESS_ALL_ROW_GROUPS option,
    239, 240, 242

Compressed rowgroup, 42, 241, 242
Compression delay, nonclustered
    columnstore indexes,
    189–195, 198
Constraints, 60, 212
Cost of modifying data, 123, 124
Covering indexes, 180, 182, 183, 204

D

Database maintenance tasks, 160
Data growth, 28
Data load, 30
    columnstore reorganize
        operations, 120–122
    drop nonclustered indexes, 119
Data movement/migration, 158, 159
Data reads, 253, 254
Data set, 33, 35, 36
Data space, 149, 151
Data warehouse, 6, 7
Delete bitmap, 41, 125, 153, 225
Deleted rows, 42, 75, 228, 229
Delete operations
    columnstore index, 128
    delete bitmap, 125
    delta store, 125
    rowgroup metadata, 126, 127
    rowgroups, 125
Delta rowgroups, 94, 201, 227
Delta store, 40, 41, 50, 118, 120–122, 134
Dictionaries consume space, 257
Dictionary compression, 55, 57, 60
Dictionary encoding, 54–60, 257
Dictionary metadata, 56, 58, 59
Dictionary pressure, 237, 239,
    241, 257–259
Disk-based execution plan, 272

E

Execution modes, 98, 101

F

Filegroup, 161
Filtered index, 195–198
Filtered nonclustered columnstore
    indexes, 195–199
Filtered nonclustered rowstore
    indexes, 214, 215
Fragmentation
    cause, 226
    delete bitmap, 225
    quantifying deleted rows, 228, 229
    unordered data, 230, 231, 233,
        234, 236
    unordered inserts, 227
    UPDATE operation, 227

G

Global dictionary, 56–58

H

Hot data, 43, 196
Huffman compression
    algorithms, 69

I, J, K

Indexed views, 218–220
Index maintenance, 160, 170, 247
INSERT operation, 132, 174, 236, 240
Integer data compressed, 52, 53
Internal columnstore index
    objects, 93–95

L

Large objects (LOB), 67
Linear approximations, 29

M

Memory-optimized columnstore
    indexes, 63
    caveats, 273
    durability setting, 268
    enabling, 264
    error message, 267
    execution plans, test analytic query, 272
    MAX length columns, 266
    nonclustered columnstore indexes, 269
    performance benefits, 273
    SCHEMA_ONLY, 268
    table creation, 265, 267, 270
    test analytic query, 271
Memory-optimized indexes, 25
Memory sizing, 254, 256
Metadata reads, 249, 250, 252, 253
Microsoft Xpress compression algorithm, 69

N

No-maintenance columnstore index, 236
Nonclustered columnstore indexes
    architecture, 42
    benefits, 185
    code changes, 199
    compression delay, 188–194
    creation, 186
    DELETE and UPDATE operations, 185
    execution plan, 186
    filtered, 195–199
    hot, warm, and cold transactional
        data, 187
    index maintenance, 247

Nonclustered columnstore
    indexes (*cont.*)
  index usage statistics, 204, 205
  rowgroups, segments, and
    compression, 185
  STATISTICS IO, 187
  testing, 203, 204
  transactional table, 186
  vertipaq optimization, 199,
    201–203
  workloads, 186
Nonclustered index, 23, 83, 95, 119
Nonclustered rowstore indexes
  analytic query, 182, 208
  benefits, 211
  columnstore segment metadata, 210
  compression, 220, 222
  enforcing constraints, 212, 214
  filtered, 214, 215
  guidance, 222, 223
  index creation query, 211
  indexed views, 218–220
  query execution plan and IO, 211
  Statistics IO output, 208
  stock item key column, 209
  vertipaq optimization
    add filters, 216
    periodic index maintenance,
    216, 218
Nonclustered rowstore primary
    key, 98, 214
Normalization, 14, 60, 62
Normalizing wide columns, 258

O

OLAP
  architects, 17
  challenge, 180
  workloads, 18, 184
Online order tracking system, 188
ONLINE rebuilds, 242, 243
Online transactional processing (OLTP)
  challenge against rowstore tables, 180
  data and processes, 183
  vs. OLAP data access patterns, 16
  query retrieving, 22
  storing analytic data, 7, 8
  workloads, 18
Operator properties
  columnstore and rowstore index
    scans, 102
  rowstore clustered index scan, 104
Optimal analytic workloads, 154
Optimization strategies, 274
Ordered data, 228, 233, 234
Over-indexing, 183

P

Page header, 44
Page structure, SQL Server, 44
Partition functions, 160, 165, 176
Partitioning
  add files to filegroup, 162
  boundary configuration, 165
  columnstore index maintenance, 246
  configuration, 164
  database files, 163
  database maintenance, 160
  data modification, staging data, 174
  data movement/migration, 158, 159
  data types, 167
  elimination, 159
  filegroup, 161
  guidelines

column choice, 176
   partition and rowgroup sizing, 175
   storage choice, 176
hot/warm/cold data, 157, 158
INSERT operation, 174
narrow analytic queries, 169
partition scheme, creation, 165
query execution plans, 170
query optimizer, 170
rebuild operation, 171
staging table, switching operation, 172
STATISTICS IO, 169
storage speed and cost, 158
table partitioning, benefits, 177
table with ordered data set, 168
Partition scheme, 165–167, 173, 250
Partition switching, 161, 172, 175
Performance
   data reads, 253, 254
   memory sizing, 254, 256
   metadata reads, 249, 250, 252, 253
Periodic index maintenance, 216, 218
PowerPivot, 24, 63

Q

Query execution plan, 105, 170, 211
Query optimizer, 76, 159, 170

R

REBUILD operations, 171, 242, 244, 247
REORGANIZE operation, 237–240,
   242, 247
Row batch structure, 105, 106
Rowgroup elimination, 155, 253
   data space, retrieve, 149
   DELETE operations, 153

invoice date key column,
   144, 149
metadata, 143
metadata query, 149
narrow analytic query, 146
ordered and unordered columnstore
   index, 151
power, 146
row counts, 152
SQL Server, 153
STATISTICS IO, 145, 153
Rowgroup metadata, 240, 241
   columnstore index, 74, 127
   Deleted_rows, 75
   Delta_store_hobt_id, 75
   Partition_number, 74
   Size_in_bytes, 75
   State and State_Description, 75
   Total_rows, 75
Rowgroup operational statistics
   columnstore index, query, 84
   delete_buffer_scan_count, 86, 88
   index_scan_count, 85
   returned_row_count, 88
   scan_count, 85
Rowgroup physical metadata
   created_time, 84
   has_vertipaq_optimization, 83
   query, 79
   state_desc, 80
   sys.column_store_row_groups, 80
   transition_to_compressed_state_
      desc, 82
   trim_reason_desc, 81, 82
Rowgroups, 36–39
Rowgroup sizing, 175
Row mode execution, 97–99
Row offsets, 44

Row order (vertipaq) optimization, 62–65

Rowstore indexes, 47

    analytic query, 180

    covering index, 183

    execution plan, analytic query, 182

    OLAP and OLTP queries, 180

    STATISTICS IO, 181, 182

    threshold, 180

Run-length encoded data, 124

S

Segment elimination, 78, 154, 253

    columnstore index, 138

    filter and aggregate, 140

    optimization technique, 140

    query, 140

    query for two columns, 139

    reducing resource consumption, 142

    rowstore tables, 140

Segment metadata

    base and magnitude, 78

    columnstore index, 77

    encoding_type, 77

    has_nulls, 78

    Min_data_id and Max_data_id, 78

    null_value, 78

    on_disk_size, 79

    query, 76

    row count, 78

Segment reads, 253

Segments, 36–39

SELECT query, 130

Sorting column, 259

Spatial indexes, 25

SQL Server Analysis Services, 1, 24, 63

SQL Server storage, 22

Statistical metrics, 4

T

Table partitioning, 157, 159, 177

Text-based data types, 4

Third-party analytics software, 6

Third-party tools, 184

Time-based units, 145

TOMBSTONE rowgroup, 202, 239, 241

Transactional data, 11–14

Transactional data storage,
        limits, 21–23

Transactional order query, 13

Transactional queries, 22

Transactional sales order table, 3

Transactional tables, 181, 187

Transactional workloads, 18, 19, 264

U

Unordered inserts, 227, 233, 235

Unstructured data, 1, 6

Update operations, 128–135, 233, 247

V

Value-based encoding, 77, 78

Value compression, 53, 57, 60

Value encoding, 51–54

Vertipaq compression, 63, 66

Vertipaq optimization, 63, 65, 66, 83, 119,
        124, 199, 201–203

W

Workloads, 18, 83, 97, 105

X, Y, Z

XML indexes, 25

Printed in the United States
by Baker & Taylor Publisher Services